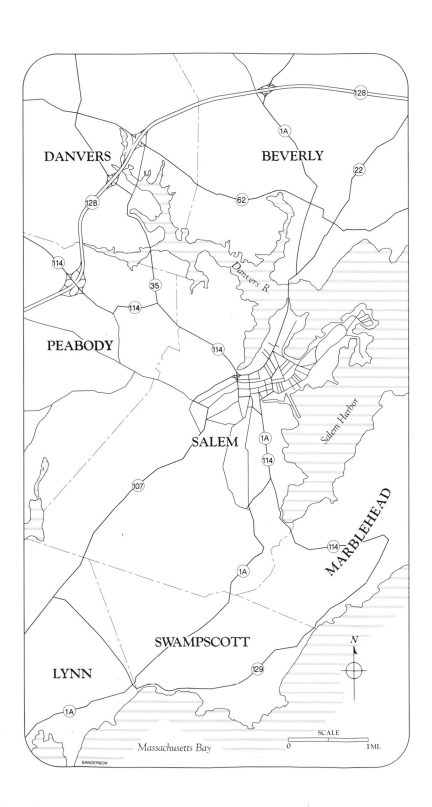

DANVERS

BEVERLY

PEABODY

SALEM

Danvers R.

Salem Harbor

MARBLEHEAD

SWAMPSCOTT

LYNN

Massachusetts Bay

128

1A

22

62

128

114

35

114

114

1A

114

107

114

1A

129

1A

N

SCALE

0   1 MI.

SANDERSON

ARCHITECTURE IN SALEM

An Illustrated Guide

By Bryant F. Tolles, Jr.

with Carolyn K. Tolles

Foreword by Paul F. Norton

ESSEX INSTITUTE

with the cooperation of Historic Salem, Incorporated

SALEM, MASSACHUSETTS

1983

Library of Congress Catalogue Card Number
83–80763

International Standard Book Number
0–88389–084–4 (cloth)
0–88389–085–2 (paper)

Text design by Sandra Rigney
Maps by Dick Sanderson

Produced by The Book Department, Inc.,
Boston, Massachusetts

Composition by Foster-Bush Studio,
Wellesley, Massachusetts

Printed by Edwards Brothers, Inc.,
Ann Arbor, Michigan

Publication expenses have been met by the
James Duncan Phillips Fund of the Essex Institute,
and by a generous grant from the McCarthy Family
Foundation Charity Fund.

Printed in the United States of America

To my wife, Carolyn K. Tolles,
without whose encouragement and research assistance
this book would not have achieved
its final form

CONTENTS

FOREWORD

The intelligent way to visit a city is to acquaint oneself with its most important aspects either before or upon arrival. For this purpose nothing is better than a friendly guidebook. It may be of the general, all-inclusive type, like the European Baedekers and Blue Guides; or, it may be like this guide to Salem architecture, a guide written specifically to explain the history of its buildings. Naturally one cannot expect to find here mention of every building in the city. The author, Bryant Tolles, who is a well-known architectural historian and executive director of the Essex Institute, has made a selection of approximately 350 buildings and complexes which for various reasons he considers the most important. He sees beauty and perfection of workmanship in some, while others are good examples of historic styles of architecture, and a few are chosen for largely historic importance (e.g., the residence of a Salem worthy).

The art of writing accurate, interesting architectural guidebooks is fast becoming perfected in the United States. Tolles has already published an excellent guide to New Hampshire architecture (1979), resolving the problem of organization by grouping the buildings by counties. In the smaller area of Salem he decided to arrange the guide as a series of seven walking tours plus notation of a few buildings in outlying areas. This scheme lends interest which otherwise might be lacking if one were confronted by an endless list of buildings. If you find yourself in the center of town and can spare three-quarters of an hour at lunch time, you may take the "City Center" tour, and so on.

It should be pointed out that writing architectural guidebooks has not been an exclusively American occupation. In fact, the great architectural historian Nikolaus Pevsner, after emigrating to England, began a long county series in 1951 called the *Buildings of England*. These quickly became popular because they were informative without being pedantic and had few but well-chosen photographs. Although the idea of such a series has never caught on in America, the inspiration for writing architectural guides seems to have come from the English effort.

Reading a guidebook may not seem to be the most stimulating of occupations. However, I suspect that all Salem citizens and visitors to the city will find that a well-written guide like this will give them more pleasure than they might foresee. Buildings once ignored by the casual tourist or passer-by may, through literary acquaintance, become objects of great interest and real aesthetic satisfaction.

PAUL F. NORTON
Professor of History of Art
University of Massachusetts–Amherst

Architecture in Salem: An Illustrated Guide had its beginnings in 1975, early in my term as executive director and librarian of the Essex Institute. Upon my arrival in Salem, I quickly became conscious of the dearth of recently published literature treating Salem architecture, long recognized as one of the richest concentrations of 17th century, Georgian Colonial, Federal, and Victorian eclectic buildings in the United States. Not since 1940, when the Institute published Fiske Kimball's *Mr. Samuel McIntire, Carver* . . . has a major illustrated volume on the architectural history of Salem appeared. No comprehensive architectural guidebook for the city has ever before been published, although interest in doing so has been expressed for many years.

This volume has been compiled for a general audience and is intended as a field guide rather than a general history; hence, it exclusively focuses on the surviving architecture of Salem. It is the primary aim of the book to serve as a reference for the identification and appreciation of Salem's unique building heritage. In this connection it is hoped that the volume will supply new data and critical evaluation to foster future local preservation efforts. If it proves a useful preservation tool to the Essex Institute, Historic Salem, Incorporated, the Salem Historical Commission, the Planning Office of the City of Salem, the Salem Redevelopment Authority, and other local groups and individuals, then the publication, in one major respect, will be successful.

The title of the book aptly and succinctly describes its subject matter. Over 350 buildings and complexes have been selectively chosen for inclusion, and approximately 230 of these are illustrated. The architecture is broadly representative, but by necessity, some buildings of merit have not been included due to size limitations of the volume. The building entries are arranged in a systematic fashion according to seven walking tour districts, which conform to historically and/or geographically identifiable areas of Salem. There is a separate section for buildings located outside of these districts. In each tour district section, the building entries are numbered so that the reader may use them in logical sequence and proceed easily from one tour district to the next. At the beginning of each section there is a map on which building locations are shown, making use of the entry numbers. Outlying buildings may be found by consulting the general Salem map at the end of the book. Map scales vary in order to conform to the page size of the book.

Architecture in Salem . . . treats a wide spectrum of residential, ecclesiastical, commercial, educational, industrial, and civic architecture. Engineering structures, such as bridges, wharves, and fortifications, have been intentionally omitted. Chronologically, the entire span of Salem's architectural history has been covered, but with an emphasis on Federal-era buildings for which the city is internationally renowned. At the back of the book is a bibliography in which the substantial literature pertaining to Salem architecture is selectively published for the first time.

Like most architectural guides that are published today, this volume does not contain an illustrated glossary of architectural terms. For those readers who wish full definitions of terms employed in the text, consult standard dictionaries of English usage, and such reference works as: Nicholas Pevsner, John Fleming, and Hugh Honour, *A Dictionary of Architecture*, revised edition (Woodstock, N.Y.: The Overlook Press, 1976), also published by Penguin Books, 1966, and subsequent printings and editions; Henry H. Saylor, *Dictionary of Architecture* (New York: John Wiley and Sons, Inc., 1952, and subsequent printings); and John J.-G. Blumenson, *Identifying American Architecture: A Pictorial Guide to Styles and Terms, 1600-1945* (Nashville, Tennessee: American Association for State and Local History, 1977).

Financial backing for the production and printing of this volume was provided by the James Duncan Phillips Fund of the Essex Institute, and by a generous matching grant from the McCarthy Family Foundation Charity Fund, which has previously supported other Institute publications. Under the terms of the McCarthy Foundation grant, 35% of the proceeds from sale will be returned to a special revolving fund, established to help finance future printings and/or editions of the book. The Hurdle Hill and Atwater Kent foundations and two individuals donated funds for photography and compilation.

Virtually all of the photographs were taken by the author, with developing services provided by the Essex Camera Shop (Salem), Peter Zaharis, proprietor. Mark Sexton of the Peabody Museum of Salem photography department deserves particular credit for his excellent enlarging and printing work. Photographs were also supplied by Richard Merrill (Institute files) (A-3 and A-5), the House of Seven Gables Settlement Association (B-14 and B-15), David Matt of the *Salem Evening News* (G-15), and the Park Department (D-49, taken in c. 1950, and F-16, taken in c. 1931), and the Planning Department (H-3) of the City of Salem. Historic photographs at the beginning of each tour section are owned by the Institute.

Of the many individuals who have assisted me in my research and granted access to collections, none deserve more thanks than the staff of the Essex Institute. Particularly helpful in making vital materials available were Irene Norton, Marylou Birchmore, and Caroline Preston of the library staff. Mrs. Norton also read and critiqued the entire manuscript. Other Institute staff members who have contributed to the project are Curator Anne Farnam, Associate Curator Dean Lahikainen, Assistant Curator John Wright, Education Coordinator David Goss, Administrative Receptionist Carolyn Farley, and Assistant to the Director Katherine Richardson, who copyedited the manuscript and offered much useful advice. Paul Norton, professor of history of art, University of Massachusetts–Amherst, and the editor of the Papers of Samuel McIntire at the Institute, has been both a helpful friend and consultant during the project. The Institute will publish Professor Norton's completed work in 1984.

I would also like to acknowledge with gratitute the assistance of several other individuals, and library and archival staffs, most based in Salem. Joyce King, the current researcher for the Historic Salem house marker program, offered innumerable research leads and important data that contributed greatly to the book. Allison Crump, formerly of the Planning Department, City of Salem, read parts of the manuscript and offered research advice on the business center of the city. Edward Stevenson, director of the House of Seven Gables, reviewed the materials for the Gables Association houses, while Peter Fetchko, director of the Peabody Museum of Salem, reviewed the entry for the Peabody Museum complex. Elizabeth Wheaton, the clerk of the Salem Historical Commission, supplied data on National Register properties and local historic districts. City Clerk Josephine Fusco and her staff were most kind in granting us access to the city archives. Also due my appreciation are the staffs of the Essex County Registry of Probate and Registry of Deeds (Salem), where much essential research was conducted. Additional useful information was gleaned from the local building survey forms maintained by Historic Salem and the Massachusetts Historical Commission, and I wish to recognize the efforts of those who compiled them over many years. Thanks is also due the staffs of the Boston Athenaeum and the Harvard Graduate School of Architecture and Design (Cambridge) where research in periodicals was carried out. I also wish to extend my appreciation to Bruce Shatswell of Salem who lent constant encouragement and contributed advice for the drafting of the maps.

Lastly, and most significantly, I would like to express my gratitude to Frederick S. Allis, Jr., chairman, and the other members of the Institute's Publications Committee for their interest in and support of the project. They share with me a belief in the great significance of Salem's distinctive architectural heritage, and in the need to maintain an appreciation and knowledge of this heritage through this publication.

B.F.T., Jr. *with* C.K.T.
Salem, Massachusetts
August 1982

MAPS OF TOUR DISTRICTS

A map showing the principal automobile routes into Salem will be found opposite the title page of the book. A street map of Salem, including the locations of outlying buildings (Section H), may be found on the inside back cover of the book.

Salem, Massachusetts, a thriving small city of just under 38,000 residents today, had its origins in 1626 when Roger Conant located here with a group of settlers from nearby Cape Ann. First called Naumkeag, from the Indian word meaning "fishing place," the new settlement was the earliest town established in the Massachusetts Bay Colony. Soon the name Salem, from the Hebrew word for "peace," was adopted. The fledgling community was quick to take advantage of its proximity to the sea, and by the early 19th century, Salem was one of North America's major mercantile ports, trading with Europe, Africa, and the Far East. The development of Salem as a regional financial center followed directly from successes in international commerce. After the decline of trade in the 1830s and 1840s, the textile, leather, and other industries assumed prominence in the local economy. Later in the century, this economy became more diversified. Despite the setback caused by the disastrous 1914 fire, the city has maintained its regional importance as a center for industry, business, education, medicine, law, and county government.

Geographically the village of Salem was at first concentrated on a long, narrow peninsula jutting into Beverly Harbor and between the North and South rivers, with Essex Street the principal east-west artery. The original political boundaries of the town, however, encompassed a much larger area, including what is today much of central Essex County. Gradually other towns were split off from Salem, so that by 1810 available land was at a premium. This led to the filling in of small streams, swamps, coves, the Mill Pond, and much of the North and South rivers, thereby transforming the original configuration of the shoreline, especially the old commercial wharf and shipbuilding districts. The center of Salem became physically linked with the north and south portions which had traditionally been separate social entities. Such a topographical history has influenced the physical growth of the community, dictating the street layout and the placement and function of its buildings.

Salem's architectural development has been influenced by geographical as well as economic and cultural factors. Over the years, the city's building heritage has achieved a high status, particularly that of the so-called "First Period" (c. 1626–c. 1715), and the Federal era (c. 1780–c. 1830). In more recent times Salem's outstanding collection of Victorian buildings (c. 1830–c. 1910) has received attention. Extensive literature (see "Bibliography" below) exists describing the architecture of the city and the history of individual districts, streets, buildings, architects, and builders. Throughout the United States and abroad, Salem has established its reputation as possessing one of this country's most significant architectural legacies. Of the older, smaller, eastern seacoast communities, Salem exhibits the richest and most comprehensive variety of styles, building types, and building practices. Urban renewal efforts of the past decade have added luster to this distinguished heritage.

FIRST PERIOD ARCHITECTURE, c. 1626–c. 1715

Salem is blessed with one of the largest and richest extant collections of 17th-century houses of any town or city in New England. When the first settlers arrived in 1626 they erected small, rude wooden shelters and houses, conjectural replicas of which may be seen today at Pioneer Village (1930) off Lafayette Street on Salem Harbor. By mid century two basic types of wood-frame residences were being constructed locally—two-room, two-story houses with end chimneys, and four-room, two-story houses with central chimneys, the latter type simply an expansion of the former. Salem's two oldest surviving dwellings, the Pickering (c. 1651, etc.) and Retire Becket (c. 1655) houses originally consisted of two rooms in two stories, but were subsequently doubled in size. Certain of these houses later acquired rear leantos, as we may see today in the Gedney (c. 1656) or John Ward (after 1684, etc.) houses, or featured prominent front gables, good examples of which are present in the Ward, Hooper-Hathaway (c. 1682), or Jonathan Corwin (c. 1675) houses. The House of Seven Gables (1668; c. 1678, etc.) illustrates with its multigables the larger type of residence, of which there are only a few surviving examples in New England.

Characterized by a natural, direct appearance, these 17th-century buildings were box-like in construction with medium or steep-pitched roofs and were supported by carefully hewn and fitted (pegged) timber frames expertly crafted by skilled artisans. Devoid of architectural detail, the simple house form was most frequently relieved by a massive chimney of brick or stone. Entrances were customarily placed on the long front sides, with little attention to formal symmetry. Randomly positioned and small, the windows were usually of the casement type, with diamond-shaped, leaded panes. In several of Salem's 17th-century houses, the upper floor projects beyond the lower creating an overhang or jetty. Occasionally windows were placed in the gable end under the eaves, creating functional attic half-stories. Wall surfaces consisted of narrow unpainted clapboards and trim. Originally an outgrowth of the English Elizabethan (late medieval) rural house form, these buildings were adapted to changing styles, demands, and financial resources over the years and, like so much New England architecture of more recent vintage, were modified in size and decoration. The examples that we may view in modern-day Salem reflect various methods and degrees of historic restoration and were barely recognizable as 17th-century buildings before such restoration was carried out.

THE GEORGIAN COLONIAL ERA, c. 1720–c. 1780

During the 18th century, Salem prospered economically, and there was extensive building activity throughout the community. To this day,

with the sole exception of Newport, the city possesses the largest con-
centration of Georgian Colonial domestic architecture among New
England's old seacoast communities. Virtually all of this building,
however, is of the vernacular variety with local adaptations, as most of
the high style Georgian Colonial residences, many formerly along Essex
and Washington streets, have been razed. Examples of other building
types from this era have also disappeared.

Situated largely in the Derby, Broad, and upper Essex street areas,
the plain vernacular houses of early and mid century tend to be small,
two-story symmetrical wood-frame structures with central chimneys,
double-sash windows, and gambrel or pitched roofs. Frequently they were
erected with one end facing the street in order to take full advantage
of the building lots with their limited frontage. Simple in form and lacking
in architectural detail, these houses customarily feature classical doorway surrounds of the basic post-and-lintel or pedimented types. Good
local examples are the Jonathan Neal house (1767) on Broad Street, the
Lindall-Gibbs-Osgood house (1755) on Essex Street, and the Crowninshield-Bentley house (1727–1730, etc.) at the Essex Institute. A rare
specimen in brick is the Derby house (1761/62; 1790) on Derby Street.

More characteristic of the high-style Georgian Colonial, with its predominant richness in ornamentation and bold classical details, are several
large gambrel-roofed residences which have survived on upper Essex
Street. Primary examples are the Lindall-Barnard-Andrews (c. 1740),
Cabot-Endicott-Low (c. 1744–1748, etc.), and Capt. Thomas Mason (c.
1750) houses. These are distinguished by pedimented roof dormers and
doorway surrounds and, in the two newer buildings, by corner quoins,
and molded and dentiled cornices. Still, even these impressive buildings lack the roof balustrades, pedimented projecting pavilions, large
pilasters or columns, and Palladian windows so often associated with the
most sophisticated architecture of the Georgian Colonial era. There is
only modest evidence in these houses of the influence of English Palladian architecture and the numerous English builders' handbooks and
design books which guided master builders and artisans in the American colonies.

After 1765, almost in anticipation of the principal Salem house form
of the Federal period, many local Georgian Colonial dwellings were constructed three stories high with hipped roofs. Typical examples of this
type in wood are the Webb-Briggs-Whipple (1770 or before), Capt. Edward Allen (c. 1768), Mason-Roberts-Colby (1768, etc.), and Ropes-
Waldo (c. 1768, etc.) houses. These possess many of the same decorative features as their lower gambrel-roof counterparts, with center
chimney floor plans.

THE FEDERAL STYLE AND THE ERA OF McINTIRE,
c. 1790–c. 1830

After the end of the Revolutionary War, Salem entered an era of
maritime commercial prosperity unparalleled in its history. With the success of the local economy came a period of remarkable architectural
achievement during which the Federal style, derived from English and

American design books, was the predominant planning mode. Throughout this country as well as abroad, Salem became known for its outstanding and unusual collection of Federal-style buildings. Largely responsible for this impressive heritage was the local architect, master carpenter, and carver, Samuel McIntire (1757–1811), famed for his distinctive and delicate version of the English Adamesque style. Working in Salem at the same time as McIntire were a number of other master builders and skilled artisans whose talents also contributed to this notable architectural legacy. Synonymous with this period is the name of Chestnut Street, considered by many scholars of American architecture to be the nation's most magnificent residential street.

Of the several varieties of Federal residential architecture present in Salem, the three-storied, four-square, low-hipped-roof mansion is the most common. Constructed of wood as well as brick, these grand buildings, in most instances, preserve the formal and elegant symmetry of the Georgian Colonial era, with a central hall plan and a smooth five-bay facade arrangement with a central doorway the main visual focal point. Most often the doorway is topped by a semicircular or semielliptical traceried fanlight with flanking rectangular sidelights. Protecting the doorway is a rectangular or semicircular flat-roofed portico supported by columns and pilasters in a variety of Greek and Roman orders. Other common features are narrow double-sash windows with splayed lintels, Palladian windows, a light molded cornice, tall end chimneys, and porch and roof balustrades. Early Federal examples which bridge the gap between the Georgian Colonial and the Federal styles are McIntire's Peirce-Nichols (1782, 1801, etc.) and Simon Forrester (c. 1790/91) houses, and the Hosmer-Townsend-Waters (1795), the Joshua Ward (c. 1784-1788), the Benjamin Hawkes (1780; 1801), the Joseph Felt (1794/95), and the Capt. Nicholas Crosby (1800) houses. Also quite prevalent in Salem is the smaller-scale vernacular Federal house which is characterized by a wood frame and siding, pitched roof, central chimney, rectangular floor plan, and modest detail confined largely to the main doorway.

Lighter in feeling, less robust, and more refined in embellishment than Salem's early Federal architecture is the architecture of the mid-Federal period dating from c. 1800 to c. 1815. Corresponding with the years of McIntire's greatest achievement, this era produced Salem's most outstanding group of buildings. These display the genius of McIntire as well as the creative influence of Boston's Charles Bulfinch (1763–1844) and several other prominent New England designers and master builders. Locally, the Adamesque Federal reached its greatest height in such structures as McIntire's Gardner-Pingree (1804–1805), Clifford Crowninshield (1804–1806), and Cook-Oliver (1802–1803; 1808) houses, McIntire's Hamilton Hall (1805–1807), the Old Custom House (1805), the Old Town Hall and Market House (1816), and the Amos and Solomon Towne (c. 1804), the White-Lord (c. 1811), the Dodge-Barstow-West (c. 1802), and the Capt. Stephen Phillips (1804–1805) houses. These all feature attenuated, chaste, sometimes meagre but finely executed classical elements, often geometric in nature, with the free use of curved moldings, surfaces, and arches. Not only is this ornamentation free and flexible, but so are the floor plans and proportions. Salem architecture of the years c. 1800–c. 1815 possesses a quiet coherency and beauty that is approached in no other period in the city's history.

Although McIntire died in 1811, his influence on local architecture persisted for over two decades afterwards, and the Adamesque Federal building tradition remained strong until c. 1835. This style reached its most advanced stage of development in such ornately articulated buildings as the new Custom House (1818/19; 1853/54), and the Andrew-Safford (1818/19), Loring-Emmerton (1818; 1885), Forrester-Peabody (1818/19), and Dodge-Shreve (1822–1825) houses. More subdued Federal mansions such as the Pickman-Shreve-Little (c. 1819), the Devereux-Hoffman-Simpson (1826/27), and the George Nichols (1817/18) also continued to be erected during this era. The brick housing or commercial row became popular at this time in many American cities, and Salem has excellent examples in the Bowker block (c. 1830), the Varny-Reynolds-Ropes building (1845), the Shepard block (c. 1850/51), the Roberts-Shepard-Thorndike double house (c. 1830), and the Allen-Osgood-Huntington triple house (c. 1828/29, etc.). Certain structures (East India Marine Hall [1824/25] is the best local example) presaged the coming of the Greek Revival in both form and decoration.

FROM THE GREEK REVIVAL TO THE MID VICTORIAN ECLECTIC, c. 1830–c. 1870

During the twenty years (c. 1825–c. 1845) which it took for Salem to make the transition from a predominantly maritime commercial economy to an industrial one there was diminishing prosperity and hence less construction activity than in the previous three decades. As a consequence, the earliest of the Romantic era styles, the Greek Revival, did not have a deep impact here as in many other New England seacoast communities, and there are few high style examples. Those that exist, however, are of extremely high quality. One would be hard pressed to find anywhere finer Greek temple-form granite buildings than Richard Bond's City Hall (1836/37) or Old Essex County Courthouse (1839–1841). The most extensive local evidence of the Greek Revival style may be seen in the Ionic and Corinthian-columned porches appended to older residences (cf. Chestnut Street) or brick housing rows (e.g. West triple house, c. 1833/34), and in the wooden vernacular temple-form houses of the type found on Howard, Winter, Summer, upper Federal, and upper Essex streets.

The early Gothic Revival, almost the antithesis of the Greek, left its picturesque mark on very few Salem buildings. Of the local Gothic examples, however, two stone churches (St. Peter's, 1833/34, etc., and First [North], 1835/36, etc.) and one wooden house (Henry M. Brooks, 1851) are among the finest examples of this style surviving in America. Characteristic of the substantial stone ecclesiastical type are a symmetrical plan, central square tower with large entry, large pointed-arch windows with tracery and colored glass, and wall and tower battlements. The more fragile wooden houses or cottages, customarily modeled on design book plates (e.g. Andrew Jackson Downing, Alexander Jackson Davis, Richard Upjohn, etc.) usually featured steep-pitched roofs, open verandas, wall dormers, bays, complex chimneys, pointed-arch doors and windows, hood molds, gingerbread bargeboards, clustered columns, and in some instances, corner quoins, rusticated or board and batten walls, crockets and pinnacles, and wheel, trefoil, or quatrefoil windows.

While there are few Salem buildings in which the Italian Revival style appears in its purest form, there are numerous examples in which it is dominant. In scores of other structures, mainly houses of the Georgian Colonial, Federal, or Greek Revival styles, the characteristic bracketing was added to provide an Italian Revival flavor. Other features common to this style are round-headed windows (occasionally paired), corner quoins, rusticated or flat-board wall surfaces, bay windows, towers, roof balustrades, low pitched or hipped roofs, balustraded balconies, heavy and ornate window and door moldings, flat and segmental-arch hoods, and asymmetrical floor plans. Certainly the most fully developed local examples, all built of brick and brownstone, are the Downing block (1858), the State Normal School (1853/54; 1870/71), the Bertram-Waters house (1855; 1888/89; 1911/12), and Plummer Hall (1856/57) and the John Tucker Daland house (1851/52) at the Essex Institute. Noteworthy Italian Revival buildings of wood are the William B. Parker (c. 1851/52), Emery S. Johnson (1853), Ives-Putnam (1850/51), Ives-Webb (1855/56), Francis Cox (c. 1846) houses, and the Rogers/Russell (1875) and Curwen/Gillis (c. 1854) double houses. The Italian Revival became almost a national style in the decade before the Civil War.

Although it was prevalent in the United States from c. 1860–c. 1890, the French Academic (Second Empire) style was hardly used in Salem until after 1870, and it only lasted for about ten years. Popularly known as the "mansard" because of the presence of a double-pitched French roof enclosing the top floor on all sides, the style also is distinguished by tall arched and pedimented windows, asymmetrical floor plans, ornate roof dormers, verandas, eaves brackets, and boldly stated classical moldings, quoins, cornices, and belt courses. French Academic houses are usually three stories tall (including the mansard roof story) and square-shaped, and occasionally possess a projecting front central pavilion rising above the house proper. Fine examples of this style may be seen along Lafayette, upper Essex, and upper Federal streets.

Of the other American architectural styles in vogue before 1870, only the Romanesque Revival made any headway in Salem, with the Church of the Immaculate Conception (1857–1864; 1880/81) and the Superior Court of Essex County (1861/62, etc.) the best extant examples. There are no local buildings conceived in the Octagon, Egyptian Revival, or Moorish Revival styles. A number of local houses are eclectic combinations of several mid-Victorian styles and illustrate the creative imaginations and expert contracting skills of the era's carpenter builders.

LATE VICTORIAN AND EARLY MODERN STYLES, c. 1870–c. 1930

While Salem is most widely known for its outstanding First Period and Federal-style architecture, the decades from the end of the Civil War to the Great Depression also produced some outstanding buildings. Particularly noteworthy are the numerous structures conceived in the Queen Anne, late Gothic Revival, Victorian Gothic, and Colonial Revival styles. Other design vernaculars represented are the late Romanesque Revival, the High Victorian Italianate, the Byzantine Revival, the Bungaloid, the Neoclassical Revival, and the Neo-Romanesque Revival. A few houses and commercial buildings combine several styles of the period, and are most appropriately described as "late Victorian Eclectic." Curiously, Salem possesses no buildings of note designed in such popular Gilded Age styles as the Stick, Shingle, Chateauesque, or Richardsonian Romanesque.

Salem's half dozen outstanding Queen Anne houses share in common irregularity in plan and mass, and variety in building materials, wall textures, and color. Windows and doors are of many forms, with either flat or round-arched headings. Often present are tall, modeled brick chimneys, bays, corner towers, turrets, intersecting pitched roofs with pronounced gables, large porches, and projecting upper stories. Architectural detail, small in scale and usually classical, is employed in an unrestrained manner. The best Salem examples of the Queen Anne are situated in the Lafayette Street area and adjacent to the Salem Common.

Of the Gothic-derived styles postdating the Civil War, Salem is most fortunate to have several variations. Best representative of the Victorian Gothic, with its polychromatic exterior finish and lavish decoration, are the remodeled First Church (Daniel Low buildings) (1826; c. 1874) and the Dickson Memorial Chapel and Conservatory (1892–1894) at Greenlawn Cemetery. St. James Church (1891–1900), Blake Memorial Chapel (1904–1905) at Harmony Grove Cemetery, Grace Church (1926/27), and St. Thomas the Apostle Church (1930) embody the principles of the late Gothic Revival, which is characterized by simpler silhouettes, quieter wall surfaces, less obtrusive color effects, and more refined detail than the earlier Victorian Gothic.

Originating in Boston, the American Colonial Revival borrowed from both the Georgian Colonial and Federal style vocabularies. Largely due to the powerful legacy of Samuel McIntire's work, the Colonial Revival made a deep impression in Salem, and there are numerous fine local examples of this popular architectural vernacular. Buildings of this style are usually a combination of pre- and post-Revolutionary and contemporary elements which are often overplayed or in improper relationship to each other. Great emphasis is placed on a rectangular plan, strict symmetry, grand scale, and classical correctness, with few distracting projections. Colonial Revival buildings are further noted for their elaborate pilastered or columned doorways, semicircular and multistoried bays, roof dormers and balustrades, Palladian windows, and other familiar historic features. The earliest local examples of this style were erected in the upper Essex and Chestnut streets area between 1889 and 1910. Expressing a strong Neo-Adamesque flavor, Salem's finest Colonial Revival houses appeared in the Warren and Lafayette street areas after the disastrous 1914 fire destroyed older dwellings. The third and final wave of construction in this style occurred between 1915 and 1933, and resulted in such outstanding public buildings as the Masonic Temple

(1915/16), the Lydia E. Pinkham Memorial (1922), and the U.S. Post Office building (1932/33). Over the years, numerous Salem Federal-era mansions have received Colonial Revival modifications, both exterior and interior.

THE TWENTIETH CENTURY, c. 1930 TO THE PRESENT

For most of the past half-century of its history, Salem has exhibited little representative modern architecture of marked quality. But for a few commercial structures and special function buildings at Salem State College and the Salem Hospital, the preeminent styles of thirties, forties, fifties, and sixties are noticeably absent. During this period some residential work continued to be produced in the Colonial Revival style, but this architecture is of marginal importance.

This unproductive trend was reversed in the 1970s, however, largely due to the impetus of urban renewal and a drive for expanded educational and health care facilities. A new influx of federal and private money into the community resulted in a surge of construction and renovation activity. Throughout the downtown area, older 18th- and 19th-century structures were creatively rehabilitated and assigned adaptive uses under the direction of local architects James Ballou, Oscar Padjen, Jonathan Woodman, Robert Scagliotti, Staley McDermet, John Emerson, David Jacquith, and others. New contemporary construction appeared based on designs by several noted architects and firms, including Padjen, Scagliotti, Philip W. Bourne (Boston), Stahl, Bennett (Boston), Nelson W. Aldrich and Maxwell Pounder (Boston), Arland A. Dirlam (Marblehead, Mass.), John Collins (Philadelphia), Henry A. Frost and Associates (Boston), James Walker (firm of Whitman and Howard, Boston), Phineas Alpers, Architects (Boston), Stephen Tise Associates (Brookline, Mass.), and Philip M. Briggs of Architecture Design Development (Cambridge, Mass.). Particularly outstanding are the Ernest S. Dodge wing of the Peabody Museum (1974/75) by Bourne, with Stahl, Bennett, the East India Mall and Parking Garage (1973–1975; 1977–1979) by Aldrich and Pounder, the Salem Five Cents Savings Bank addition (1972/73) by Padjen, the extension to the Registry of Deeds and Probate (1979–1981) by Phineas Alpers, Architects, the Pickering Wharf development (1977–1980) by Briggs, and the Federal Street condominiums (1978–) by Stephen Tise Associates. New condominium units are presently in various stages of planning or construction, and promise to augment significantly the new architecture of the city in the immediate future. The renovation of old commercial blocks continues.

Salem's most dramatic and monumental contemporary building projects have been designed for Salem State College, the Salem public school system, and the Salem Hospital. At Salem State College Edward A. Tedesco Associates' (Winchester, Mass.) Richard B. O'Keefe Physical Education/Athletic Center (1973–1976) and Desmond and Lord's (Boston) College Library (1969–1974) are definite standouts. The massive low-rise complexes of the new Salem High School (1972–1976) by Haldeman and Goransson (Boston), and the Witchcraft Heights Elementary School (1971/72) by Coletti Brothers (Hingham, Mass.) represent major contributions to present-day educational design. Among the recent additions to the Salem Hospital complex, the Davenport building (1972/73) by Tom Payette (Boston), and the Shaughnessy Hospital (1976) by James Fitzgerald (Boston) command the most attention. These products of modern technology and design perpetuate the distinguished building tradition established by Salem's oldest 17th-century wood-frame architecture.

LIST OF SYMBOLS

NHS National Historic Site

NHL National Historic Landmark

HABS Historic American Buildings Survey

NR National Register of Historic Places

MHL Massachusetts Historic Landmark

HSI Historic Salem, Incorporated (historic marker program)

WSHD Washington Square Historic District (local)

MHD McIntire Historic District (local)

DSHD Derby Street Historic District (local)

NATHAN READ house (1793; demolished, 1857) by Samuel McIntire (1757–1811) and formerly at 134 Essex Street. Photograph, c. 1857.

A

SALEM COMMON

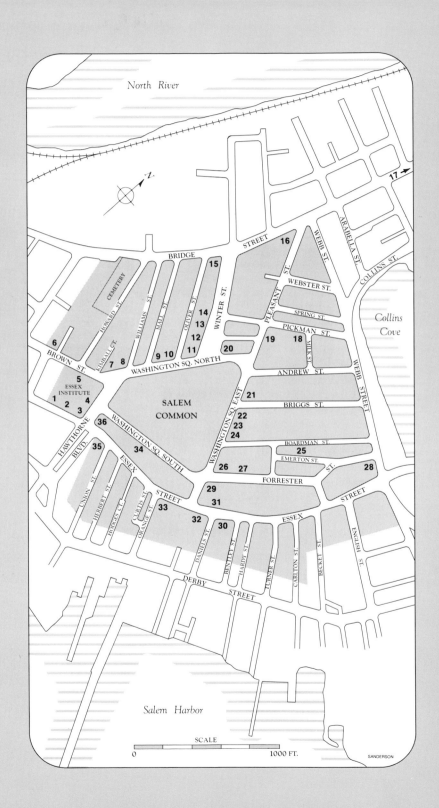

North River

17 →

BRIDGE STREET

16

WEBB ST.

ARABELLA ST.

COLLINS ST.

15

WEBSTER ST.

Collins Cove

CEMETERY

HOWARD ST.

KIMBALL CT.

WILLIAMS ST.

MALL ST.

OLIVER ST.

WINTER ST.

PLEASANT ST.

SPRING ST.

14

13

12

PICKMAN ST.

19 18

MILK ST.

WEBB STREET

6

BROWN ST.

7 8

9 10

11

WASHINGTON SQ. NORTH

20

ANDREW ST.

5

ESSEX INSTITUTE

1 2 3 4

SALEM COMMON

WASHINGTON SQ. EAST

21

BRIGGS ST.

36

WASHINGTON SQ. SOUTH

22

23

24

HAWTHORNE BLVD.

35

34

BOARDMAN ST.

25

EMERTON ST.

28

26 27

FORRESTER

ESSEX STREET

UNION ST.

HERBERT ST.

HODGES CT.

CURTIS ST.

ORANGE ST.

29

31

33

32 30

DANIELS ST.

BENTLEY ST.

HARDY ST.

TURNER ST.

CARLTON ST.

BECKET ST.

STREET

ESSEX

ENGLISH ST.

DERBY STREET

Salem Harbor

SCALE

0   1000 FT.

SANDERSON

INTRODUCTION

Originally the area that now constitutes Salem Common was a swampy, uneven, undeveloped nine-acre parcel of land containing several ponds. Over the years it has alternately been referred to as the "Town Swamp," the "pen," the "training field," "Salem Common," and "Washington Square." In the 17th and 18th centuries it was used to graze livestock and train the local militia, and was also the location of the Salem almshouse, a gunhouse, and a school building. Inspired by the completion of the Beverly Bridge (reached by Bridge Street) in 1788, and the reorganization of the militia in 1801, Elias Hasket Derby, Jr. led a subscription campaign to grade and fill the area, plant poplar trees and shrubs, lay out walkways, and construct a surrounding wooden fence with four ornamental gates. The western gate was embellished by Samuel McIntire (1757–1811) with a carved wooden medallion portrait of George Washington. A small-scale replica of this gate (a 1976 bicentennial project) may be seen today in the southwestern corner of the Common.

Renamed Washington Square in 1802, the Common, one of New England's largest, has continued in use as a military training ground, a recreational area, and a site for public events. Shedding older names, the four streets around the Common became known as Washington Square East, Washington Square North, Washington Square West, and Washington Square South. The poplar trees were eventually supplanted by elms and maples, and c. 1850 the wooden fence and gates were replaced by an ornate cast iron fence, sections of which still stand. At the center of the Common is an octagonal reinforced-concrete Neo-classical Revival bandstand, designed by architect Philip Horton Smith (1890–1960) and built in 1926 as part of the Salem Tercentenary Celebration. In 1928 the Salem Park Department assumed management of the tract.

The formal development of the Common made the land surrounding it highly desirable for residential use, and up to 1820 many prosperous merchant families—Forresters, Whites, Silsbees, and others—erected spacious and extravagant Federal-style mansions overlooking the pleasing expanse. The majority of these were the hipped-roof, three-story brick type considered synonymous with fine Salem architecture of the period. On the north and east sides of the Common these grand houses displaced older industrial activities (ropewalks, tanyards, etc.) and small wooden dwellings and shops. Later in the 19th century the areas behind the Common mansions were completely developed for residential use, and the streeets which extend out to the north and east feature numerous examples of Victorian eclectic architecture reflecting a variety of styles—

Greek Revival, Italian Revival, Gothic Revival, French Academic (Second Empire), and Queen Anne. The houses along Bridge and lower Essex streets, two of the oldest and most important thoroughfares of the town, illustrate earlier styles and building practices. The Essex Institute, with its superb collection of period houses, highlights the Salem Common area at its west end.

A-1

A-1 ESSEX INSTITUTE   1851/52; 1856/57, etc.
132 Essex Street
NR; MHL; WSHD

This massive brick-and-brownstone edifice is the headquarters of the Essex Institute (established 1848), one of the oldest, largest, and best-known privately endowed regional historical societies in the United States. Salem's best example of mid-Victorian Italian Revival-style architecture, this versatile facility, while preserving much of its exterior and interior decoration, has accommodated a variety of functions over its long history. It exists as a powerful and dignified visual statement of mid-Victorian cultural taste.

The west portion of the complex, Plummer Hall (photo, left), was built in 1856/57 for the Salem Athenaeum, a private proprietary library, from a bequest made by Miss Caroline Plummer in memory of her brother Ernestus Augustus Plummer. The architect was Enoch Fuller (1828–1861) of Salem. Reserving the upper floor for its own use, the Athenaeum rented the lower floor to the Essex Institute, and additional space to the Essex South District Library and the Essex Agricultural Society for their libraries. Architecturally Plummer Hall is most noteworthy for its tall round-arch second-story and segmental-arch first-story windows, its thick bracketed cornice, its arched central doorway (now closed), and its paneled and molded brickwork. No longer present are the original roof and porch balustrades, and the front fence with its round sculptured balusters. The Institute purchased Plummer Hall in 1906 when the Athenaeum constructed a smaller, more modern building at 337 Essex Street (see D-41). Today the hall contains museum galleries, an auditorium, storage areas, administrative offices, and a museum store.

The John Tucker Daland house (photo, right center), the east portion of the complex, was erected as a residence in 1851/52 from plans drafted by Boston architect Gridley J.F. Bryant (1816–1899). One of the best examples of cube-type, one-family Italianate residential architecture surviving in New England, it is among the last detached brick houses to be erected in Salem. It is distinguished by its fine bracketed cornice, rusticated corner quoins and foundation stones, segmental-arch and flat-entablature window frames, and heavy rectangular front porch supported by two sets of paired Corinthian columns and topped by a modified Palladian window. At one time the building possessed roof and porch balustrades, and paneled brick chimneys, a Bryant trademark. Constructed for Daland, a prosperous local merchant, this three-story, symmetrical structure was inhabited by his family until 1885, when the Institute acquired it as its first permanent home. It was promptly remodeled, primarily for library and office use, under the direction of North Salem architect William Devereux Dennis (1847–1913). Upon the acquisition of Plummer Hall (see above), the Daland house was attached to it by means of a Renaissance Revival connector section (1907) designed by Boston-based architect William G. Rantoul (1867–1949). The next major alteration was made in 1913/14 when the rear bookstack ell was enlarged. Then from 1966 to 1968, based on plans submitted by Campbell, Aldrich & Nulty, architects of Boston, a plain, functional five-story brick bookstack ell was constructed, and the connector section was enlarged to accommodate new office and gallery space. The original Fuller and Bryant plans, as well as those for the rest of the complex, are preserved in the Institute's archives. The Institute is open to the public at least six days a week all year, except for the Christmas holidays.

A-2

A-2   GARDNER-PINGREE HOUSE   1804–1805
Essex Institute
128 Essex Street
NHL; HABS; NR; MHL; WSHD

Erected in 1804 and 1805 for the prosperous Salem merchant John Gardner, Jr., this beautifully proportioned and precisely detailed mansion is generally regarded as one of the most outstanding Adamesque Federal town houses in the United States and perhaps the premier example in New England. It stands as an appropriate symbol of Salem's early maritime success in world markets. Not surprisingly, the house has been featured prominently in the published literature of American architectural history, and many scholars have extolled its finest qualities. In the estimation of the late Talbot Hamlin, the house met the highest ideals of "restraint, refinement and delicacy" (*The American Spirit in Architecture*, p. 95), while William H. Pierson considers it a masterpiece "remarkable for its combination of austerity and grace" (*American Buildings and their Architects: The Colonial and Neoclassical Styles*, p. 222).

Based on certain stylistic characteristics and documents at the Essex Institute, the Gardner-Pingree house has been traditionally attributed to Salem's talented master builder and carver, Samuel McIntire (1757–1811), and is considered to be the finest example of his most mature design work. Recent research in Gardner's daybook (1801–1808) (Peabody Museum of Salem), however, suggests that the attribution of the house plan to McIntire, while in all likelihood correct, is not yet and may never be concretely documented (Dean T. Lahikainen, "New Insights into the Early History of the . . . Gardner-Pingree House . . .," *Essex Institute Historical Collections* 116, p. 234). Despite this uncertainty, it may be safely assumed that the fine ornamentation of the exterior, as well as the lavish wood carving and applied composition decoration of the interior was executed by McIntire. The daybook entries make reference to several other local suppliers and artisans involved with the construction of the house—Jeremiah Page (bricks), David Robbins (master mason), Joseph Fogg (lumber), Epes Cogswell (housewright), Samuel Hood (carpenter), John Warden and his son (interior finish), and William Luscomb, III (painter and glazier) are among those named.

A superb design achievement, the balanced rectangular facade of the three-story brick structure "relies for its success on a rhythmic repetition of a window motif, on its decorative stringcourses, accentuated in . . . [red brown], emphasizing fine vertical proportions, and on its elaborate semi-circular portico at the front door" (Gerald W.R. Ward, *The Gardner-Pingree House*, p. 8). Bound to the facade where the cornice meets the lower stringcourse, this portico is typical of McIntire's late work, possessing Corinthian columns and flanked by Corinthian pilasters. A wooden balustrade crowns the three-section facade and conceals a low-hipped roof. Projecting to the rear is a brick and wooden ell, adjacent to which is a two-story brick barn of the same date as the house.

In 1811 financial circumstances forced Gardner to sell his house to Nathaniel West, who transferred title to Joseph White just three years later. The property passed to the first David Pingree (1795–1863) in 1834, commencing nearly a century of unbroken Pingree family ownership. Finally, in 1933, the house was donated to the Essex Institute by the heirs of the second David Pingree (1841–1932), and since then has been restored, furnished with high-style regional Neoclassical furniture and decorative arts objects, and opened to the public. It may be visited a minimum of five days a week throughout the year.

Directly behind the Gardner-Pingree house in the Louise DuPont Crowninshield Gardens is the quaint Clement-Derby-Beebe summer house (c. 1800), formerly in Wakefield, Massachusetts—it is one of the finest Adamesque Federal buildings of its type in the Essex County region. Across the street at 129 Essex Street is the former Gideon Tucker house (1818–1809; plans and carvings by McIntire) (HSI) which, before its remodeling by the Father Matthew Catholic Total Abstinence Society in 1910, closely resembled the Gardner-Pingree house. Its original handsome semicircular Neoclassical entrance porch has been preserved by the Essex Institute and is attached to the rear of Plummer Hall (see A-1). In 1981/82 the Tucker house was partially restored and rehabilitated for apartments, under the direction of Newburyport architect Jonathan Woodman (Woodman Associates).

A-3 CROWNINSHIELD-BENTLEY HOUSE   c. 1727–1730, etc.
Essex Institute
126 Essex Street at Washington Square West
NR; MHL; WSHD

Built c. 1727 to 1730 ,for fish merchant and sea captain John Crowninshield and formerly located at 106 Essex Street (behind the
Hawthorne Inn), this modest, chaste, gambrel-roof wooden dwelling
epitomizes a local middle-income Georgian Colonial house. Consistent with Georgian Colonial principles, the five-bay facade is symmetrical, with three evenly spaced closed-gable dormers piercing the
front roof plane. The front central doorway (reconstruction), with
its flat Doric pilasters, transom light, and closed pediment is the
primary visual attraction on an otherwise plain clapboarded wall surface. Scholars who have studied the house believe that it may have
originated as a "half-house" (east side), was enlarged by 1761, and
was again expanded in 1794. In 1959/60 the building was stripped
of its extended modern ells, moved to the grounds of the Institute,
and meticulously restored by subscription as a memorial to preservationist Louise DuPont Crowninshield.

Although it was lived in by four generations of Crowninshields
until 1832, the house has gained its principal fame from its association with the noted clergyman, diarist, and scholar, the Reverend
William Bentley, who boarded here from 1791 and 1819 while he
was minister of the East Church. The interior woodwork is a
fascinating compendium of American classical styles of the 18th
century, from their "earliest bold beginnings," to their "mid-
century refinements," to "the final changes which form a transitional bridge to the Adamesque style of the Federal period" (Abbott

Lowell Cummings, *Antiques* 76 (October 1959): 329). Based on
documentary research, the house is furnished in a manner that por-
trays an era in Salem's history that to date has received limited attention from social and cultural historians. The interior rooms may
be seen by the public from June through October.

A-4

A-4 ANDREW-SAFFORD HOUSE   1818/19
Essex Institute
13 Washington Square West at Brown Street
HABS; NS; MHL; WSHD

Dominating the west side of Salem Common, this monumental,
three-story-plus-hipped-roof brick Neoclassical mansion is one of
the most important late Federal-era houses in New England. The
house was built in 1818/19 for John Andrew, a merchant who made
his fortune trading in Russian furs, and it is Salem's most extravagantly conceived and flamboyantly detailed early 19th-century
dwelling. The weight and mass of certain elements foreshadow the
advent of Victorian eclecticism. Commanding primary attention are
the deck and lower roof balustrades, the four massive free-standing
fluted columns on the south garden side, the elaborately executed
Corinthian-columned front entrance porch with balustrade, and the
elliptical-arched Palladian window above, resembling that of the
Dodge-Shreve house (see E-18) at 29 Chestnut Street. Based on

stylistic similarities, Gerald W.R. Ward (*The Andrew-Safford House*, pp. 14–16) has speculated that David Lord (1783–1845), the documented builder of the Dodge-Shreve, may also have constructed the Andrew-Safford house. Lord's close associate, the master mason David Robbins, may also have had a hand in the building project. The serenely beautiful interior moldings and other woodwork of the house bear the mark of carver Joseph True (1785–1873), an apprentice in his youth to Samuel McIntire.

In 1860 the house left the possession of the Andrew family and for a decade was occupied by the Smith and Creamer families. It was then purchased by James O. Safford, a prominent Salem leather dealer, and remained in his family until it was acquired by the Essex Institute in 1947. Presently the house is the home of the director of the Institute and his family and is open to visitors on a limited schedule. The main building is supplemented by a south garden (with gazebo), and a north side stable which together create an imposing horizontal composition that has no equal in Salem. The Andrew-Safford house is a dramatic "product of . . . [an] era of building made possible by Salem's success in commercial ventures" (Ward, p. 13).

A-5

A-5 JOHN WARD HOUSE   After 1684, etc.
Essex Institute
Brown Street opposite Howard
NHL; NR; MHL; WSHD

The John Ward house is one of New England's finest wood-frame-and-clapboard 17th-century dwellings, and it has received extensive exposure in books, pamphlets, and articles in the field of American architectural and social history. Originally situated at 38 St. Peter Street, this asymmetrical dark-stained and gabled Elizabethan building dates from no earlier than December 1684, when the land on which it initially stood was acquired by John Ward, a local currier. Soon thereafter he built a one-room-plan house (the parlor and chamber above, the large chimney, and the porch and stairway), the south (left) half of the present structure. This first-phase dwelling possessed an overhang (without drops) both on the front and south end, an unusual feature for its day. Under a steep-pitched roof, the attic space was expanded and illuminated by a wide cross gable (now restored) on the front facade. Architectural historian Hugh Morrison believed that in this form the house strongly resembled the Hooper-Hathaway house (c. 1682, etc.) (see B-15) at its earliest stage.

By the time John Ward's estate was probated in 1732, the house had been enlarged by the addition of a one-room plan (with second cross gable) on the north (right), and a rear leanto. Structural evidence and old photographs show that a wing was added to the right end during the 19th century but was removed by 1905. After many years as a bakery and tenement, the building was acquired by the Essex Institute in 1910. Over the ensuing two years, it was moved to its present site and restored under the supervision of historian and preservationist George Francis Dow. It is one of the first restorations of its kind in the United States.

In the two front first-floor rooms of the Ward house, one may observe Dow's interpretation of 17th-century New England architecture, furnishings, and domestic life. The leanto contains a later apothecary's shop, a weaving room, and a small cent shop. When viewed on the exterior, the entire structure clearly demonstrates the builder's subconscious recollections of "the moving surfaces and shifting accents, the dynamic silhouettes and vertical aspirations of Gothic England" (Morrison, *Early American Architecture*, p. 64). The public may visit the interior from June through October.

Adjacent to the house on Institute grounds are the Lye-Tapley shoe shop (c. 1830, originally in Lynn, Massachusetts), and a small pitched-roof structure containing the frame of Salem's first Quaker meetinghouse, c. 1688.

A-6   IVES-WEBB HOUSE   1855/56
18 Brown Street opposite Liberty
NR

The wooden building at 18 Brown Street, erected for Stephen B.
Ives in 1855/56, is one of Salem's grandest and most ornate Italian
Revival houses. Two-and-one-half stories with a medium pitched
roof, it exhibits smooth, rusticated wall surfaces, projecting eaves,
paired, scrolled cornice brackets, segmental-arch roof dormers,
varied window trim (flat hoods with side brackets, hood molds with
corbel stops, and segmental-arch hoods with drop moldings), and a
side entrance porch with arched openings, square columns, and
fancy, curvilinear brackets. The overall composition is an asymmetrical balancing of forms resulting in a picturesque appearance.
The original low cast-iron fence survives along the front sidewalk.
After Ives owned the house, Capt. Stephen Webb lived here; in
this century, the Salem Young Women's Association was head-
quartered here until it was disbanded in 1980.

   Down Brown Street toward Salem Common at number 8 is the
Howard-Downing house (NR; HSI), a three-story brick building with
one narrow end facing forward. The cornice consists of molded
bricks, and, curiously, there are no lintels above the windows.
According to tax records this dwelling was built c. 1808, but the
off-center, recessed front doorway, with its Ionic pilasters and flat,
corniced lintel, is clearly a later Greek Revival modification. This
doorway is one of the best articulated for its period in Salem.

A-7

A-7 EAST CHURCH (Salem Witch Museum) 1844–1846
19½ Washington Square North at Brown Street
NR; WSHD

This fine brownstone-and-brick Gothic Revival structure was erected between 1844 and 1846 for the East Church (organized 1718), the oldest branch of the First Church of Salem. Local historians have long differed as to who drew the plans for this imaginatively conceived building. There is no question, however, based on East Church records at the Essex Institute, that the design should be credited to Minard Lafever (1798–1854), a nationally renowned New York City architect known primarily for his Gothic Revival churches but also for his work in the Greek, Egyptian, and Italian Renaissance Revival styles. Lafever also made his mark as the author of several highly influential architectural handbooks, the best known being *The Modern Builders' Guide* (1833) and *The Beauties of Modern Architecture* (1835). The masons for the East Church were Henry Russell and Benjamin R. White, and the head carpenter was William Lummus.

The attribution of the East Church to Lafever represents an exciting research discovery. His recently published biography (Jacob Landy, *The Architecture of Minard Lafever*, 1970) fails to mention the building but does describe and illustrate three others—the First Baptist Church (1841/42), New York; the Pierpont Street Baptist Church (1843/44), Brooklyn; and the Church of the Saviour

(1842–1844), Brooklyn—which are similar and were built about the same time. In each case a rich, broad, crenelated brownstone facade is broken by three pointed-arch entrances and a large, central, traceried, pointed-arch window flanked by two smaller windows of the same type. In the East Church facade, multistage octagonal towers, cut down from their original heights c. 1925, are the chief visual reference points. Other evidences of the Gothic may be seen in the corner buttresses topped by battlements, crenelated belt courses, and smaller pointed-arch windows. Serious fires damaged the building in 1902 and in 1969 (when it housed the Salem Auto Museum), but since 1972, with its interior entirely rebuilt, it has been the home of the Salem Witch Museum.

Just to the west (left) of the East Church on Kimball Court are two plain but noteworthy gambrel-roof wooden houses—at number 4, the Asa Wiggins house (formerly at 29 St. Peter Street) (by 1836) (HSI), and the John Crowninshield house (formerly at 14 Brown Street) (c. 1755) (HSI), the birthplace in 1773 of the famed mathematician and navigational scholar, Nathaniel Bowditch.

A-8

A-8 NATHANIEL WESTON HOUSE   1837/38
21 Washington Square North at Williams Street
NR; WSHD

Somewhat overshadowed by the flamboyant East Church (see A-7) just to the west (left), this simple but strongly stated Greek Revival wooden dwelling was erected for merchant Nathaniel Weston in

1837/38. Two stories under a pitched roof, this house departs from the customary Greek temple form with a long side wall instead of a narrow gable end serving as the principal street facade. This shingled facade displays five bays in a perfectly balanced arrangement, and is enframed by a plain frieze, wide corner boards, and a high granite block foundation. A typical recessed entrance, positioned in the center and facing Salem Common, contains a doorway with transom and side lights. The trabeated entrance surround with its pronounced cornice is similarly characteristic of the Greek mode. Other details of interest are the ornate snowrail at the edge of the front roof plane, and the decorated metal drainpipes attached by scrolls to the facade corner boards.

Two streets to the east (right) at 5 Oliver is another wooden Greek Revival dwelling (NR) of the same type as the Weston house, but slightly more elaborate. Erected for bank cashier Nathaniel B. Perkins c. 1847, it features molded window frames, trapezoidal window lintels (second story), a gouged belt course, and a lovely recessed front doorway framed by sets of paired Ionic columns and surmounted by a heavy protruding cornice with modillions. This doorway is a late Colonial Revival modification made c. 1976.

A-9

A-9 FORRESTER-PEABODY HOUSE   1818/19
29 Washington Square North at Mall Street
HABS; NR; WSHD

Greatly admired by the Reverend William Bentley (see his *Diary* . . ., vol. 4, pp. 53, 624; 3 July and 21 October 1818), this tall, three-story, Flemish-bond brick residence is the most ornate and ostentatious of the Federal mansions bordering the north side of Salem Common. Erected in 1818/19 for John Forrester, the son of merchant Simon Forrester (see B-6), the building occupies the site of the Mason house (see D-3), now at 91-93 Federal Street. The Forrester family lived at number 29 until 1834 when the property was bought by Col. George Peabody, the son of Capt. Joseph Peabody. Peabody remained here until 1892, entertaining such notables as Longfellow, Lowell, and Agassiz. Later the building accommodated the Salem Club, a defunct men's social organization, and the Bertram Home for Aged Men, which is still there today.

Typical of Salem residences of its period and type, the Forrester-Peabody house is protected by a medium hipped roof surmounted by a wooden balustrade and pierced by towering brick chimneys. The windows of the structure are capped by handsome splayed lintels with molded and beaded keystones as in the White-Lord (see A-10) and the White-Silsbee/Hodges-Mott (see A-11) houses nearby. The most beautifully articulated elements of the house, however, are the molded and beaded cornice with curved profile modillions and the rectangular front porch supported by four Corinthian columns which shields a magnificent doorway. The Corinthian motif is repeated in narrow flanking pilasters of the doorway. While he owned the house, George Peabody added the one-story ballroom wing on the east side, and the three-story bay in the large north ell. Other modifications have since been made to the house and to the two-story carriagehouse (1818/19) behind it. Still intact is the original ironwork of the front fence, porch balustrade and stair rails, and ballroom balcony—this is among the finest fabricated for an early 19th-century Salem house.

A-10

A-10   WHITE-LORD HOUSE   c. 1811
31 Washington Square North at Oliver Street
NR; WSHD

Another of Salem's magnificent Federal-period brick mansions, this
three-story-plus-hipped-roof structure was erected for Stephen White
c. 1811. The contractor was Joshua Upham (1784–1858) who was
responsible for the construction of several other local buildings of
the same era. This handsome and dignified dwelling was the home
of merchant John W. Rogers from 1831 to 1844, and merchant
Thomas P. Pingree from 1844 to 1858. For the next ninety years,
until 1948, members of the Lord family occupied the house. President Monroe and Sen. Daniel Webster were both entertained here.

On its exterior the White-Lord house is little changed from its
original appearance but for the substitution of Victorian 2/2 double
sash windows for the traditional 6/6 windows, probably by the
Lords. Like number 35 (see A-11), the building has an irregular
floor plan created by the presence of a northeast corner ell, the east
wall of which is flush with Oliver Street. Particularly lovely is the
broad front doorway shielded by a rectàngular porch canopy supported by slender Corinthian columns and embellished by a wooden
balustrade trimmed with unusual flame-like finials. Facing Salem
Common in the protruding jog of the ell is a beautifully articulated
narrow entrance flanked by engaged Tuscan Doric columns and
capped by a semicircular fanlight set under a broken pediment.
Other decoration includes a roof-top balustrade and a molded cornice with pronounced brick modillions. The front window lintels
are splayed with molded and beaded keystones. Behind the house is

a rectangular brick carriagehouse with a clock set into the arch above the main doors.

A-11 WHITE-SILSBEE/HODGES-MOTT   c. 1811/12; 1840/41
DOUBLE HOUSE
33-35 Washington Square North between Oliver and Winter streets
NR; WSHD

Erected c. 1811/12 and 1840/41, the White-Silsbee/Hodges-Mott double house has long interested students of architecture because of its irregular massing and fine Federal decorative detail. Situated on an odd-shaped corner lot, this rambling three-story brick structure consists of two separate but adjoining residences.

The west (left) and oldest of the dwellings at number 33 (formerly 2 Oliver Street) was built for Joseph White, Jr., the brother of Stephen White. Documents tell us that the contractor was Joshua Upham (1784–1858), also the builder of Stephen's house (c. 1811) (see A-10) next door. After Joseph's death in 1816, his wife Eliza remained here until 1831, when the property was sold to the Silsbees, who held title to 1880. For a time the house served as a parsonage for the Tabernacle Church, but then in 1924 passed to the Clarks who owned it until 1969. L-shaped in plan, the house features tall chimneys above a low hipped roof, a cornice with ball molding, stone splayed window lintels with beaded keystones, and a flat-roofed entrance porch with a plain entablature and Ionic columns. Above the porch is a full-length window seldom seen in a house of this period.

The east (right) house at number 35 was built for the Misses Hannah and Betsy Hodges c. 1840/41. Hannah acquired the house outright in 1851, and after her death it was purchased by John N. Mott in 1871. The Motts retained ownership until 1924 at which time it (along with number 33) was bought by the Clarks, the owners until 1969. Rectangular in plan, this dwelling possesses the same general embellishment as number 35, including the main south doorway and porch, save for the reproduction balustrade. The off-center placement of the doorway gives the Salem Common side of the entire structure a balanced, unified appearance. In the yard behind is a two-story, hipped-roof brick carriagehouse which was probably raised at the same time as number 33.

A-12

A-12 JOSEPH STORY HOUSE   1811
26 Winter Street facing Washington Square North
NHL; NR; WSHD

This large, somewhat modified Federal-period dwelling was erected in 1811 for Judge Joseph Story, the highly esteemed United States congressman, associate justice of the United States Supreme Court, and a founder of the Harvard Law School where he became the first Dane Professor. Steeped in history, the house was the scene of receptions for many dignitaries, including President James Monroe in 1817 and the Marquis de Lafayette in 1824. In 1819 it was the birthplace of Judge Story's son, William Wetmore Story, the noted poet and sculptor. On the north side of the property, Judge Story formerly maintained offices from which he established a broad reputation as a great jurist, legal writer, and teacher.

The Story house is comparable in size, scale, and style to the other brick Federal mansions around Salem Common. Constructed by the talented Joshua Upham (1784–1858), the builder of the neighboring White-Lord (see A-10) and White-Silsbee/Hodges-Mott (see A-11) houses, this three-story-plus-hipped-roof residence is rectangular, with its narrow east end facing Winter Street, and a two-stage wing on the opposite west end. In 1901 the present deep Colonial Revival entrance porch was added by then owner George C. Vaughn, replacing the original porch which had previously been removed. Vaughn was also responsible for the balustraded first-story bay window, and the balustraded wing section. The handsome modillioned cornice and splayed stone window lintels are original design features.

A-13

A-13 CHARLES H. ODELL HOUSE
24½ Winter Street
NR: HSI; WSHD

1887

Tucked away behind the historic Story residence (see above), the Charles H. Odell house is a larger though less pure and exuberant example of the Queen Anne style than the Fairfield house (see A-27) on Forrester Street. Nonetheless, it should not be ignored.

Built in 1887 for Odell, a local auctioneer and real estate and insurance agent, this rambling, two-story-plus-hipped-roof wooden
dwelling displays an irregular plan, varied gables, bays, a paneled
chimney, an open veranda, textured wall surfaces, and diverse window shapes and sizes, all of which are associated with Queen Anne
architecture. Signs of the then-popular Eastlake decorative influence
are evident in the base latticework and turned spindles, posts, and
balusters of the front porch, and the scrolled support brackets of the
dormers and first-floor corner window. The form and elements of
the building suggest a handmade look, and represent a reaction
against the mechanization and standardization of the new American
industrial revolution.

A-14

A-14 PAYSON-FETTYPLACE HOUSE   c. 1845
16 Winter Street
NR; HSI

This pleasantly scaled two-story wooden house with ell, erected
c. 1845 for bank cashier Edward H. Payson, is one of the best local
examples of vernacular Greek Revival architecture. With one gable
end facing the street in imitation of the Greek temple form, the
building is embellished by a closed gable pediment with boxed cornices, a thick, plain entablature, and four Doric pilasters on the
front matched-board facade. Breaking the predominance of these
Greek elements, and reflecting the influence of a concurrent style—
the Italian Revival—are a front off-center, segmental-arch doorway,

and a gable segmental-arch window. The house was occupied by the Fettyplace family from 1850 until 1911.

On the opposite side of Winter Street at number 11 is a two-story wooden dwelling (NR) built c. 1850 for Ephraim Brown, Jr. in the Italian Revival vernacular. Displayed on the symmetrical, matched-board facade are numerous features characteristic of this style—richly molded window frames; first-story flat window caps with brackets; a modillioned porch canopy with large side brackets; a second-story bay window; a modillioned cornice with paired brackets; and a center gable incorporating a small round-arched window.

A-15

A-15 KINSMAN-COLE HOUSE
2 Winter Street at Bridge
NR

c. 1870/71

Situated on the site of the old Howard house, this two-story rectangular brick Italian Revival dwelling was built c. 1870/71 for John Kinsman, the superintendent and collector of the Salem and Danvers Aqueduct Company. Kinsman and his heirs occupied the house until 1901, at which time the Cole family commenced a long period of ownership lasting to 1950. Capped by a truncated hipped roof broken by closed gable dormers, the building possesses unusually delicate second-story window hood molds with medallions and brackets carved from brownstone. On the first-story level the windows are bounded by molded brownstone frames and are topped by

bracketed cornice heads. A segmental-arch doorway is protected by
a square-columned porch featuring carved curvilinear modillions
which echo the shape of the main roof cornice modillions. In the
Kinsman-Cole house, light and heavy elements are successfully combined, and are crisply set off against ample, uniform wall surfaces.
Virtually all embellishment is concentrated on the front facade to
produce maximum visual effect, noticeable from the east end of
Bridge Street.

A-16

A-16 CAPTAIN ISAAC SMITH HOUSE   1800
121 Bridge Street at Pleasant and Webb
HSI

The lot on the corner of Bridge and Pleasant streets was an advantageous location for Capt. Isaac Smith to have his new "Mansion
House" erected in 1800. Smith had purchased the land in 1798
from Cornelius and Grace Bartlett. When he died just two years
after occupying this dwelling, it passed to his wife, Elizabeth. After
1804 a series of other owners followed, none of whom held title for
very long, with the exception of the Hodgkins family, which had
partial and then full stake in the property between 1851 and 1921.
    The Smith house is a conventional three-story, hipped-roof, rec-
tangular wooden structure, largely with Federal-period adornment.
The primary visual feature is a front enclosed entrance porch with a

closed-pediment roof gable, a molded entablature with a narrow dentil strip, and six fluted Doric pilasters. On the west side of the building is a plain Federal doorway with a flat cornice, while on the east wall there is a Greek Revival open entrance porch and doorway with corner blocks. Attached to the rear of the house is a pitched-roof ell.

Just beyond the intersection of Bridge and Pleasant streets is Webb Street, on the west side of which (at number 121) is the former Hose No. 2 firehouse (c. 1855). A two-story, pitched-roof wooden structure, it has lost some of its original Italian Revival features (open pyramidal-roof belfry; paneled front sliding doors), but has retained its paired cornice brackets and round and segmental-arch windows with hood molds.

A-17

A-17 THOMAS MARCH WOODBRIDGE HOUSE   1809/10
48 Bridge Street at March
NR

An examination of local tax records for the period reveals that this square, three-story, brick Federal mansion, so typical of Salem, was built in 1809/10 on two parcels of land acquired in 1801 and 1805 by tannery owner Thomas March Woodbridge and his wife, Mary. Somewhat of a landmark in its area because of its isolation from similar local buildings (cf. Washington Square and Chestnut Street), the house has traditionally been ascribed to Samuel McIntire (1757–1811) owing to the "character and details of the carved interior finish" (Fiske Kimball, *Mr. Samuel McIntire, Carver . . .*, p. 126), and to its marked similarity to his other late, austere designs. After Woodbridge's death in 1822, the building had a long succession of owners until its acquisition in 1939 by the Society for the Preservation of New England Antiquities (Boston), which maintained it for a time. In 1955 it was bought by its present occupants, the Children's Friend and Family Service Society of the North Shore, Inc., which cares for it through a special committee known as the "Preservers of Woodbridge House." Though it lacks its original Doric balustraded front entrance porch, the Woodbridge house is largely intact on its exterior, displaying identical, delicately articulated, broken pediment east and west doorways (from William Pain's *The Practical House Carpenter . . .*, London, 1794), and a boldly stated, modillioned cornice. Most of the original McIntire interior woodwork has also survived.

A-18

A-18   COOK-KIMBALL HOUSE   c. 1807–1808
14 Pickman Street
NR; HSI

This square, three-story-plus-hipped-roof brick Federal house is of the type present on Chestnut Street and Washington Square North. Salem tax records reveal that the building was erected c. 1807–1808 for Robert Cook, Jr., a local painter. Upon his death in 1815 the property continued in the Cook family until 1839, when his daughter sold it to James S. Kimball, a sea captain. Kimball's daughter, Sarah, lived here until her death in 1923.

On the basis largely of style, Fiske Kimball (*Mr. Samuel McIntire, Carver* . . ., pp. 52, 53, 135) attributed the exterior and interior carving of the house to Samuel Field McIntire (1780–1819). The most outstanding exterior feature is the slightly recessed front doorway with sidelights ornamented by delicately carved Adamesque husks and ribbons and protected by an Ionic columned rectangular porch with a modillioned cornice. Above is a modillioned roof cornice; the first- and second-story window lintels are of reeded stone. On the interior are a hung spiral staircase and impressive fireplace carvings.

Robert Cook later constructed the three-story, hipped-roof wooden house (1813–15) (NR) next door (west) at number 12. Fiske Kimball also attributed the embellishment of this building to Samuel Field McIntire. After Cook's death the house passed successively to Nathaniel Weston, John Bertram, and Charles Millet. The house has been altered, but still displays on its front facade an attractive doorway (below a Victorian canopy) with sidelights, a semicircular fanlight, and fluted pilasters on either side.

Two other brick Federal residences on Pickman Street are of the same period and type as the Cook-Kimball house. To the east (left) at number 16 is a double house (NR) (photo, left) with two fanlighted entrances and "plank frame" windows; it was built in 1816/17 as a real estate venture by master builder David Lord. Across the street at number 17 is a dwelling (before 1810) (NR) with bold belt courses, "plank frame" windows, and a reconstructed arched front doorway surround with pilasters—this building formerly served as the headquarters of the Mack Industrial School for girls which was disbanded in the 1920s.

A-19

A-19 WILLIAM B. PARKER HOUSE

c. 1851/52

33 Pleasant Street
NR

The center building in a row of three striking wooden mid-
Victorian eclectic residences, this two-story-plus-pitched-roof Italian
Revival dwelling was erected for sea captain and merchant William
B. Parker c. 1851/52. It was owned by his heirs until the late
1920s. Rising above a high granite foundation is a tall, formal,
perfectly balanced facade with a slightly projecting central pavilion
topped by a closed gable pediment. Projecting from this pavilion is
a rectangular entrance porch exhibiting a plain entablature with a
modillioned cornice supported by round, fluted Doric columns.
Modillions are also present in the flat entablature caps of the first-
story windows, and in the main roof and pavilion raking cornices.
The repetitious use of this motif, along with the extensive employ-
ment of corner quoins serves to unify the many classical elements of
the building.

The two-story, truncated mansard-roof house to the right (35
Pleasant) is believed to have been constructed for clothing manufacturer James Trefren c. 1870, and was owned by banker Charles
Odell from 1879 to 1910. In 1851/52 the large, boldly articulated
square dwelling to the left (31 Pleasant) was constructed for naval
captain Charles Millett. Shoe dealer Daniel A. Varney and his heirs
held title to the propety from 1878 until World War I. The heavily

detailed front porch canopy and full-length square bay windows are unusual in a Salem house of the early fifties.

A-20

A-20 ROBERTS-SHEPARD-THORNDIKE DOUBLE HOUSE

c. 1830

39-41 Washington Square North at Winter Street
NR; WSHD

The land upon which this tall, three-story brick double house stands was acquired by William Roberts, a local master mason, in 1825. Approximately five years later, as a speculative venture, he completed the construction of numbers 39-41 Washington Square North, apparently with the intention of developing a row of identical, attached houses continuing eastward to Pleasant Street. This project was never completed. In 1830 number 39 was conveyed to Stephen Shepard, and then changed hands twice prior to 1848 when it was acquired by Francis Brown, whose family owned it until 1944. Number 41 was sold to Larkin Thorndike, also in 1830, and remained in his family until 1870, when the Willard Browns bought it.

Bearing a close similarity to "The Studio" double house (c. 1826–27) (See E-2) at 2-4 Chestnut Street, the Roberts-Shepard-Thorndike double house is a transitional work of architecture, largely Federal-style in form and details, but also reflecting the impact of the new Greek Revival. Both halves of the building have recessed, arched entrance portals, with a fanlight and sidelights around each doorway, and full-length French windows with cast-iron balconies (a popular Greek Revival feature) on the first-story level. The building is set on a high stone foundation which encloses a windowed half-basement. White-painted rectangular window lintels and sills provide repetitive decorative accents on the front facade and the parapeted end walls. Attached to the rear of each half is a two-story brick service ell.

A-21

A-21 NATHANIEL SILSBEE HOUSE

1818/19

94 Washington Square East at Briggs Street
NR; HSI

This unusual, much altered, three-story brick mansion was erected in 1818/19 for Nathaniel Silsbee, a prosperous Salem shipmaster and later U.S. senator from Massachusetts. Famous visitors to the house included Daniel Webster, James Monroe, and Henry Clay. In planning his place of residence, Silsbee dreamed of exceeding in size and grandeur the other great Washington Square mansions built for John Forrester (see A-9) and John Andrew (see A-4) at about the same time. Because of the extensive renovations made in the Italian Revival style by Nathaniel Silsbee, Jr. when he moved into the building c. 1850, it is difficult to tell what the house, especially the front facade, looked like when it was constructed. Thanks to Bentley's diary and other sources, however, we do know that there was a modified Palladian window (like that of the Andrew-Safford house) over the front central doorway, which probably was protected by a rectangular, Federal-style columned porch. The Federal south side entrance has survived, as have the rectangular, reeded lintels over the side wall windows. The c. 1850 facade changes produced the varied Italianate window treatment and square-columned, balustraded porch that one may view today. From 1866 to 1907 the Kimball family owned the house, at which time the Knights of Columbus, the current occupants, purchased the property. Modern additions have been made to the rear.

The white-painted, pitched-roof Greek Revival house (NR) to the north (left, corner of Andrew Street) at number 96 was built in 1832 for Nathaniel Silsbee, Jr., an early mayor of Salem, and he lived here before occupying his father's house (see above). Typical Greek Revival details include the front facade matched boarding, the long French windows with cast-iron balustrade, and the closed gable pediment with lunette.

A-22

A-22 BALDWIN-LYMAN HOUSE

92 Washington Square East at Briggs Street
HABS; NR

1809–1812

Based on style characteristics, architectural historian Fiske Kimball (*Mr. Samuel McIntire, Carver . . .*, p. 127) believed that Samuel McIntire (1757–1811) "had some connection" with the design and construction of this fine three-story brick Federal mansion. It stands on the site of Thomas Briggs's house and ropewalk, which once ran all the way to Collins Cove. According to valuation books, the building date may be securely fixed at 1809, with finishing work continuing after McIntire's death. The first owner of the house was Jabez Baldwin, a wealthy Salem watchmaker and jeweler and a member of the firm of Baldwin and Jones. In 1881 this substantial residence was willed by Baldwin's daughter to her cousin, Dr. Jabez B. Lyman, and it remained in the Lyman family until 1920.

In Kimball's words, the exterior design of the Baldwin-Lyman house "conforms to that of the McIntire houses of his late period, such as the [Thomas March] Woodbridge house" (see A-17). The Corinthian-columned porch (two columns are replacements) resembles McIntire's other local work, but the interior embellishment was largely executed by his son, Samuel Field McIntire (1780–1819), and others. The house is further impressive for its five, tall, bevel-capped chimneys, its bold, modillioned cornices, and its splayed window lintels with double keystones. The north-and-south-side Italianate porches with their second-story bay windows are the only obvious changes in the original building.

A-23

A-23 DR. HARDY PHIPPEN HOUSE

84 Washington Square East
NR

1900

The grand, imaginatively conceived Colonial Revival mansion built in 1900 for Dr. Hardy Phippen was based on plans by an as yet unidentified architect. It is the only house of its period and style overlooking Salem Common. This two-story, hipped-roof wooden dwelling is on the site of Joseph Vincent's former house and ropewalk, which once extended to Collins Cove. It served as a single-family residence until 1953, when it was converted to a funeral parlor.

Derived from the work of Charles Bulfinch and Samuel McIntire, the Phippen house brings together a variety of Georgian Colonial and Federal elements. Though there are differences in scale and decoration, the form of the facade is obviously based on that of McIntire's Assembly House (see D-15) at 138 Federal Street. The semielliptical relieving arches on the first story are borrowed directly from Bulfinch's brick architecture. Other features deserving notice are the ornate cornice with mutules, the full Doric frieze, the wide belt course, the first-story French windows with cast iron balconies, the rectangular front porch with tapered Ionic columns, and the pedimented side doorway flanked by Ionic pilasters. An elegant McIntiresque wooden fence formerly stood in front of the house.

A-24

A-24 FRANCIS BOARDMAN HOUSE   1782–1789, etc.
82 Washington Square East at Boardman Street
HABS; NR
HOSMER-TOWNSEND-WATERS HOUSE   1795
80 Washington Square East at Boardman Street
NR; WSHD

Begun for Capt. Francis Boardman in 1782, but not completed until 1789, the three-story, hipped-roof, wooden residence at 82 Washington Square East (photo, left) was the first great mansion on Salem Common and was formerly one of the most elegant architectural showpieces in Salem. Originally the building possessed a delicate upper roof balustrade, bold corner quoins, a distinguished columned front porch, and a beautifully articulated closed south-side porch with details like those on the west-side porch of the Peirce-Nichols house (see D-1) at 80 Federal Street. These fine features, however, have been lost to renovations made since the late 19th century, and the current front porch and upper bay window are turn-of-the-century Victorian eclectic additions. Building accounts in the Essex Institute archives refer to the brothers Joseph and Samuel McIntire, thereby connecting them with the house and suggesting that Samuel may have conceived the design (see Fiske Kimball, *Mr. Samuel McIntire, Carver* . . ., p. 59). This possibility is given further credence by the similarity of certain details to those present in other known McIntire houses of the period. More recent owners include members of the Silsbee and Bowdoin families.

Across Boardman Street at 80 Washington Square East is the square, three-story, central-chimney dwelling (photo, right) erected for Captain Joseph Hosmer in 1795. Unlike its predecessor next door, it displays most of its original exterior embellishment, highlighted by a well-scaled, off-center Doric doorway on the west facade and a picturesque closed Doric entrance porch on the east garden side. The designer/builder of this unusual house remains unknown, but Kimball (*Mr. Samuel McIntire, Carver* . . ., p. 50) does ascribe to Samuel McIntire an interior fireplace surround, which he believed McIntire carved and installed in c. 1807 when Samuel Archer owned the property. Archer also is supposed to have added the long east ell running flush with Boardman Street. The house was later the home of Capt. Penn Townsend, Judge Joseph G. Waters, and Henry FitzGilbert Waters, the noted genealogist.

A-25 BOARDMAN STREET HOUSES
Between Washington Square East and Webb Street

1879–1890, etc.

To the east of Salem Common, extending from Washington Square East to Webb Street, are several parallel streets, one of which, Boardman Street, was almost entirely developed between 1879 (when it was laid out) and 1890. It is one of Salem's most fascinating residential neighborhoods. Lining the north and south sides for the full length of the street are a strikingly uniform collection of late Victorian eclectic single and two-family wooden houses which have more architectural significance as a group than individually. Together they form a handsome streetscape fostered by similarity in height, mass, shape, roof configuration, materials, and fenestration. These "elements of repetition and rhythm" (*The Salem Handbook* . . ., p. 54) combine to create an environment in which the individuality of small details (architectural elements, colors, planting, fences, etc.) stands out. According to the Salem directories and building permits, the south side of the street was almost completely occupied by 1884, while the north side was sparsely settled until 1888, when a flurry of building activity quickly filled up available lots. For the most part, these stylistically diverse houses were built by individual landholders, although there were some instances of real estate speculation when two or more buildings were financed by one investor.

A-26

A-26 WEBB-BRIGGS-WHIPPLE HOUSE
1 Forrester Street at Washington Square East
NR; WSHD

1770 or before

The origins of this quaint three-story, central-chimney wooden dwelling are somewhat shrouded in mystery. Believed to be the oldest surviving residence on Salem Common, it may contain structural members dating from the late 17th or early 18th century. Records show that the house plot was acquired by Capt. Benjamin Ives in 1720, and was conveyed to Capt. Samuel Webb in 1767. Most sources for the house claim that it was built in 1770, an assertion supported by its form, plan, and decorative detail. Enos Briggs, the famed master shipbuilder (the second *Grand Turk* and the frigate *Essex*), lived here from 1808 until his death in 1819. In 1879 the house was sold to Stephen Whipple, a dealer in gum copal, and his descendants have occupied it ever since. Over the years the house has retained most of its pre-1800 features including the "penny shop" in the northwest corner, and the enclosed pedimented entrance porch in the center of the five-bay south facade. The upper-story windows contain unusual nine-pane solid sashes.

Behind the Webb-Briggs-Whipple house at 78 Washington Square East is a modified, two-story, mid-Victorian eclectic dwelling, (NR; WSHD) built for Gilbert G. Newhall in 1846/47 from drawings by the noted Boston architect Gridley J.F. Bryant (1816–1899), designer of other Salem buildings. Opposite the Webb-Briggs-Whipple house at 2-4 Forrester Street is a large, wooden, late-Victorian eclectic double house (NR) which tax records and city directories tell us was constructed c. 1872/73 for occupancy by Charles H. Bates and Emery K. Benson. Its ornate and elegant details include Italianate paired cornice brackets, Gothic Revival drop pendants, a variety of window frame treatments, and heavily framed, recessed and paired front entrances.

A-27

A-27   CHARLES E. FAIRFIELD HOUSE   c. 1891–92
9 Forrester Street
NR

Certainly the most provocative Victorian building on Forrester Street is this modest but nicely articulated single-family Queen Anne-style residence. According to Salem city directories and other documentation, it was erected c. 1891/92 for Charles E. Fairfield, clerk at the James Fairfield Lumber Company on Central Street. The Forrester family later assumed ownership of the property and retained it into this century, renting it to several tenants.

Typical of the Queen Anne style, the Fairfield house is asymmetrical in composition and is rich and varied in its decorative forms, textures, materials, and colors. Present are the characteristic conical corner tower, veranda, dissimilar wall surfaces, pedimented dormers, bays, pronounced gables, irregular-shaped and -sized windows, and high, multiple roofs intersecting at right angles. The detail is classical (e.g. columns, pilasters, cornice modillions) and small in scale, much as it is in the larger Queen Anne houses of Lafayette Street (see section F).

A-28

A-28 ST. NICHOLAS RUSSIAN ORTHODOX CHURCH

1908

64 Forrester Street at Webb

The intriguing wooden church erected for the St. Nicholas Russian Orthodox parish in Salem ranks as one of the finest Byzantine Revival ecclesiastical buildings surviving in New England. Completed in December 1908, it initially served a group of skilled leather workers from Poland and southern Russia who settled in this area to work in the leather and shoe factories of Salem and Peabody. Bishop Alexander of New York City formally dedicated the church in services held on 6 November 1910. Architecturally the building is distinguished by the five onion domes (topped by patriarchal crosses) on its main tower, side towers, and cupolas. Other interesting features are the corbel tables, ornate front entrance porch canopy, and semicircular and flat (with ears) window hood-moldings.

A-29   CLIFFORD CROWNINSHIELD HOUSE   1804–1806
74 Washington Square East at Forrester Street
HABS; NR; WSHD

Impressively sited at the southeast corner of Salem Common, this magnificent wooden, three-story, hipped-roof Federal mansion is one of a very few buildings in the city that can be securely credited to Samuel McIntire (1757–1811). According to a Crowninshield family account book (Peabody Museum of Salem), the house was erected for merchant Clifford Crowninshield at the time of his marriage. Upon his premature death in 1809, the property passed to his sister, who resided there with her husband, James Devereux, the captain of the *Franklin*, the first American vessel to trade with Japan. Subsequent owners were members of the Waters and Goodell families. In 1892 Zina Goodell moved the former north wing to the rear (thereby increasing the depth of the building) and had the entire structure relocated closer to the corner of Forrester Street.

The same account book contains several entries for work performed by McIntire which were the basis of Fiske Kimball's attribution (*Mr. Samuel McIntire, Carver . . .*, pp. 109–10) of the house to him. Also listed are several local materials suppliers and tradesmen active at the time, including William Luscomb, Joshua Ward, James Nichols, Daniel Galencia, Asa Flanders, Joseph Newhall, and Daniel Farrington. In plan, proportions, and details, the house is typical of McIntire's mid-career work, particularly its roof balustrade and semicircular and balustraded front porch, which resemble those of his Gardner-Pingree house (see A-2) at 128 Essex Street. Although it has been partially remodeled, the interior still contains a lovely spiral staircase, and exquisite mantel carving illustrating the

impact of Asher Benjamin's design books on McIntire's craftsmanship.

To the rear of the house is the original wooden hipped-roof
stable, on the north end of which is an arcaded shed, once used for
an office and shop.

A-30 DANIELS HOUSE   1667; 1756
1 Daniels Street at Essex
HABS; NR

Presently serving as a small inn and dining establishment, this
three-story, wood-frame-and-clapboard homestead was originally
built as a single-family residence by Stephen Daniels, a shipwright,
in 1667. It was later enlarged in 1756 by Daniels's great grandson,
Samuel Silsbee, and assumed its present appearance. The oldest
parts of this building are the lower two stories of the southern half,
which contain interesting interior structural timbers and finishing.
The northern half, the third floor, and the large leanto ell were
added by Silsbee, a carpenter by trade. Originally the main doorway
to the house was on the south side, but the five-bay Daniels Street
facade now has the principal entrance, protected by a reproduction
enclosed pitched-roof porch. During the 19th century the ownership
of the house was divided, and at various times members of the
Reed, Hodges, and Russell families held half interests.

The plain, two-story, pitched-roof wooden house (HSI) east on

Essex Street at number 10 was raised in 1798 for David Murphy, a ropemaker who had immigrated from Ireland. In 1808 another Irishman, James Dalrymple, a watchmaker, acquired the property and it remained in his family for the next century. This practical, well-built structure is a representative vernacular Federal-era dwelling with no overt stylistic pretense except for the enclosed, pilastered front entrance porch covered by a half-hipped roof.

A-31

A-31   SAGE-WEBB-WILKINS HOUSE   c. 1800
52 Essex Street
NR

This unusual three-story, medium-pitched-roof dwelling was built c. 1800 for Daniel Sage, a Scotsman who married into the Silsbee family. Upon Sage's death, Benjamin Webb, an Essex Street apothecary, bought the property. During most of this century it was owned by the Wilkins family. The building has attracted much local attention over the years as the only house in Salem with brick ends incorporating paired chimneys. It also features a nicely proportioned enclosed, pedimented front entrance porch with a modillioned cornice, a plain entablature, and square, fluted pilasters; in the Derby Street-Salem Common area a number of porches exist of the same type and period. The western brick end is penetrated by windows, but the eastern end has none, very likely because it is the "weather" side.

Two lots to the east (right), beyond the Gardner Maynard Jones Memorial Library (formerly the first story of the Bentley School) and behind the apartment building at number 48, is the Christopher Babbidge house (46½ Essex Street) (NR; HSI), built c. 1715 and probably before. This simple, wooden, gambrel-roof, Georgian Colonial dwelling formerly stood on the street but was moved back to its present site in 1914 when number 48 was constructed. According to Sidney Perley (*History of Salem* 2: 309–10), the house was cut in half in 1859, and only the western portion remains.

A-32

A-32 NARBONNE HOUSE

c. 1672, etc.

Salem Maritime National Historic Site
71 Essex Street
NHS; NHL; HABS; NR

Acquired in 1964 by the National Park Service, the Narbonne house is the most recent addition to the buildings comprising the Salem Maritime National Historic Site. It is one of Salem's oldest surviving dwellings and though altered somewhat from its original appearance, it is a valuable historical resource. Partially restored and unfurnished, it serves today as a "study" house reflecting late 17th- and 18th-century structural design, building practices, and interior finishing. It may be visited by special appointment.

Abbott Lowell Cummings (*Architecture in Colonial Massachusetts*, pp. 176–77) credits the building of the oldest portion of the house to Thomas Ives, a slaughterer, who was in possession of it by January 1676, "and perhaps at the time of his marriage on April 1,

1672." The facts are unclear as to the exact initial form of the house and its structural development, but it is known that as built it "consisted of a room with chamber and garret and chimney bay (left-hand portion) and an original leanto with a fireplace of unusual size and character." The one-and-one-half story, gambrel-roofed ell at the right, along with the central portion of the leanto, are believed to have been attached to the original two-story steep-pitched-roof dwelling when Capt. John Hodges owned the property between 1750 and 1780. These additions doubtless replaced older construction. The northern and southern parts of the leanto were added later. The home of fishermen, mariners, and shipwrights, the house belonged to John Andrew after 1800, and his niece, Mrs. Sarah Narbonne, later inherited it.

A-33

A-33 JOHN HODGES HOUSE   c. 1788
81 Essex Street and 1 Orange Street
HABS; NR; HSI

One of several Hodges family houses in this section of Salem, this formal, two-story-plus-gambrel-roof wooden residence adds distinction to the lower Essex Street neighborhood. Research conducted at the time it was awarded a Historic Salem marker suggests that the house was originally built c. 1788 for merchant John Hodges, who conveyed it to his son, Benjamin, a mariner, upon its completion. For much of the 19th century it was owned by members of the Hodges, Webb, and Meek families.

The Hodges house possesses the form as well as the details of a fashionable late Georgian Colonial dwelling. This is illustrated by its symmetrical facade, three evenly positioned, closed-gable dormers, corner quoins, bold modillioned cornice, and handsome front central doorway with broken pediment, semicircular fanlight, and Ionic pilasters. Originally the front lower story windows displayed cap moldings, but these have been removed. The building is roughly U-shaped, with an ell facing on Orange Street and probably dating from the time of construction, and a wing with small ell of more recent vintage on the east end.

Across Essex Street at numbers 76-78 is the Joseph Danforth house (NR; HSI), an outstanding example of a Greek Revival two-family wooden dwelling. Erected in 1832 by Danforth, a housewright, it has a symmetrical, two-story, matched-board facade broken by 6/6 double sash windows, and a central pedimented doorway with recessed entrances framed by square pilasters decorated with fretwork. The front plane of the pitched roof is penetrated by an unusual trap-door monitor, which is most common in industrial architecture of the period.

A-34

A-34 OAKES-GRAY-PERKINS HOUSE   c. 1809/10
38 Washington Square South
NR; WSHD

With one end towards the street, this rectangular, one-room-deep wooden house was erected c. 1809/10 by Joshua Oakes, a ship joiner. It is one of the best local examples of a simple, hipped-roof,

Federal-style dwelling. Among its sparse but delicate details are a narrow cornice with beaded molding and a plain side-yard entrance with sidelights and a semielliptical fanlight. The rectangular porch canopy above this entrance is held up by square incised columns, which are mid-19th century replacements of the originals. Inside is a graceful hung spiral staircase that runs to the third floor. The third story displays unusual 3/3 double sash windows. Attached to the rear is a three-story service ell in which a second entrance probably existed at one time beneath a small semicircular fanlight. Members of the Perkins family have lived in the house since 1892.

A-35

A-35   BROWN BUILDING   1808–1809
(Merchant's Building; Union Building)
2–4 Union Street and 105–107 Essex Street
NR

According to references in Rev. William Bentley's diary (see bibliography), this elongated, three-story, hipped-roof structure was constructed in 1808–1809 on land formerly owned by the Brown family. It is the oldest surviving commercial/residential brick row building in Salem and one of the first to be built locally. Over the years it has been variously referred to as the Brown, the Merchant's, and the Union building, and has housed the Merchant's Bank, William Stearns Apothecary store, other retail outlets, professional offices, and religious and educational facilities.

The Brown building has suffered from some alteration and neglect since it was built, but it is still largely intact except for the obviously modern commercial fronts on the north end. Particularly interesting is the fine masonry work, evident in the curved brick dentil cornice, the Flemish bond brick walls, the reeded brownstone belt course, the brownstone splayed and keystoned lintels, and the granite foundation steps, foundation, and sidewalk surface drains. On the long twelve-bay Union Street facade are four original narrow doorways with semicircular fanlights. The designer/builder of the row is still unknown, but considering his connection with the construction of the nearby Archer block (see A-36) and certain design similarities, Samuel McIntire (1757–1811) is a reasonable possibility.

A-36

A-36 HAWTHORNE INN (Hawthorne Hotel)   1924/25
18 Washington Square West at Essex Street
NR; WSHD

The strategic corner lot (formerly Andrews's corner) on which the Hawthorne Inn is situated has been important in the history of Salem's central business district for over 170 years. In 1809/10, the Archer block (known as the Franklin building after 1818) was constructed here under the direction of Samuel McIntire (1757–1811). From his elevation and floor plans at the Essex Institute and an engraved view, we know that this rectangular, hipped-roof brick structure accommodated retail stores, offices, and residential apartments. Damaged by fire in 1845 and again in 1859, it was finally destroyed by fire in 1860. Soon thereafter, in 1863/64, a new Franklin building was erected in the same location and served many of the same functions as its predecessor. Owned by the Salem

Marine Society (which has its headquarters today on the top of the inn), this unusual Italian Revival structure featured extraordinarily fine brickwork, especially in the arcaded first story.

The Hawthorne Hotel, as the inn was initially titled, took the place of the Franklin building in 1924/25. Funded by a $750,000 subscription raised by Salem-area residents, this impressive, U-shaped, Colonial Revival-style, brick-and-stone-trim edifice was erected by H.C. Stephens Company of New York City utilizing plans prepared by Wenham and Boston architect Philip Horton Smith (1890–1960) of the firm of Smith and Walker. Six stories tall, the inn possesses numerous typically Colonial Revival components, including a solid-wall roof balustrade, a modillioned cornice, quoined corners, splayed window lintels, recessed arched and pedimented window headings, belt courses, and modified Palladian windows.

JOSEPH WATERS house (later Bertram Home for Aged Men)
(1806/1807; greatly modified after 1929) at 114 Derby Street and
Turner. Photograph, 1891, by Frank Cousins.

B

DERBY STREET

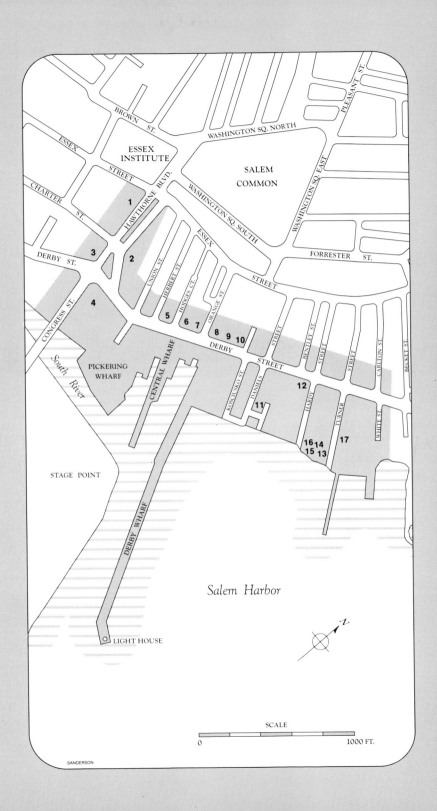

BROWN ST.

WASHINGTON SQ. NORTH

ESSEX INSTITUTE

ESSEX

STREET

SALEM COMMON

CHARTER

ST.

HAWTHORNE BLVD.

WASHINGTON SQ. SOUTH

WASHINGTON SQ. EAST

PLEASANT ST.

1

3

2

DERBY ST.

ESSEX

STREET

FORRESTER ST.

UNION ST.

HERBERT ST.

HODGES CT.

ORANGE ST.

CONGRESS ST.

4

5

6 7

8 9 10

STREET

BENTLEY ST.

CARLTON ST.

BECKET ST.

South River

PICKERING WHARF

CENTRAL WHARF

DERBY

STREET

KOSCIUSKO ST.

DANIELS ST.

HARDY ST.

TURNER ST.

WHITE ST.

12

11

STAGE POINT

16 14

15 13

17

DERBY WHARF

Salem Harbor

LIGHT HOUSE

N

SCALE

0   1000 FT.

SANDERSON

INTRODUCTION

The development of Derby Street postdates that of lower Essex Street, and many of the streets that extend east from lower Essex to the Salem harbor waterfront existed before 1762, when local historians believe that Derby was first laid out. The subsequent growth of Derby Street was closely linked to the history of the wharves nearby, particularly Union (Long) and Derby wharves. Between 1790 and the War of 1812, at the height of Salem's worldwide maritime trade activity, the street was a busy commercial and popular residential section of the town. After 1830, due to new trade restrictions and the inadequate depth of its harbor, Salem lost the bulk of its commerce to Boston, and the Derby Street area declined in economic and social significance.

In 1790, when Salem was the sixth largest town (@ 8,000 inhabitants) in the United States, much of the population had resided proximate to the one-half mile stretch of the Derby Street waterfront. Servicing the wharves reaching out into the harbor and the South River were warehouses, shops, and sail lofts interspersed with older wooden houses dating from as early as the late 1600s—the House of Seven Gables Settlement Association owns and maintains the most impressive and architecturally significant group. Many of the town's merchants, ship captains, and artisans lived along Derby Street, and on the side streets running north to lower Essex Street. As maritime prosperity increased, successful mercantile families such as the Derbys, Forresters, Crowninshields, and Wards erected splendid Georgian Colonial and Federal-style mansions, the last of which rivaled those on Chestnut Street and around Salem Common. The architectural jewel of the area was then and still is the Custom House, an imposing Adamesque Federal edifice perfectly positioned at the head of Derby Wharf; the Custom House is the centerpiece for the Salem Maritime National Historic Site.

Despite the decline of Salem's international commerce, the port remained active in the coastal trade and shipbuilding, and as late as 1836, the year that Salem was incorporated as a city, there were still over thirty wharves along the waterfront. As time passed, however, most of these disappeared or became part of land-filled tracts accommodating new industrial and commercial facilities. Pickering Wharf, the city's modern waterfront residential/commercial village, occupies a large portion of the old wharf district where the South River joins Salem harbor.

The Derby Street area has remained one of the most densely populated parts of Salem, with many older converted dwellings or newly constructed tenements and apartment buildings. The city's expanding 19th-century industries attracted a variety of immigrants, mainly Irish and Eastern European, to the area, and it continues to exhibit a rich ethnoreligious heritage.

B-1 JOSEPH FENNO HOUSES
(Woman's Friend Society)
12-14 Hawthorne Boulevard

1809-1812

According to the architectural historian Fiske Kimball, this plain, rectangular, three-story brick Federal double house was commenced in 1809 for Joseph Fenno, a local feltmaker, but was not completed until 1812. Protected by a low-hipped roof above which tall, slender brick chimneys rise, the building is conservatively adorned with a narrow roof cornice molding, and double-keyed, splayed lintels over the windows. Each side wall has a main entrance, one topped by a semicircular fanlight, and the other surmounted by a semielliptical fanlight and flanked by sidelights. Kimball believed that Samuel Field McIntire (1780–1819), Samuel's son, was responsible for the overall design and some of the interior carving (two parlor mantel-pieces) of the house (see *Mr. Samuel McIntire, Carver . . .*, pp. 135–36).

Today, under the name of "Emmerton House," the Fenno double house is used by the Woman's Friend Society (established 1876) as a home for business women and students. One half of the building was donated to the Society by Jennie Bertram Emmerton in 1884, and soon afterwards the other half was purchased and expanded by the addition of a large ell.

B-2

B-2 CHURCH OF THE IMMACULATE CONCEPTION (Roman Catholic)   1857–1864; 1880/81
15 Hawthorne Boulevard opposite Charter Street

Salem's oldest surviving Roman Catholic ecclesiastical structure, the Church of the Immaculate Conception is a rough but interesting example of Romanesque Revival-style architecture. Erected between 1857 and 1864 to replace the first Catholic church in Essex County, St. Mary's Church (c. 1821; razed, 1877) on Bridge Street, this massive pitched-roof brick edifice originally possessed a symmetrical front facade above which was positioned an hexagonal bell tower with a concave spire roof and gold cross. In 1880, while a general interior remodeling was in progress, efforts were made to repair the belfry, but these proved futile and it was replaced by the present multistage square side tower with tall spire roof. Characteristic of the Romanesque Revival, the round-arch form is present everywhere —in the linked front entrance portals, random-sized stained-glass windows, tower ventilators, and in miniature in the arcaded corbel tables under the roof gable eaves. The wall surfaces are broad and smooth, displaying painted sandstone-trim accents over the front facade doors and windows. The architect was Enoch Fuller (1828–1861), the contractors Russell and White, and the supervising carpenter Enoch P. Fuller (1803–1886) (father of the architect), all of Salem.

B-3

B-3   LYDIA E. PINKHAM MEMORIAL   1922
264 New Derby Street at Hawthorne Boulevard

The Pinkham Memorial building was erected in 1922 for Mrs. Aroline C. Gove in memory of her mother, Lydia E. Pinkham, the founder of the famed Lydia Pinkham Medicine Company of Lynn, Massachusetts. Established to serve as a baby clinic and head-quarters for health agencies, it was designed by the Boston architectural partnership of Parkman B. Haven (1858–1943) and Edward A. Hoyt (1868–1936). Covered by a gambrel slate roof, this distinctive two-story, brick-and-limestone-trim Colonial Revival edifice features parapet end walls, each with paired chimneys and a large round-headed window screened by a small balcony. The symmetrical front facade is graced by three pitched-roof wall dormers, with round-arch windows, and a heavily framed front central doorway topped by a broken segmental-arch pediment set on console brackets. Splayed limestone window lintels and rectilinear sills provide additional decorative accents.

B-4a

B-4b

B-4 PICKERING WHARF
Derby and Congress streets on the South River and Salem Harbor

1977–1980

A major part of Salem's recent urban revitalization, the $5 million Pickering Wharf waterfront development is a fascinating mixture of housing, offices, retail and restaurant space, a museum/theatre, a marina, and public walking areas. It has received national recognition from architectural critics. Prior to the creation of this village-like complex, an oil tank farm, warehouses, and other buildings occupied the five-acre site. The imaginative plan was drafted by Philip M. Briggs of the firm of ADD (Architecture Design Development) of Cambridge, Massachusetts. Derby Construction Company served as contractor.

A self-contained neighborhood, Pickering Wharf enjoys a physical separation from other areas of downtown Salem—this is announced at the main entrance by the square wooden tower bearing the development's name and logo. The area's pedestrian nature is emphasized by cobblestone pavement, brick and concrete walkways, and shops easily accessible from the sidewalks. Varied in shape and materials, the free-standing structures "suggest the distinctive quality of New England. . . . The architects refer to historical Salem with steeply pitched roofs, dormer windows, brick and clapboard siding" (*Architectural Record*, March 1980). The form and character of long-ago waterfront buildings are vividly recreated in a contemporary architectural setting.

B-5

B-5 DERBY-WARD HOUSE
27 Herbert Street at Derby
NR; DSHD

c. 1738, etc.

This substantial plain gambrel-roofed wooden residence was erected c. 1738 for Richard Derby, a prosperous sea captain and ship owner, and it was here that his distinguished sons—merchant Elias Hasket, statesman Richard, and ship captain John—were born and raised.

One of the oldest Salem dwellings of its type, the Derby-Ward house has paired interior chimneys, simple boxed roof cornices, double-sash windows (originally 18/18 pane) and returns on the gable ends. On the north side is a "Beverly jog" with a separate doorway. The central enclosed entrance porch, with its closed pediment, fluted Doric pilasters and side-wall oval windows was almost certainly added some twenty or more years after the house was built, and is nearly identical to that of the Capt. Edward Allen house (see B-12), and others in the city. After the Revolutionary War the Derbys sold the property to the Ward family, which occupied it well into the 19th century.

B-6

B-6   SIMON FORRESTER HOUSE

c. 1790/91

188 Derby Street at Hodges Court
NR; DSHD

Acquired in an unfinished state by Capt. Simon Forrester in 1791, this three-story, five-bay, hipped-roof house, while impressive in its massing and siting, has retained little of its original architectural detail. Alterations made since World War I have resulted in the removal of corner quoins, the shortening of chimneys, the elimination of molded window caps, and the substitution of 2/2 for 6/6 double-sash windows. Even more drastic has been the modification of the Roman Doric front entrance porch, from which the entablature details (triglyphs and mutules) have been stripped and the support columns replaced with what Fiske Kimball graphically referred to as "barbarous square posts" (*Mr. Samuel McIntire . . .*, p. 67).

Based on stylistic and detail similarities to the Peirce-Nichols (see D-1), Joshua Ward (see C-21), and Francis Boardman (see A-24) houses, Kimball has attributed the design of the Forrester house to Samuel McIntire (1757–1811). It is because of this attribution, and the evidence of McIntire's consummate skill in the interior woodwork, that the house deserves notice. The east parlor mantelpiece, removed c. 1895, is at the Essex Institute and is believed to be the only significant example of McIntire's carving from his early career.

B-7

B-7 BENJAMIN W. CROWNINSHIELD HOUSE   1810–1812
180 Derby Street at Orange
NR; DSHD

This chaste and commodious three-story Federal brick mansion was built between 1810 and 1812 for Benjamin W. Crowninshield, a member of a local merchant family, a U.S. congressman, and secretary of the navy under Presidents James Madison and James Monroe. In 1817 President Monroe used the house while visiting Salem. Gen. James Miller, a hero in the War of 1812, also lived here while serving as collector at the Custom House from 1825 to 1849.

Fiske Kimball has conjectured (*Mr. Samuel McIntire, Carver . . .*, p. 128) that Samuel McIntire may have planned the house just before his death in February 1811—the design and interior woodwork are reminiscent of his last residential commissions. The woodwork, though, was probably completed by his son, Samuel Field McIntire.

The most prominent features of the house are the white-painted splayed-and-reeded window lintels and the front central Doric Greek Revival porch (added after 1820) shielding a broad doorway with semielliptical fanlight and sidelights. Set in the front wall between the second and third stories is a brownstone panel bearing the inscription "Home for Aged Women presented by Robert Brookhouse in 1861"—the building serves this same purpose today. In 1906 and again in 1916 the original house was greatly expanded to the rear, but these additions nicely complement the older portion. Architect William G. Rantoul (1867–1949) drafted the plans on both occasions.

B-8

B-8 CUSTOM HOUSE

1818/19; 1853/54

Salem Maritime National Historic Site
178 Derby Street at Orange
NHS; NHL; HABS; NR; DSHD

The principal building of the Salem Maritime National Historic Site (established in 1938), the Custom House is an imposing symbol of Salem's former preeminence in world-wide maritime commerce, as well as a superlative example of American Federal public building architecture. It was here that import duties used to finance the federal government were collected. The Custom House is steeped in history and has added significance because of Nathaniel Hawthorne's presence here from 1846 to 1849 as surveyor of the port of Salem. While serving in this post, the renowned author gathered material for his greatest novel, *The Scarlet Letter*, the introduction of which eloquently describes the Custom House, its occupants, and its activities.

This gracious Flemish-bond brick structure, erected where the elegant residence of George Crowninshield once stood, is set on a high granite foundation and may be entered through a beautifully adorned front central doorway serviced by a sweeping flight of granite steps. Combining delicate restraint and rich detail in the best tradition of Salem Federal architecture are the balustraded front entrance, with its four attenuated Ionic composite columns and fully developed entablature, and the modified Palladian window above in which the porch column entablature elements are repeated. Perched high on the roof balustrade rests, in Hawthorne's words, "an enormous [gilded] specimen of the American eagle, with outspread wings, a shield before her breast, . . . a bunch of intermingled thunderbolts and barbed arrows in each claw. . . ." Surmounting the hipped roof, with its tall brick chimneys, is an octagonal Italianate cupola that dates from alterations (mostly interior) made in 1853/54. A three-story bonded warehouse ell is attached to the rear. Although the construction of the Custom House occurred several years after Samuel McIntire's death, it shows McIntire's influence, perhaps in large part because four of his contemporaries— nephew Joseph McIntire, Jr., David Lord, Joseph Edwards, and Joseph True—are known to have labored on the building. Perley Putnam (1778–1864) of Salem supervised construction. The building is open to the public all year.

Behind the Custom House is a one-story brick scale house, raised in 1829 as a storage place for weighing and measuring apparatus formerly used by custom officials. Across Derby Street is the 2,000-foot-long Derby Wharf (1760s; enlarged 1806). The small U.S. Coast Guard lighthouse at the tip was built in 1871. Just to the right of Derby Wharf is the smaller Central Wharf, constructed about 1789 and operated by Simon Forrester whose house (see B-6) overlooks it, and later owned by John Bertram. At the head of this wharf are the brick foundations of the former Forrester warehouse (before 1832), and a wooden warehouse (c. 1800), relocated from Front Street in 1977.

B-9 BENJAMIN HAWKES HOUSE

1780; 1801

Salem Maritime National Historic Site
Off Derby Street at 4 Custom House Court
NHS; NHL; HABS; NR; DSHD

Sandwiched between the Custom House (see above) and the
Richard Derby house (see below), this substantial three-story wooden
Federal-style dwelling was commenced for merchant Elias Hasket
Derby in 1780, but was left in an unfinished state when in 1782
Derby abandoned the project and purchased the Pickman house on
Washington Street. The building was described in William
Bentley's diary as "an uncomely mass" and a "monument of folly"
and sat untouched for almost twenty years, until it was acquired by
boatbuilder Benjamin Hawkes in 1801. Hawkes immediately under-
took major renovations which produced today's structure. The
house was reduced in size, the fenestration and roof profile changed,
tall brick chimneys added, and the original cupola replaced by a
balustraded roof deck. Simultaneously the floor plan was modified to
accommodate two families. The handsome east and west enclosed
entrance porches, with their closed pediment roofs, paired Doric
pilasters, and side-wall oval lights, are markedly similar to that of
the Capt. Edward Allen house (see B-12).
    Documentation assembled by Fiske Kimball and National Park
Service historians suggests that the original 1780 building was
planned by Samuel McIntire—in fact, three drawings for a Derby
house "near the Wharf" are in the McIntire papers at the Essex Institute. Only in recent years has it been established that this am-

bitious first residence was not demolished, but was transformed for Hawkes's use. Whether or not McIntire had anything to do with the 1801 work, however, is still open to speculation. The property was restored in 1938/39 and 1959, and is administered by the Park Service. It is not open to the public.

B-10 DERBY HOUSE
Salem Maritime National Historic site
168 Derby Street
NHS; NHL; HABS; NR; DSHD

1761/62; 1790

The oldest surviving brick house in Salem, this outstanding two-and-one-half-story Georgian Colonial residence was erected in 1761/62 by Capt. Richard Derby for his son, the millionaire merchant Elias Hasket, and his new wife, Elizabeth Crowninshield. During the late 18th and early 19th centuries the house was owned by members of the Nichols, Prince, and Ropes families before it fell upon hard times. In 1927/28 it was rescued by the Society for the Preservation of New England Antiquities, which initiated restoration under the supervision of George Francis Dow. Additional interior restoration has been completed by the National Park Service since it assumed control of the property in 1938.

In the words of architectural historian Hugh Morison, the Derby house "bespeaks the typical Georgian house of good quality" (*Early*

American Architecture . . ., p. 500). This is reflected in every detail of the exterior—the gambrel roof with its three dormers, the paired end chimneys, the five-bay symmetrical facade, and the delicate classical doorway with its closed pediment and Tuscan Doric pilasters set against imitation jointed-stone wood trim. Additional decoration in brick is provided by the dentiled cornice, string courses, water tables, and segmental-arch window headings. Like the exterior, the interior is less pretentious than those of the largest New England Georgian houses (e.g., the Jeremiah Lee mansion, Marblehead, 1768), but does contain fine early dark-painted molded paneling, fireplace surrounds, and stairway balusters and rails. The kitchen ell dates from c. 1790. Fully furnished, the house is open for public visitation.

Just to the east (right) of the Derby house is the wood-frame-and-clapboard West India Goods Store (Rum Shop) (NHS; NHL; HABS; NR; DSHD), built before 1815 by Capt. Henry Prince and moved to this spot from the head of Derby Wharf. Also maintained by the Park Service, this simple structure typifies Salem waterfront commercial buildings of its time.

B-11

B-11 SARAH SILSBEE HOUSE   1807
35 Daniels Street
NR; HSI

This modest two-story, hipped-roof Federal residence was built in 1807 by Nathaniel, William, and Zachariah Silsbee for their mother Sarah, the widow of Capt. Nathaniel Silsbee (1748–1791), and their sister Sarah Wellman. With one end facing Daniels Street, the house is entered on its long north facade through an enclosed Roman Doric entrance porch. Striking in its proportions and details, this porch is decorated with a full entablature (containing dentil molding and mutules), and matching fluted pilasters and sidelights on either side of the doorway. Two unusual features of the house are the long south brick wall (all other walls are clapboarded) and the thick flat-board second-story window lintels. The two-story ell rising above the principal building mass was a later addition.

Next door to the north (left) at 27 Daniels Street is Capt. Silsbee's own residence (HSI), built in 1782/83 when he retired from the sea to become a ship owner and merchant. Devoid of much architectural detail, this three-story, pitched-roof dwelling is just one room deep with a two-story ell.

B-12

B-12 CAPTAIN EDWARD ALLEN HOUSE

c. 1768

125 Derby Street at Hardy
NR; DSHD

Erected in c. 1768 for Capt. Edward Allen, this three-story, hipped-roof Georgian Colonial house has passed to the present generation with few exterior modifications. In a 1788 entry in his diary, Rev. William Bentley noted that a "windy day . . . destroyed the Turret upon the house of Captain Allen"; otherwise, the building looks much as it did when it was built. Like other Salem dwellings of its period and type, the Allen house possesses corner quoins, classical cornice molding, and graduated window heights. Laid out around a large central brick chimney, the rectangular floor plan is traditional, following the pattern of 17th- and early 18th-century New England houses. A common local feature of the time is the front central enclosed entrance porch, covered by a closed molded pediment roof, and embellished with a thick entablature, fluted Doric pilasters, and side-wall oval lights. In the interior are an unusually fine stairway with carved balusters, and an Adamesque mantelpiece, installed some time after the house was completed.

B-13

B-13   HOUSE OF SEVEN GABLES   1668; c. 1678, etc.
(Turner House)
House of Seven Gables Settlement Association
54 Turner Street
NR; MHL; DSHD; HABS

Because of its association with Salem's famed author Nathaniel Hawthorne and his celebrated novel *The House of the Seven Gables*

(1851), this much-remodeled, rambling old mansion has become one of America's most cherished historic sites and hence one of the city's most popular visitor attractions. It is also an important example of 17th-century New England domestic architecture, and as such has received notice in the literature of American architectural history.

The House of Seven Gables was erected in 1668 for Capt. John Turner, a successful merchant, and remained in his family for three generations. Facing south toward the harbor, it was at first a two-room, two-and-one-half-story, central-chimney plan with two "Gothic" cross-gables in front (see portion at right of photograph), and probably looked very much like the John Ward house (see A-5) at the Essex Institute. A few years later Turner added a kitchen leanto. As his personal fortunes improved, he built (c. 1680) the south wing (single-room plan) with a separate brick chimney, as well as the two-story porch. Hiding most of the former weathered-clapboard facade, this new wing contained a second parlor, a chamber, and a garret with three gables, and displayed double casement windows and an overhang with carved pendants.

Alterations continued when John Turner, Jr. inherited the house and in 1692 added a new north kitchen ell (subsequently removed and then replaced in 1908–1910) and installed the renowned "secret staircase" in the rebuilt main chimney. In c. 1725 he introduced more new stairs, Georgian-style interior paneling, double sash windows, and boxed in the overhang of the parlor wing. During the late 18th and 19th centuries the building underwent further modifications by several owners, including the Ingersolls, Hawthorne's relatives—the front porch was rebuilt, gables were removed, and Victorian trim was added. Finally in 1908 the house was purchased by the House of Seven Gables Settlement Association's founder, Caroline O. Emmerton, who entrusted its restoration (particularly the steep-pitched gables, of which there are actually eight) to Boston architect Joseph E. Chandler (1864–1945), an early expert in historic preservation. It is open (furnished to 1840 when Hawthorne knew it) to the public, whose admission fees help support the Association's nearby settlement house (Caroline Emmerton Hall, formerly the Captain Joseph Waters house, 1806–1807, at 114 Derby Street).

Hawthorne always professed that any similarities between the picturesque dwelling at 54 Turner Street and the dwelling featured in *The House of the Seven Gables* were coincidental. The book commences, however, with a passage that unmistakenly connects the two:

> Half-way down a by-street of one of our New England towns stands a rusty wooden house, with seven acutely peaked gables, facing towards various points of the compass, and a huge, clustered chimney in the midst. . . .

B-14   RETIRE BECKET HOUSE

c. 1655

House of Seven Gables Settlement Association
54 Turner Street, adjacent to the House of Seven Gables
NR; MHL; DSHD

Named for Retire Becket, the best-known member of the distinguished shipbuilding family, this small, plain house was built c. 1655 for Retire's great-great grandfather, John Becket. Originally located on Becket Street adjacent to the family shipyard, it was acquired in 1916 by Miss Caroline O. Emmerton. In 1924, it was moved to its present site for use as a tearoom and antique shop, and more recently a gift store. Architect Joseph E. Chandler supervised the move and the subsequent restoration.

When John Becket first owned the house, it was a simple single-room plan, containing a large living room on the first floor and a large bedroom on the second, with a staircase entry at the western end. A structural overhang, still present, extended across the front exterior. It is believed that upon the marriage of Becket's son, the house was doubled in size, and acquired a central brick chimney. In 1682 a leanto was attached to the rear. Later, Retire Becket inherited the house, and after he died in 1831, it ultimately passed to two of his sisters. One of the sisters proceeded to sell her (eastern) half in 1850 to the Eastern Marine Railway Company, which promptly demolished it and the chimney. The building today is comprised of the old western half, and an archway section and leanto added by Miss Emmerton.

B-15   HOOPER-HATHAWAY HOUSE   c. 1682, etc.
House of Seven Gables Settlement Association
54 Turner Street, adjacent to the House of Seven Gables
NR; MHL; DSHD

Originally located at 23 Washington Street, this important 17th-century dwelling was erected for Benjamin Hooper, a cordwainer. Like the Becket house (see above), it started as a single-room plan with a chimney bay, but after 1784 it was doubled in size, and a leanto was attached to the rear. This leanto was later enlarged from one to two stories in height. The Hoopers occupied the house until 1795, when it was sold to Henry Rust. It then passed to the Gardner family, and finally c. 1864 to the Hathaways, who were bakers. It was while the Hathaways owned it that the building became a familiar landmark known as "The Old Bakery." When it was threatened with possible demolition in 1911, Miss Caroline O. Emmerton purchased it, and had it moved to the grounds of the House of Seven Gables, where it was restored by architect Joseph E. Chandler.

As we view it today, the house possesses an interesting front elevation, with asymmetrical window placement, a large cross-gable, an overhang with ornamental pendants on the oldest (left) side, and a "Beverly jog" on the right end. A massive off-center brick chimney subtly balances the cross-gable, adding to the Gothic verticality of the facade. The house features unusually fine cut and chiseled exterior overhang support timbers and interior shouldered

posts. The fenestration is varied, with restored diamond-pane casement windows in the c. 1682 side, and double sash types in the
newer addition. The house may be visited during the summer
months.

B-16

B-16 NATHANIEL HAWTHORNE BIRTHPLACE

Between 1730 and 1745

House of Seven Gables Settlement Association
27 Hardy Street, accessible from 54 Turner Street
HABS; NR; MHL; DSHD

Formerly situated at 27 Union Street, this modest two-and-one-half-
story gambrel-roof house was the birthplace, on 4 July 1804, of
Nathaniel Hawthorne, America's great Romantic-era author. Moved
to its present site (minus its ell) in 1958, it now stands next to the
House of Seven Gables which Hawthorne immortalized in his novel
of the same name. The front of the house no longer faces the street
as it once did, but is oriented with its gable end toward the street
like so many Salem houses of its period and type.

According to Abbott Lowell Cummings (see *Essex Institute
Historical Collections* 94: 196–204), it was probably built sometime
between 1730 and 1745 for Joshua Pickman, "Mariner" of Boston,
possibly making use of structural timbers taken from a 17th-century
Pickman family dwelling which once stood on the Union Street
site. Right from the start, it was framed as a typical mid-18th-
century, central-chimney house with a classical post-and-lintel front
doorway. Hawthorne's grandfather purchased this dwelling in 1772.

Most of the original interior has been preserved intact and may be viewed by the public in season.

At 25 Hardy Street, behind the Hawthorne birthplace, is the Joshua Phippen house (1782–1784), (NR; MHL; DSHD;), a large three-story-plus-hipped-roof wooden building with enclosed pedimented entrance porches on each side wall. It is also owned by the House of Seven Gables Settlement Association, but is not open to the public.

B-17

B-17   JONATHAN WHIPPLE HOUSE   c. 1843
49 Turner Street
NR; HSI

Built c. 1843 for Jonathan Whipple, a manufacturer of gum copal, this small one-and-one-half-story cottage illustrates the best qualities of the simple vernacular Greek Revival style. Giving the house its unmistakable stylistic character are a medium pitched roof, tall slender chimneys, Doric corner pilasters, heavy cornice molding, full side-wall entablatures, and a recessed doorway with thick border molding and "bull's-eye" corner blocks. The modest one-story ell to the rear appears to have been a later addition.

To the north (left) of the Whipple house at number 45 is a recently restored three-story-plus-hipped-roof early Federal residence (c. 1785) long known as the Capt. John Collins house. The little dwelling to the left of this building at number 43 was raised for Penn Townsend, a cooper, c. 1773, and displays a nicely developed Doric front doorway and an unusually tall central brick chimney.

BOSTON AND MAINE RAILROAD DEPOT (1846/47; demolished, 1954)
by Gridley J.F. Bryant (1816–1899) and formerly at the junction of
Washington and Norman streets (Riley Plaza). Photograph, 1891, by
Frank Cousins.

C

CITY CENTER

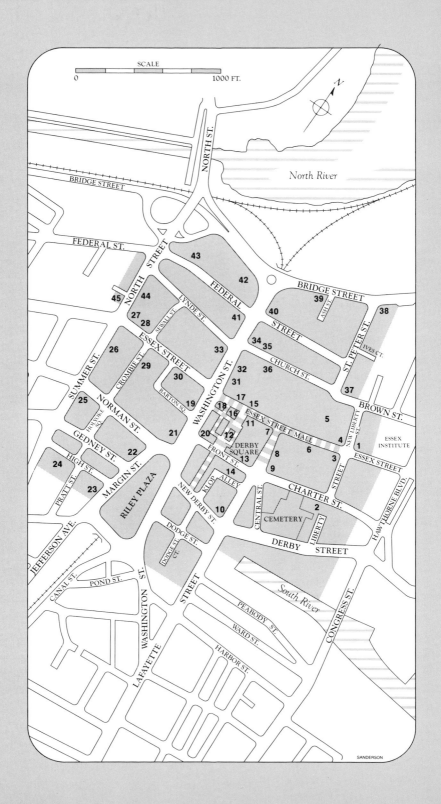

SCALE

0   1000 FT.

N

North River

BRIDGE STREET

FEDERAL ST.

NORTH ST.

NORTH STREET

43

FEDERAL

42

BRIDGE STREET

45   44   27   28
39
40   INLET
38

STREET

LYNDE ST.

SEWALL ST.

41

ST. PETER ST.

IVES CT.

34   35

26   ESSEX STREET
33

CHURCH ST.

SUMMER ST.

CROMBIE ST.

29

WASHINGTON ST.

32   36

BROWN ST.

31   37

30

BARTON SQ.

19

17   15

NEW LIBERTY ST.

25   NORMAN ST.

HOLYOKE SQ.

21

18   16   ESSEX STREET MALL
20   12   11   7   5   4   1

ESSEX
INSTITUTE

GEDNEY ST.

22

MARGIN ST.

FRONT ST.

DERBY
SQUARE

6

ESSEX STREET

24   HIGH ST.

PRATT ST.

23

RILEY PLAZA

13   14   8   3

9   CENTRAL ST.

LIBERTY STREET

HAWTHORNE BLVD.

NEW DERBY ST.

KLOP ALLEY

10   CHARTER ST.

2   CEMETERY   DERBY   STREET

DODGE ST.

INDGE ST. CT.

JEFFERSON AVE.

CANAL ST.

POND ST.

WASHINGTON STREET

STREET

South River

CONGRESS ST.

LAFAYETTE

PEABODY ST.

WARD ST.

HARBOR ST.

SANDERSON

INTRODUCTION

The central portion of the City of Salem is roughly square in shape, and is bounded by Summer and North streets on the west, Bridge Street on the north, Howard Street, the Essex Institute, and Liberty Street on the east, and New Derby Street, Riley Plaza, and Endecott Street on the south. Since 1626, when Salem was officially founded, this area has served as a major economic and political center for the entire Essex County region. The first impetus to commercial development here was provided by Salem's highly successful maritime trade in the 18th and early 19th centuries. The decline of shipping in the mid-19th century corresponded with the growth of local industrial enterprise which fostered the further physical expansion of downtown Salem, culminating in the construction of substantial commercial blocks along Washington Street in the 1880s and 1890s. The disastrous 1914 fire, although it devastated other sections of the city, spared the center and diverted investment and the pressure for modern development elsewhere. As a result of the fire and of the urban renewal of the 1970s, the 19th-century character of this area has been preserved, and the economic core of Salem, with its impressive array of commercial, civic, religious, and cultural structures, supplied with new vitality and significance.

The city center area is bisected by Essex Street (see Section D), one of the oldest streets in Salem, and its principal business thoroughfare. At the intersection of Essex and Washington streets is Town House Square, the historic focal point for the city's economic, social, political, and religious life. For most of Salem's history, the local population has been concentrated within walking distance of the square, and since 1836, when the city was officially incorporated, most local commercial activity has been carried on here. In the middle of the square, at the head of Essex Street Mall, is the site of the old Town Pump (made famous by Nathaniel Hawthorne), where a modern commemorative fountain has recently been constructed. At the east end of Washington Street (named in 1796) where Riley Plaza is now situated was the broad tidal basin of the South River, which first accommodated wharves and warehouses but later was filled in for a railroad yard and Gridley J.F. Bryant's famous railroad station (1846/47; destroyed, 1954).

Early in its history Essex Street became one of the busiest streets in Massachusetts, serving both residential and commercial purposes. By the mid-19th century the street was lined with stores, restaurants, hotels, theatres, meeting halls, and office blocks, with all architectural styles from the Federal to the Italian Revival in evidence. Many of the older structures have been restored under the urban renewal program and have been supplemented by modern construction in East India Square. Between Washington and Liberty streets, Essex Streeet has been turned into a brick-and-stone pedestrian mall, bringing an entirely new sense of urban life to the city. At the Liberty Street end are the Peabody Museum of Salem (see C-3) and the Essex Institute (see A-1), the two major museums of Boston's North Shore.

A couple of blocks east of Town House Square on the site of Elias Hasket Derby's magnificent mansion is the Old Town Hall and Market House (1816) (see C-12), the focal point of activity for the surrounding district (known as Derby Square). During the early and mid 1800s, the hall was the scene of political and temperance rallies, lectures, and other cultural events, while the area outside was used as a public market place. Fine brick Federal commercial blocks were erected adjacent to the Town Hall and along Front Street, which formerly bordered the original South River waterfront. Rehabilitated in the 1970s, the remaining commercial buildings in the Market Square district form Salem's most important early group.

In the buildings of these and other (Central, North, Church, lower Essex) streets in the city center, Salem's architectural heritage securely rests. A partial list of master builders and architects associated with the preurban renewal establishment of this heritage includes an impressive array of professional talent—Samuel McIntire (1757–1811), Charles Bulfinch (1763–1844), Thomas Waldron Sumner (1768–1849), Solomon Willard (1788–1862), Peter Banner (n.d.), Richard Bond (1797–1861), Isaiah Rogers (1800–1869), Richard Upjohn (1802–1878), Gridley J.F. Bryant (1816–1899), Enoch Fuller (1828–1861), Clarence H. Blackall (1857–1942), the firm of Robert S. Peabody (1845–1917) and John G. Stearns (1843–1917), Lester S. Couch (1866–1939), the partnership of Franklin H. Hutchins (1871–1934) and Arthur W. Rice (1869–1938), and Philip Horton Smith (1890–1960). It is because of the work of these and other men, as well as the fortunes of history that downtown Salem has remained a compendium of American architectural styles and building practices.

C-1

C-1 SECOND CORPS CADETS ARMORY 1908
136 Essex Street at Liberty
NR

This massive brick-and-stone-trim edifice is one of Salem's most
visible architectural landmarks. Erected in 1908, it stands on the
site of the former Joseph Peabody house (c. 1820), which, with a
drill shed attached to the rear, served as an armory from 1890 until
it was razed to make way for the present building. A fine example
of turn-of-the-century, tradition-bound armory architecture, this
structure exhibits many characteristic features—octagonal crenelated
corner towers, a wide Tudor-arch front entrance, narrow windows
with double pointed-arch, Tudor-arch, and hood-mold headings of
early Gothic Revival inspiration, and a front facade corbel table in
the Romanesque Revival vernacular. In February 1982 a devastating
fire rendered the facility temporarily useless.

Contained in the interior of the "head house," nearly destroyed
by the fire, were officers' headquarters, offices, social areas, and
storage rooms; at the rear is a large 170-by-86-foot drill shed. The
architect for the building (the plans are at the Essex Institute) was
John C. Spofford (1854–?) of Boston, well known for his twenty-
year partnership with Charles Brigham and his other public buildings in Maine and the Boston area. The contractor was Pitman and
Brown Company. The armory is owned by the Commonwealth of
Massachusetts and for years was the home base of the 1st Battalion

102nd Field Artillery (formerly Second Corps Cadets) of the Massachusetts Army National Guard. The building's future is presently undetermined.

Directly opposite the armory at 133 Essex Street is the Empire Clothing Company store, a one-story, low-keyed Art Deco-style building, erected in 1949 (extended, 1954) from plans by Sumner Schein and Associates of Boston.

C-2

C-2   SAMUEL PICKMAN HOUSE

Before 1681

20 Liberty Street at Charter
NR

Long hidden beneath a mansard roof added in the Victorian era, this small two-story wooden building was identified as a 17th-century Elizabethan house for the Salem Historic District Study Committee Report in 1968. The "unimproved" land on which this dwelling is situated was acquired by Samuel Pickman, a mariner, in 1657, and his estate inventory of 9 May 1687 included mention of a house on this tract. Structural evidence suggests that the house originally consisted of a large right-hand hall with a chamber and attic above and a chimney bay. According to architectural historian Abbott Lowell Cummings (*Architecture in Colonial Massachusetts . . .*, pp. 179–80), the "room at the left with leanto roof at right angles may have existed at the outset, and was later raised to a full two stories about 1725," at which time a new chimney was constructed. The one-story projecting porch was added c. 1800. The embellished (with carved "chevron" and "lamb's tongue" motifs) shouldered posts and summer beams of the interior timber frame are considered by Cummings to be among the most unusual he has observed in a house of this period. The builder may well have been Nathaniel Pickman, Samuel's father and a housewright, but this has not been documented. The house was purchased by Historic Salem in 1964, and was conveyed to Philip A. Budrose of Marblehead in 1969, under whose ownership it was restored. For a time it was a historic house museum, but today it is occupied by professional offices.

C-3

C-3 PEABODY MUSEUM OF SALEM
161 Essex Street Mall at Liberty and Charter streets
NHL; HABS; NR

1824/25; 1885/86;
1904; 1906; 1952/53;
1959; 1961; 1974/75

This low asymmetrical complex accommodates the Peabody Museum of Salem, internationally recognized in the fields of maritime history, ethnology, and regional natural history and the oldest continuously operated museum in the United States. The physical plant, which has evolved over 150 years, is a collection of styles and building practices predominant at various times in American institutional architecture.

The oldest and most important portion of the complex (photo, right) is East India Marine Hall, erected in 1824/25 for the East India Marine Society (established 1799), the forerunner organization of the Peabody Museum. Long presumed to be the work of Boston designer Alexander Parris (1780–1852), the building has in recent years been ascribed to masterbuilder Thomas Waldron Sumner (1768–1849), a professional associate of Parris's, based on an analysis of original drawings owned by the museum (Sumner also planned the Independent Congregational Church at Barton Square, Salem, now demolished). As originally conceived, East India Marine Hall was intended to have third floor pavilions at both ends, and a main entrance on its west side. Ultimately these were eliminated, and a two-story, pitched-roof, granite-facade-and-brick structure constructed, with business rental space at ground level and a commodious exhibition and meeting hall above. A late Federal-style edifice presaging the Greek Revival, it possesses seven bays on its front granite gable end, with rectangular windows on the first floor and a string of tall arched windows on the second. In the closed pediment gable above is an unusual round window with a square surround punctuated by radiating keystones. The contractor was William Roberts, who also did work on several other Salem buildings.

Additions to this first structure have failed to compromise its original appearance. In 1885/86 Academy Hall (incorporating East Hall) was appended to the southeast corner, with Stone, Carpenter, and Willson of Providence, Rhode Island, drafting the plans. This was followed in 1904 by the conversion of the first floor to museum space, and the construction of the west side entrance corridor with its classical trabeated entranceway (a matching entrance corridor, removed c. 1973, was erected on the east side in 1929). Two years later, under the supervision of architects Peabody and Stearns of Boston, Weld Hall was built behind Academy Hall. Additional gallery space was provided in 1952/53, with Andrew Hepburn (of Perry, Shaw, and Hepburn, Boston) as architect. In 1959 and 1961, Boston architect Philip W. Bourne designed the library wing and the Crowninshield Room respectively, both in the Colonial Revival vein. Then in 1974/75, Bourne, working with Stahl, Bennett of Boston, planned the new Ernest S. Dodge wing (photo, left), a granite-faced structure of the contemporary (Brutalist) school of architecture that is notable for its massiveness, rectilinearity, and broad, quiet wall surfaces, interrupted by deep-shadowed penetrations and plate-glass window apertures.

C-4 **BOWKER (Manning) BLOCK**   c. 1830
144-156 Essex Street Mall at Liberty Street

With its west end facing the new East India Square, the Bowker
(originally Manning) block is an outstanding example of early 19th-
century commercial architecture. Although it was erected c. 1830,
this handsome structure displays the fine smooth brickwork, tall
brick chimneys, granite window sills and lintels, molded cornices,
and overall rectangular form of earlier Federal-style buildings. The
builder was William Roberts of Salem. The store front is believed
to have been created by virtue of alterations made c. 1894. Over
the years the block has housed the local police court, the Second
Corps Cadets (see C-1), the Merchants Bank, and the retail outlets
of James F. Almy, William Filene, and David Conrad, three of
Salem's most prominent businessmen. The building was rehabilitated in 1973–1975 for L.H. Rogers, an exclusive women's clothing store.

C-5   EAST INDIA MALL   1973–1975; 1977–1979
AND PARKING GARAGE
Essex Street Mall; Brown and Liberty streets and St. Peter Square

The East India Mall and Parking Garage were developed as two distinct but functionally and aesthetically related projects starting in 1973. In both cases the firm of Mondev International, Limited of Montreal, Canada, was involved, serving as general planner for the parking garage and as principal developer (see C-36) for the mall in cooperation with two French companies, Sorimet (a subsidiary of Renault) and Sefrius (a subsidiary of U.I.I.).

Despite its massive bulk and contemporary design, the parking garage (see photo C-51) fits comfortably into the historic environment of downtown Salem. Accommodating up to 1,000 automobiles in enclosed space, this rectangular reinforced-concrete, four-level structure is in many respects a flashback to International Style architecture of the forties and fifties. Reminiscent of this style are the flat roof, smooth and uniform wall surfaces, asymmetrical elevations, square support columns, and general horizontality fostered by the parking level apertures. The parking garage was developed by the City of Salem and designed by the engineering firm of Zaldastani Associates, with Nelson W. Aldrich Associates (with Maxwell Pounder) of Boston serving as consulting architects.

The core of this new retailing complex is the East India Mall (see photo C-5r), containing space for fifty stores, three movie theaters, offices, and restaurants, some of which occupy space on the first level of the parking garage. Erected between 1977 and 1979, this striking reinforced-concrete, brick, metal, and plate-glass "mixed-use" structure was designed by Nelson W. Aldrich (see above) with his partner Maxwell Pounder (the firm name was changed to Aldrich, Pounder, and Associates) acting as project architect. Situated on the Essex Street Mall, the main artery of Salem's revitalized business district, the mall is a forceful visual statement of the New Formalism pioneered in this country by Philip Johnson, Edward D. Stone, and Minoru Yamasaki. Appropriate to this style, the roof-line is level, the arch motif is prominent, the principal facade is symmetrical, the wall surfaces are composed of mixed materials, and the column supports are thick and modeled.

C-6

C-6 DOWNING BLOCK

173-175-177 Essex Street Mall
HSI

1858

Built in 1858 (date stone) for dry-goods merchants Thomas W. and
John H. Downing, this three-story, brick-and-brownstone Italian
Revival commercial building (photo, left) is the most outstanding
structure of its period and type surviving in Salem. In 1973/74 it
was beautifully restored under the supervision of local architect
Oscar Padjen. Attracting visual notice are the arched front entranceway and arcaded storefronts, the segmental-arch windows with
molded hoods and drops, and the bracketed broken cornice with
segmental arch. Because of the construction date and the similarity
of the facade details to those of Plummer Hall (see A-1) at the
Essex Institute, it is conceivable that Enoch Fuller (1828–61), the
architect of Plummer Hall, may also have designed the Downing
block.

The three-story commercial block (photo, center) to the west
(right) at number 179 appears to have been built c. 1865, and was
also used by the Downings for their business. The front facade was
restored in 1980/81 with Salem architect Staley McDermet in
charge of the project. The two-story brick block (photo, right) at
number 181 was constructed c. 1875 and restored in 1979/80 with
Oscar Padjen as architect. Many diversified businesses have occupied the three buildings over the years.

C-7 OLD CUSTOM HOUSE   1805
4-10 Central Street and Essex Street Mall

Formerly the "Central Building," but today the "Old Custom
House," this rectangular three-story, hipped-roof brick structure was
erected in 1805 as a block of stores for William S. Gray and Benjamin H. Hathorne. John Chandler and Joseph McIntire provided
materials and labor. Joseph's brother Samuel (1757–1811), the
designer of the neighboring Stearns block (1792; demolished, 1902),
may have planned the building, but this is unsupported by documentation. Architectural historian Fiske Kimball believed, however,
that the carved gold eagle (the original is at the Essex Institute)
over the front central trabeated doorway was by Samuel McIntire,
and this fact plus his brother's association clearly links him with
the building.

Simple and well-proportioned, the Old Custom House may be
admired for its slightly projecting central pavilion containing a
semicircular fanlight, and for a recessed Palladian window above the
doorway. Its familiar name stems from the fact that the U.S.
Custom Service was here in 1805–1807 and 1813–1819. As part of
Salem urban renewal, the building was restored in 1975/76, with
John Emerson and Oscar Padjen providing architects' services. It
was then that the first-floor arched windows were introduced.

Across Central Street at number 1 (also 185-189 Essex Street
Mall) is the two-story brick Naumkeag block, which has recently

been attributed to Gridley J.F. Bryant (1816–1899), architect of a number of other Salem buildings. Greek Revival in inspiration, it was built for Benjamin Creamer in 1847. The contractor was Albert Blaisdell of Boston. The architectural firm of Larkin, Glassman, and Prager was responsible for its restoration c. 1975.

C-8

C-8 ESSEX BANK BUILDING   1811; 1899
11 Central Street

The former Essex Bank building is believed to be the only surviving structure in Salem designed by the distinguished Boston master-builder Charles Bulfinch (1763–1844). Accommodating the first bank (1792) in Essex County, the building follows a domestic plan adapted to commercial purposes. Although extensive interior modifications were made in 1899 when the Salem Fraternity (the oldest boys' club in the United States) acquired the building, much of Bulfinch's initial conception is still present. The built-up granite base with double stairways originally supported a tall portico of four Ionic columns, sheltering a wide doorway with fanlight. The windows are largely authentic, including the reeded stone surrounds and wood-tracery lunettes on the first-floor front facade. Unusual for Salem architecture of the period are the four stone belt courses on this facade. The building features a fine wrought-iron balustrade by Joseph Cheketty, and superb interior ceiling stucco decoration (today concealed), assumed to have been the work of Bulfinch's chief plasterer, Daniel Raynerd. Mid-19th-century alterations, executed in the Italianate vein, produced the ornate front cornice brackets and the closed entrance porch. Ernest M.A. Machado (1868–1907) served as restoration architect for the 1899 work.

Displaying excellent late-Victorian brickwork is the Newcomb block (1886) (photo, left) designed by William D. Dennis (1847–1913) at 1-3-5-7 Central Street, to the north (left) of the Essex Bank. Architect David Jacquith recently supervised its restoration. The small three-story, pitched-roof wooden house to the south (right) at numbers 13-15 was built c. 1766 as a residence, very possibly for Joseph Scott, though this has not been adequately documented. Charles Osgood, the portrait painter, later lived there. The house was rehabilitated in the early 1970s for commercial uses, and is owned by the Salem Fraternity.

C-9

C-9   SALEM POLICE STATION   1913
17 Central Street at Charter

Designed by local architect John M. Gray (1887–1977) and built in 1913, the Salem Police Station is a good example of the Colonial Revival style in public building design. Numerous elements in this symmetrical, rectangular, brick-and-stone-trim structure are inspired by Salem's magnificent Georgian Colonial and Federal architectural heritage. These include modillioned cornices, brick corner quoins, tall round-arched windows with keystones, splayed window lintels, a broad belt course, and matching front entrances with semicircular fanlights, doric pilasters, and flat canopies supported by ornate baroque console brackets. A wooden balustrade that formerly encircled the flat roof was removed some years ago. The building has traditionally accommodated the city marshall, the police department, and until 1977, the First District Court of Essex County before it was removed to a new building (see C-34) on the corner of Washington and Church Streets.

On the opposite corner of Charter Street at 36 Central is the Salem branch of the Century North Shore Bank, erected in 1977 from designs submitted by Lawrence Rubin, a Boston architect. The flat brick wall surfaces and crisp lines of this modest pitched-roof structure nicely complement those of the neighboring police station.

C-10

C-10 MAIN FIRE STATION   1972
48 Lafayette Street at New Derby

The Main Fire Station is a stark, functional, two-story brick Colonial Revival structure with decorative motifs fashioned in white-painted wood according to Roman Doric principles. On the second-story level, square Doric pilasters are evenly spaced across the front facade and side walls, supporting a wide smooth entablature while resting on a continuous belt course. A solid ribbon-like balustrade with Doric posts and panel inserts surrounds the flat roof above. The official seal of the City of Salem may be seen set on the front facade above the central garage door. On the first floor the building houses ladder and pumper trucks and auxiliary vehicles. Dormitories, a recreation room, a study, a kitchenette, and Civil Defense headquarters were originally accommodated on the second floor. Architectural designs were prepared by Arland A. Dirlam, a nationally known church architect who planned numerous public buildings in Marblehead while professionally based there and in Boston.

C-11

C-11 PICKMAN-DERBY BLOCK

213-215 Essex Street Mall; 1 and 7 Derby Square
NR; HSI

1817

In 1815 merchants Benjamin Pickman, Jr., and John Derby, III, purchased Elias Hasket Derby's mansion and surrounding land and in 1817 began the development of Derby Square by the construction of this fine row of attached brick commercial buildings. For their builder they chose Joshua Upham (1784–1858), a master mason, who was later to supervise the erection of the Old Market House and Town Hall (see C-12) nearby.

Two stories high with a pitched roof, the block is divided into three units by two fire walls. The brickwork is the unusual Flemish bond type and is highlighted by a cornice with square and ogee-curve dentils. Two round windows decorate the south gable end of the block. Old photographs show that the first floor doors and windows once had arched headings and fanlights similar to those gracing the Old Market House and Town Hall—most of these were reintroduced in the mid-1970s when the building was restored under the direction of architect Jonathan Woodman.

The Naumkeag Clothing Company (later Newmark) building (photo, left) at 203-209 Essex Street Mall was built in 1895 by Joseph N. Peterson (masonry) and Hamilton and Balcomb (woodwork and finishing) of Salem. Holman K. Wheeler of Lynn was the architect. The facade exhibits a heavy classical cornice and yellow-brick pilasters separated by relieving arches.

C-12

C-12 OLD TOWN HALL AND MARKET HOUSE   1816
32 Derby Square between Essex Street Mall and Front Street
NHL; NR

Derby Square was the site of the residence of Col. William Browne,
a Loyalist whose property was confiscated by the Massachusetts
legislature in 1784 and subsequently conveyed to millionaire merchant Elias Hasket Derby. It was here that Derby, from plans
prepared by Charles Bulfinch (1763–1844) and modified by Samuel
McIntire (1757–1811), had a magnificent Adamesque Federal mansion constructed between 1795 and 1799. After Derby's death in
1799, due to the expense of maintenance, his son Elias Hasket
Derby, Jr. had the mansion demolished (1815) and then transferred
the land to his brother, John Derby, III, and his brother-in-law,
Benjamin Pickman, Jr. In 1816 they donated part of this tract to
the Town of Salem with the condition that a new brick Town Hall
and Market House be built there. This unusual offer was accepted
and the building promptly erected by local builder Joshua Upham
(1784–1858), from plans by an as-yet-unidentified architect. Based
on style details and the fact that he was active in Salem at the
time (overseeing the construction of the Almshouse, 1815/16, now
demolished), some have speculated that Charles Bulfinch was the
designer. The lower floor of the building was opened as a market in
November 1816, and the upper floor was first used on the occasion
of President James Monroe's visit to Salem in July 1817. When the
new City Hall was erected in 1836/37 (see C-31), this structure
ceased being the headquarters of local government.

The restoration (extensive work was done in 1933/34 under Philip Horton Smith's direction) of the Old Town Hall and Market House was the cornerstone of the Salem Redevelopment Authority's imaginative program to revive and preserve the Derby Square sector of the downtown business district in the mid 1970s. Through the efforts of architects James Ballou and John Emerson, the Bulfinchian Federal features (i.e. closed modillioned pediment with semicircular fanlight; round-arched doors and windows; Palladian windows; brick belt course; small octagonal cupola) of the building were again highlighted. At the same time, under the direction of landscape architect John Collins (Delta Group, Philadelphia), new brick market stalls were constructed along the walkway leading south toward New Derby Street (the former South River channel), near where, as Rev. William Bentley relates in his diary, similar stalls were built in 1816.

C-13

C-13 PICKMAN AND HENFIELD BUILDINGS
c. 1816; 1844/45, etc.

6-26 Front Street
NR

In 1815 Benjamin Pickman, Jr., and John Derby, III, of Salem acquired the property of the Derby heirs and made plans for the development of Derby Square. Centered on the new Market House (see C-12), the scheme called for the construction of three brick commercial rows, one of which, the Pickman-Derby block (1817) (see C-11) also still stands. Based on tax records and structural evidence, the new Pickman building (22-26 Front Street, 15 Derby Square) is believed to have been erected c. 1816. A plain two-story structure with raised end walls, it has several distinguishing Federal-style characteristics—Flemish-bond brickwork; a gable-end (west) fanlight; a classical dentiled cornice (in wood), and arched windows and doors (north side).

At the other end of the row at numbers 6-12 is the Henfield building, a brick block erected in 1844/45 by John Henfield of Salem. City records suggest that numbers 2-4 (now demolished) were built at the same time, and, though under separate ownership (William Ball), formed a single architectural unit with the Henfield building. Samuel S. Standley was the contractor. Many different businesses occupied the store fronts over the years. In 1972 this block was connected to the Pickman building by the construction of an infill unit between the two. James Ballou of Salem was the architect for this project, as well as for the restoration of both buildings between 1972 and 1975.

Behind (north of) the Pickman-Henfield row is Central Plaza, a modern brick-and-concrete complex containing condominiums, retail stores, and a parking garage. This complex was built in 1980/81 by DeIulis Brothers Construction Company of Lynn, Massachusetts, in collaboration with Pasquanna Developers of Lynn, and Robert L. Scagliotti, architect, of Salem.

C-14

C-14   VARNEY-REYNOLDS-ROPES BUILDING   1845
17–23 Front Street
NR

OLD POLICE STATION   1859/60
15 Front Street
NR

In January 1845 the land on which this two-and-one-half-story brick commercial block (photo, center and right) is situated was acquired jointly by George C. Varney and Moses Reynolds (easterly ⅓), and William and his son John T. Ropes (westerly ⅔). Immediately Varney and Reynolds contracted with mason Samuel S. Standley to erect their portion of the building from plans and specifications prepared by one L. Putnam of Salem. The Ropes family soon followed suit, also contracting with Standley for their part of the building, and all work was completed by the middle of June. In subsequent years the block changed hands many times and was used for a variety of commercial/retail purposes. A fire badly damaged the building in 1902, but it was rebuilt. In 1972/73, under the direction of the Salem Redevelopment Authority (its first project) and local architect John Emerson, the block's fine late Federal-style lines, fenestration, brickwork, and granite post-and-lintel storefronts were restored.

The charming little two-story brick structure to the east (left) (photo, left) at number 15 was erected in 1859/60 for the Salem police department and police court. The brick masonry was by Simeon Flint, and the carpentry by Lord and Russell. The building's most outstanding architectural features are the dentiled brick cornice, the granite window lintels and sills with corbel stops, and a granite front doorway lintel with ogee-curve brackets. When restoration occurred in the early 1970s, James Ballou of Salem served as the consulting architect.

C-15

C-15   SALEM FIVE CENTS SAVINGS BANK BUILDING

1892, etc.

206–208, 210 Essex Street Mall

Initially known as the Gardner Building, the Salem Five Cents Savings Bank building was erected in 1892, with Joseph M. Parsons serving as mason-contractor and Charles B. Balcomb as head carpenter. The architect's name is unknown. The design for this Colonial Revival edifice is believed to have been influenced by the one-time presence next door (east) of Ezekiel Hersey Derby's high-style Federal house (c. 1800, altered 1908), planned by Charles Bulfinch (1763–1844), with carvings by Samuel McIntire (1757–1811). Certainly the same Federal Neoclassical feeling is expressed by the Salem Five block as was formerly by the Derby house. Among the block's most pronounced features are the classical cornice with modillions, the second- and third-story Doric pilasters (mimicking those of the Derby house), the third-story Palladian window, the splayed granite lintels with keystones, the four first-story articulated Doric columns, and the flat entablature with circular medallion over the front entrance.

The building has been considerably remodeled since it was built, starting in 1914 with alterations to the first-floor facade and interior. An ell was added in 1940, and additional interior modifications were made in that year and in 1950 under the supervision of architect Philip Horton Smith (1890–1960). Designed by Salem architect Oscar Padjen, a modern glass, steel, and white-marble-faced wing was appended to the east side in 1972/73 on the site of the Derby house, which, because of its degenerated state as a commercial block, was removed.

C-16

C-16 NAUMKEAG TRUST COMPANY   c. 1900; 1910/11
BUILDING (Hoyt Block)
217 Essex Street Mall
NR
HALE (Mercantile) BUILDING   c. 1873
221-225 Essex Street Mall
NR

The Naumkeag Trust Company building (photo, left) was built c. 1900 as a retail store for W.E. Hoyt Company, clothiers and furnishers. It was initially called the "Hoyt Block" and occupied the tract on which the Kimball block, which burned in 1899, formerly stood. The Naumkeag Trust Company purchased the property in 1910/11 and had it remodeled under the direction of Boston architects Franklin H. Hutchins (1871–1934) and Arthur W. Rice (1869–1938), specialists in the design of bank buildings. Pitman and Brown Company of Salem was the contractor. This remodeling was mostly on the interior, although some exterior changes were made—these did not, however, mar the strong Colonial Revival ambience of the structure. Of many ornamental details, the roof balustrade, the wooden cornice with modillions and dentils, and the stone-accented, round-arched window openings are most eye-catching.

Also owned by the Naumkeag Trust Company is the Hale (Mercantile) building (photo, right) to the west (right) at number 221-25. Erected c. 1873, this five-story (the fifth story was added c. 1874) commercial structure is the only local example of cast-iron front architecture, developed by James Bogardus of New York City c. 1848. Decorated with a High Victorian Italianate bracketed cornice and window-frame motifs, this unusual block introduced to Salem the building technology which eventually led to the modern skyscraper. The architect was Salem's Robert P. Bruce (1830–1887), who worked with George Copeland, a former draftsman for the architectural firm of Lord and Fuller. Also attributed to this tandem is the Arrington block (Salem Evening News building) (159-189 Washington Street), originally built as a hotel in 1873 and the only surviving local example of wood-frame commercial architecture of that time.

C-17

C-17   JACOB RUST BRICK STORE   c. 1801
216-220 Essex Street Mall

The brick store of Jacob Rust, erected c. 1801, is the only surviving commercial building of its type and period in Salem. With its raised end walls incorporating paired chimneys, a plain cornice, segmental-arch window headings, and front facade belt courses, all in brick, it creates a different visual impression than the later commercial blocks on Derby Square and Front Street. When it was first built, the Rust store was one of just fifty brick buildings in Salem, but because of the mounting threat of fire in the expanding business district, many more soon followed. About 1806 or 1807 another brick block was constructed to the west (left), and it still stands, though greatly modified.

The Rust store has undergone considerable renovation over the years, including rearrangement of the interior, closing and reopening of fireplaces and flues, and the creation of granite post-and-lintel shop fronts in the mid 1800s. With the assistance of federal funds, however, the restoration of the building was carried out in the mid 1970s under the direction of local architect Robert Scagliotti.

C-18

C-18 FIRST CHURCH (Daniel Low Building) 1826; c. 1874
121 Washington Street; 231 Essex Street Mall
NR

Situated at the old center of downtown Salem, the First Church building is the fourth religious sanctuary to be erected for the parish on the same site. According to the *Salem Gazette* it was built in 1826 from plans drafted by Solomon Willard (1788–1862) and Peter Banner (n.d.), two of Boston's most accomplished church and public building designers. As the structure was planned, the second floor was used for church activities, and the first floor for rental income-producing shops. From old photographs we know that the original building was rectangular with a pitched roof, was set on a high granite-block foundation, and possessed east and west side pavilions with closed pediment (embellished with modillions) gables and tall round-arched windows. The main north gable facade was nicely articulated, with paired Ionic pilasters flanking tall round-arched windows and supporting a plain entablature and closed pediment above.

The First Church was extensively remodeled c. 1874 along the principles of the High Victorian Gothic style, then very much in vogue. The building was substantially enlarged to the west (approximately twelve feet) by the expansion of the pavilion and the addition of twin square corner towers topped by steep pyramidal roofs (since removed). Simultaneously the church was extended on the east side and furnished with new pointed-arch windows and other pointed-arch stone motifs. Daniel Low and Company acquired the property in 1923 when the First Church merged with the North Church (Unitarian).

Across Essex Street Mall at 101 Washington Street is the Neal and Newhall (Shribman) building, built c. 1892 on the site of southern portion of Samuel McIntire's brick Stearns block (1792), which was partially torn down (it was completely razed in 1902) at that time. Next door (south) at 125 Washington Street is the Salem (Eastern) Savings Bank (NR), originally the Asiatic building (c. 1855), a four-story, brownstone-facade, Renaissance Revival-style commercial block. It was designed by William H. Emmerton (1828–1873) and Joseph C. Foster (1829–1906) of Salem and was remodeled (the top story was also removed) c. 1910 in the Colonial Revival vein by Boston architect Arthur E. French (1876–1929).

C-19 PEABODY BUILDING   1891/92
120-128 Washington Street
POWER BLOCK   1889/90
138-144 Washington Street

Facing east on Washington Street and separated by a narrow alley
(Barton Square) are two of the city's most substantial late 19th-
century business/commercial buildings.

The older of these, the Power block (photo, left), was raised in
1890/91 (it was doubled in size c. 1895) according to designs
prepared by Nathan P. Sanborn of Marblehead. The Power
brothers, home furnishers who developed the building, were also
residents of this town. The principal contractors were Joseph J.
Murphy and Company of Lawrence (masonry), Hamilton and
Balcomb of Salem (carpentry), and Joseph H. Bell of Salem
(finishing). Adorned with Romanesque Revival round and segmental
relieving arches and window headings, as well as other ornate
brickwork details, this building anticipates later plate-glass-wall commercial buildings with its large front-facade window apertures. In
1982 it was partially destroyed by fire, but it has since been
restored.

More traditional is the Peabody building next door (photo,
center), planned by Clarence H. Blackall (1857–1942), a member of
the Boston architectural firm of Blackall, Clapp, and Whittemore,
known for Boston theatre, newspaper, and commercial buildings.

The partnership of Hamilton, Balcomb, and Peterson was the contractor. Named in honor of S. Endicott Peabody, this delicately detailed Colonial Revival structure was erected in 1889/90 as the headquarters for the *Salem Evening News*. The fourth story was added after 1919. Although drastic alterations have eliminated all of the original door and window decoration on the first-floor level, a number of elements (lintels, Palladian window, cornice molding) derived from Salem Federal-era houses may still be seen in the upper stories.

To the north (right) of the Peabody building at number 118 is an early Colonial Revival, three-story brick block (photo, right) designed by Peabody and Stearns, the famous Boston architects, and constructed in 1882/83. It formerly housed the U.S. post office. Much of its original facade ornamentation has been removed.

C-20

C-20 LAWRENCE PLACE   1808–1809; c. 1817; c. 1825
133 and 137 Washington Street; 34 Front Street
NR

According to Salem tax records, Capt. Abel Lawrence, a successful local merchant and distiller, financed the construction of a "brick dwelling and store" in 1808–1809 at what is today 133 Washington Street (photo, left). A rear two-story ell was built c. 1817. For the remainder of the 19th century, the "Lawrence Place," as it was known, remained with Capt. Lawrence's children and their heirs. Evidence suggests that soon after his death in 1822, his original distillery at the corner of Front Street was demolished and replaced

by the two-story brick building at 137 Washington and 34 Front
(photo, right). During the 19th century no distinction in name was
made between this block and the older "Lawrence Place." Visually
they are very similar, with medium-pitched roofs penetrated by
open-pediment dormers and brick chimneys. In the early 1970s the
two blocks were rehabilitated for new adaptive uses with James
Boulger (133 Washington) and James Ballou (137 Washington; 34
Front Street) hired as architects.

Further down Front Street at number 32 (on Derby Square) is a
two-story, mansard-roof brick building (NR) that to date has puzzled
researchers. The roof type and the brickwork, particularly the ornate
cornice, suggest a c. 1870 date. Oscar Padjen was the architect for a
restoration in the early 1970s.

C-21

C-21 JOSHUA WARD HOUSE   c. 1784-1788
148 Washington Street facing Front
HABS; NR

Erected between 1784 and 1788, the Joshua Ward house is "a strikingly fine example of a [bold], sturdy [and] sumptuous type [of
residence] that is extraordinarily interesting to see in contrast with
the light and delicate treatment of much other Salem architecture"
(*Old-Time New England* 30 (1940): 138–39). Possessing most of its
original features, this square, three-story, hipped-roof dwelling is
Salem's oldest Federal high-style brick house, and one of the last
surviving early waterfront mansions. Laid in Flemish bond brick, it

has segmental arches above the first and second story windows, a molded watertable, broken string courses, a plain cornice, and four tall end chimneys. By virtue of a sweeping restoration supervised by Salem architect Staley B. McDermet between 1978 and 1979, the original wooden roof balustrade, front doorway surround, and front fence have been conjecturally reproduced. Much interior woodwork remains, highlighted by an imposing central staircase. Recent research into manuscript sources (it is one of the best documented houses in New England) indicates that the building was probably designed by housewright Samuel Luscomb, Jr., and built with the assistance of the McIntire brothers—Samuel (1757–1811), and Joseph (1748–1825), and Angier (1759–1803). During the 19th century the house was known as the Washington Hotel, stemming from President George Washington's overnight visit there in 1789.

C-22

C-22   UNITED STATES POST OFFICE BUILDING   1932/33
2 Margin Street between Gedney and Norman

Built in 1932/33 from designs by Wenham architect Philip Horton Smith (1890–1960) of the firm of Smith and Walker, the United States Post Office building is without question Salem's finest Colonial Revival-style civic structure. Advantageously situated overlooking the open space of Riley Plaza, this handsome two-story brick, cross-gable-roof edifice (with one-story ell) fulfills the function of U.S. post office branch, as well as federal office building. Rectangular in plan with a symmetrical front facade, it exhibits elements historically associated with both the Georgian Colonial and Adamesque Federal modes. Dominant visually is the front central pavilion with its delicately articulated closed-gable pediment, classical cornice, second-story Doric pilasters, belt course, and first-story round-arched windows and triple-arcaded entranceway, reminiscent of the work of Bulfinch. A similar pediment design is repeated in the end gables, below which are recessed balconied Palladian windows. The chief contracting company was Louis B. Cadario and Sons.

C-23

C-23 ST. MARY'S ITALIAN CHURCH
(Roman Catholic)
56 Margin Street

1925

A contemporary version of an Italian Renaissance basilica church with side campanile, St. Mary's Italian Church combines elements from Roman and Lombard Italian architecture. Designed by church architects O'Connell and Shaw of Boston and built by contractor Felix L. Siano, this buff-brick-and-granite-trim building was the product of the efforts of Father Peter M. Piemonte, who presided at the dedication and served the parish for twenty years. Attracting notice on the exterior are the canopied front porch with round window above, the round-arched Bavarian stained-glass side-wall windows, and the recessed double-arched open belfry (removed, 1981) in the campanile. The interior, which seats 500 people, contains fine stained-oak benches and woodwork, terrazzo flooring, decorative wall and ceiling paintings, and carved Italian marble altars and appointments that partially date from renovations made in 1960, 1961, 1968, and since.

C-24 GEDNEY HOUSE
21 High Street
NR

c. 1665

Owned and maintained by the Society for the Preservation of New England Antiquities (Boston), this important 17th-century wood-frame house was erected by Eleazer Gedney, shipwright and church deacon. Originally, the building (a "half-house") consisted of the left-side room with its chamber above, a garret and chimney bay, and a smaller one-story room at the right covered by a leanto roof positioned at right angles. Structural evidence suggests that extensions were erected to the rear as part of the c. 1665 residence, but these were removed long ago. After the death of Eleazer's widow in 1716, their daughter Martha inherited the house—Abbott Lowell Cummings believes that "before or about this time the right-hand parlor was raised to a full two stories with framed overhang at the first story on the street," and that "a two-story leanto at the rear with separate chimney replaced c. 1800 whatever preceded it" (*Architecture in Colonial Massachusetts . . .*, p. 174). Around 1962 the central chimney was removed and the interior stripped. Since the S.P.N.E.A. acquired the house in 1967, it has been employed as a special exhibit of early structural building practices and may be visited only by special appointment.

C-25 HOLYOKE MUTUAL (Fire) INSURANCE COMPANY BUILDING

1935–36; 1973–75

39 Norman Street at Holyoke Square and Summer Street

The modern headquarters of the Holyoke Mutual Insurance Company (established 1843) were the product of two distinct building projects. The oldest section of the complex was built in 1935/36 by contractor Lawson W. Oakes from plans prepared by the architectural firm of Philip Horton Smith and Edgar Walker of Boston. Containing three stories with a flat roof and an L-shaped floor plan, the building is typical New-Deal-era classical-revival architecture in brick, light-buff facing stone, metal, and plate glass. Brick pilasters with subtle Doric capitals separate vertical window strips under a heavy, plain parapet. Appropriately, the structure is completely fireproof, with reinforced concrete interior construction.

The attractive recent addition (including a two-level underground parking garage) on the Summer Street side of the complex was erected between 1973 and 1975 by the T.G. Driscoll Construction Company of Peabody, Massachusetts. The firm of Henry A. Frost and Associates of Boston served as architects, and Brask and Standley Engineering Company of Boston were engineering consultants. Built with fireproof materials similar to those used in the 1935/36 portion, this simple but striking structure possesses wall surfaces which are effectively broken by a series of parallel three-story, tinted-plate-glass and bronze-metal window bays. Samuel McIntire's own house (1786) formerly stood at 31 Summer Street on the site of the addition.

C-26   WEST TRIPLE HOUSE   c. 1833/34
5-9 Summer Street

This handsome three-story, pitched-roof brick housing row was built
as an investment for Capt. Nathaniel West, a privateer commander
during the Revolution. Later, at an advanced age, he lived in one
of the three residential units. Shielding the single and double doorways on the front facade are typically Greek Revival flat-roofed
porches, supported by fluted Ionic columns. Local tax records indicate that the West triple house was erected c. 1833/34.

Across Summer Street and a bit south at number 18 is the Capt.
Tobias Davis house (HSI) which recent research and structural inspection suggest was built c. 1805. Although some changes have
been made since, it possesses many obvious Federal-style characteristics—three-story cubical massing, a low hipped roof with
balustrade (a replacement of the original), and tall slender brick
chimneys. The main Palladian doorway was restored in 1982.

C-27 SHEPARD BLOCK   c. 1850/51
298-304 Essex Street at North

According to Salem tax records, Michael Shepard built this three-story row of four residential units c. 1850/51. Prominently situated on the corner of Essex and North streets, the Shepard block, as it is now known, possesses the massing and proportions of older Federal-era urban housing rows, but in its Italianate brownstone window lintels exhibits traces of the mid-Victorian period. The tall brick chimneys, pitched-roof dormers, and conical-shaped attic skylights create a busy staccato effect atop the front roof plane. A double dentil strip decorates the cornice across the main facade. The eastern three units of the building were rehabilitated in 1979/80, with David Jacquith serving as architect.

C-28

C-28   Y.M.C.A. BUILDING

284-296 Essex Street at Sewall

1897/98

When he prepared the plans for the Y.M.C.A. building in 1896, architect Walter J. Paine of Beverly was influenced by more than one of the major American architectural styles that reached their peak between 1890 and 1915. One may see evidence of Beaux-Arts Classicism in the paired Doric columns flanking the front entranceway, the broken-scroll pediment above, the three arched front doorways, the multiplanar symmetrical front facade, the cornice console brackets, and the paired, ornately decorated oval windows in the third story. Signs of the Colonial Revival are present in the splayed lintels with keystones, window balustrades, corner quoin decoration, cornice modillions, entablature swags, and lightly treated second-story oriel windows. Originally the building possessed a marvelous open fourth-story loggia for reviewing parades down Essex Street. Richly embellished, this added greatly to the "hodge-podge" aesthetic impression created by the front facade.

The contracting firm for the Y.M.C.A. building was Hamilton, Balcomb, and Peterson of Salem. Contained inside are retail stores, offices, social rooms, a swimming pool, a gymnasium, recreational rooms, an auditorium, bowling alleys, and locker areas. Between 1873 and 1876 Alexander Graham Bell developed the telephone in the Sanders homestead which formerly stood on this site—a large bronze plaque on the front facade commemorates this important experimentation.

C-29 CROMBIE STREET CHURCH
(Congregational)
7 Crombie Street

1827/28; 1934/35

This dignified Federal-Greek Revival transitional building was built
as a theatre in 1827/28 by Jabez W. Barton, the proprietor of Barton's Hotel. Daniel Bancroft, a former assistant to Samuel McIntire,
is said to have drawn the plans. The theatre venture, however,
failed to attract sufficient community support and was terminated in
1830. Two years later the building passed to a dissenting group from
the Howard Street Church which established itself as the "New
Congregational Church" and then the "Crombie Street Church."
The structure has accommodated the same parish ever since.

In 1934 a serious fire gutted the interior of the church and it
was promptly rebuilt, but the exterior has remained virtually unchanged since the time of construction. Penetrating the brick front
facade are paired and recessed side doorways topped by flat, hooded
entablatures and flanked by plain Greek Doric pilasters. The planar
surface of the facade is broken by three relieving arches into which
these doorways and three round-arched windows above are set. The
aesthetic effect produced is one of balance, lightness, and grace.

Next door to the south (right) (photo, right) of the Crombie
Street Church is the three-story dwelling historically associated with
Joel Bowker, who supposedly purchased it in 1809. Although the
Flemish bond brickwork clearly dates it as a Federal-era house, the
exterior modifications (brownstone window lintels and sills;
bracketed cornice; bracketed front doorway canopy, etc.) made
c. 1860 give it a distinctly Victorian eclectic character.

C-30

C-30 MERCHANTS NATIONAL (Shawmut Merchants) BANK
1910/11

253 Essex Street

Constructed on the former Choate property, the Merchants National (now Shawmut Merchants) Bank building is an excellent example of Colonial Revival commercial architecture. Lester S. Couch (1866–1939) was selected as architect after participating in a design competition involving his firm, Little and Brown, William G. Rantoul, and Kilham and Hopkins, all of Boston. The building contract was awarded to Joseph N. and V.S. Peterson of Salem. The structure was completed in 1911, exactly one century after the organization of the bank. The front brick facade is a successfully unified composition consisting of a slightly projecting pavilion with a trabeated doorway (with closed pediment), topped by a semicircular window, and flanked by pairs of tapered Doric pilasters terminating in full entablatures. The pavilion in turn is flanked by large arched windows. Framing the facade are a lower belt course, corner quoins, and a pronounced dentiled cornice above which is a raised wall embellished with urns, panels, and a medallion under a swag. The plain brick addition to the right (west) was erected in 1972 from plans by Symmes, Maini, and McKee of Cambridge, Massachusetts.

Across Essex Street at number 242 is the Goldthwait building (c. 1876), a small-scale Victorian eclectic commercial block, for which architect William D. Dennis (1847–1913) created an ornate facade in white marble facing. To the west (left) at number 244-248 is an interesting brick block (with a curious off-center gable) believed to have been built for Thorndike Proctor in 1834 or just before.

C-31

C-31 CITY HALL

93 Washington Street
NR

1836/37

Salem City Hall, built in 1836/37, is an outstanding example in granite of a restrained and pleasantly proportioned Greek Revival civic structure. It was designed by Richard Bond (1797–1861), an accomplished Boston architect who also did the plans and specifications for the old Essex County Courthouse (1840/41) (see C-42) on the corner of Federal and Washington streets. The contracting masons were Simon M. and Augustus M. Coburn. Curiously, this solid-looking building was erected at no cost to the taxpayers as it was funded entirely from United States Treasury 1837 surplus revenue, distributed nationally to the states and in turn to the cities and towns.

The two-story, granite-block facade (the other walls are brick) features four square Greek Doric pilasters supporting a two-stage entablature divided by a dentiled string course—on the lower portion the words "City Hall" are inscribed, while above are seven beautifully articulated laurel wreaths. Atop the roof parapet is a gilded American eagle, copied from the original by Samuel McIntire, which once surmounted the wooden gateway (removed in 1850) at the western entrance to Salem Common. On the inside of the building are the Council Chamber, the mayor's rooms, storage vaults, and the clerk's, assessor's, and other administrative offices. The building was doubled in length in 1876, and was again expanded in 1978/79 by the addition of a new city archives ell.

C-32

C-32   KINSMAN BLOCK
81 Washington Street

1882

Still one of the most imposing commercial structures in Salem, the Kinsman block was built in 1882 from designs by the Salem and Boston architectural firm of George C. Lord and George A. Fuller. It was financed by and named for John Kinsman, a Salemite, who achieved business success in railroading, banking, utilities, and real estate in Massachusetts and the Midwest. The principal contractor was Samuel S. Merrill.

Constructed of brick with granite decorative accents, the Kinsman block recalls the work of the prominent Philadelphia architect Frank Furness (1839–1912), whose influence on Victorian public building architecture was felt nationwide. Like many of

Furness's buildings, this imaginative and powerfully stated structure possesses a balanced and symmetrical front facade with boldly scaled geometrical details, very effectively interrelated, though compressed together. The Kinsman block defies specific style classification and is an amalgamation of several—principally the High Victorian Gothic, Italianate, and Romanesque modes. It was built to accommodate retail stores on the street level, and the Odd Fellows Hall, and business and professional offices above.

The history of the Heritage Cooperative Bank building to the north (left) at number 71 is less clear. Originally known as Cate's block, it was erected c. 1882 and remodeled in 1890. Then some time after 1910 (old photographs show it unchanged until then) it was completely remodeled in the Colonial Revival style. Considering the high quality of the results, a major architect was likely responsible, but his identity remains unknown.

C-33

C-33 MASONIC TEMPLE   1915/16
68-74 Washington Street at Lynde

One of the largest buildings of its kind in Massachusetts, the Masonic Temple was erected in 1915/16 from designs drafted by architect Lester S. Couch (1866–1939), the business manager of the Boston firm of Little and Brown. Later a partner in the firm, Couch also planned the Merchants National (Shawmut Merchants) Bank building (see C-30) in Salem, and several other buildings in his home town, Danvers, Massachusetts. Pitman and Brown Company was the contracting firm.

A notable Salem landmark, this massive symmetrical five-story brick and "artificial" limestone edifice in the Colonial Revival style is of unqualified architectural merit. Attracting primary attention is a slightly projecting front central pavilion in which four fluted Corinthian columns rise from a rusticated and triple-arch entrance base and terminate under an entablature (inscribed "Salem Masonic Temple") and closed gable pediment containing the Masonic symbol. When it was first erected, the building accommodated retail stores, professional and business offices, and the Masonic lodge rooms, banquet hall, and reading room (with marvelous English Gothic Revival oak woodwork removed from the Peabody residence, erected c. 1820 at 136 Essex Street—see C-1).

The Masonic Temple stands on the site of the Pickman-Derby-Rogers-Brookhouse residence (1764), which was remodeled in 1786 by Samuel McIntire for Elias Hasket Derby. It was demolished in 1915 to make way for the present building. In 1982 a major fire gutted the top two stories, but these have been rebuilt.

C-34

C-34   FIRST DISTRICT COURT   1976/77
OF ESSEX COUNTY
60 Washington Street at Church

This highly functional brick, concrete, plate-glass, and steel-frame building was erected in 1976/77 from plans drafted by James Walker of the Boston firm of Whitman and Howard. The builder was James

J. Welch Company of Salem. Although it appears austere and barren at first glance, the courthouse cannot fail to impress the onlooker with its expansive brick wall surfaces, sharply defined lines, and connected box-like geometric shapes. On the four-level (two are below ground) interior are a spacious two-story lobby and stairwell, three courtrooms, judges' lobbies, a clerk's office, conference rooms, waiting areas, jury rooms, detention cells, lounges, a small library, a vault, offices, and maintenance and utility rooms. The First District Court was formerly located in the Salem Police Station (see C-8) on Central Street at Charter.

C-35

C-35 SALEM STEAM FIRE ENGINE HOUSE 1861; 1887
34 Church Street
OLD WATER DEPARTMENT BUILDING 1879
1 and 30 Church Street

These two nicely complementary Victorian eclectic buildings are distinguished by outstanding brickwork decoration. This fact was recognized in the early 1970s by the Salem Redevelopment Authority, which saved them from demolition when the new First District Court building (see C-34) was being planned for an adjacent site. The older of these, the Salem Fire Engine House, was erected in 1861 based on plans by an unidentified architect. George Hadley served as chief engineer for the project, while B.R. White superintended the masonry work, and Hammond and Brown the carpentry. The building was remodeled in 1887 under the supervision of Salem architect William D. Dennis (1847–1913). Its principal ornamental features are the heavy dentiled cornice, the segmental-arch window hoods with drops on the front elevation, and the concave and bracketed mansard roof crowning the tower at the rear. In 1975/76 architect David Jacquith directed an adaptive use restoration which produced new retail and office space.

Next door to the west (photo, left) is the Old Water Department building, which was originally erected in 1879 but was remodeled by David Jacquith 1975/76 for retail space and lawyers' offices. Of visual interest are the segmental-arch window and door headings, the second-story square pilasters, and the fine corbel table just under the roof eaves.

C-36

C-36 ONE SALEM GREEN   1974/75
Off Church Street near Washington

Designed by Nelson W. Aldrich of the Boston architectural firm of Campbell, Aldrich, and Nulty, One Salem Green occupied an advantageous location fronting on City Hall Plaza and spanning the north-south walkway linking the Essex Street Mall with the Church Street commercial/professional district. This unadorned steel-frame, brick-and-plate-glass building is five stories high and exhibits many qualities of Miesian-style (named for the German-American architect Ludwig Mies van der Rohe) architecture—a precise rectangular form, a modular pattern established by the structural frame, broad planar wall surfaces, and ground-story walls set behind square outer piers. One Salem Green is occupied by city offices, retail stores, law firms, an insurance company branch office, and other businesses. The developer for the building was Mondev International, Ltd. of Montreal, Canada (see C-5).

C-37

C-37 ST. PETER'S CHURCH (Episcopal)

1833/34; 1845/46; 1864; 1871/72

24 St. Peter Street at Brown on St. Peter Square
NR

This ruggedly picturesque, rubble-granite masonry, Gothic Revival church succeeds the first St. Peter's Church, a wooden structure raised on the same site in 1733/34. Along with the First Church (see D-47) at 316 Essex Street, it is one of the most outstanding ecclesiastical structures of its style and type in the United States. According to the articles of agreement (May 1833) between the church proprietors and the stonemasons, Loami Coburn and William Roberts of Salem, the building was erected from plans drafted by Isaiah Rogers (1800–1869), the nationally renowned Boston architect known particularly for his pioneering hotel designs and his close associations with Solomon Willard (see C-18) and Alexander Parris. The original structure was enlarged (new chancel and vestry) in 1845/46 at which time the noted New York church architect Richard Upjohn (1802–1878) contributed altar screen and chancel window plans. In 1864 the interior was furnished with new wooden galleries, and in 1871/72 the building was further expanded by a small chapel at the rear. The architect for the chapel was George E. Harney of Cold Spring, New York.

One story high with a low hipped roof, St. Peter's Church is dominated by a square crenelated attached bell tower centered on the front facade. This tower is penetrated by a Tudor-arch doorway surmounted by a large traceried pointed-arch window, above which modified quatrefoil openings appear in each wall face. Large pointed-arch windows also flank the tower and are present in the side walls. Preserved largely in its original state, St. Peter's Church stands in stark contrast to St. John the Baptist Church (Roman Catholic) at 28 St. Peter Street (three buildings to the north) which, though dedicated as a Federal-style church (formerly the Second Baptist) in 1826, has suffered greatly from remodelings in 1867, 1877, 1909, and since.

C-38

C-38   SALEM JAIL (County of Essex)   1811–1813; 1884/85
50 St. Peter Street and Bridge
NR
JAILER'S (Sheriff's) HOUSE   1813
48 St. Peter Street

The Salem Jail has considerable architectural significance in that it is one of the oldest correctional facilities in the United States still fulfilling its original function. The first portion was erected in 1811–1813, replacing an older jail nearby. From manuscript floor plans and photographs, we know that it was a massive, rectangular (thirty-eight by sixty-four feet), granite-block structure typical of institutional architecture of its day, with a hipped roof and slightly projecting pavilions on each side wall. Financial records tell us that John Page supplied the bricks, Joseph Newhall and Henry Williams furnished stone, David Robbins was the principal mason, and Joseph Edwards superintended construction, assisted by David Lord, William Roberts, and others.

In 1884/85 the building was remodeled and greatly enlarged to the west by the addition of the section near St. Peter Street and the link with the old portion. Rockport granite was the primary building material, although much brick was also employed. On this occasion two different but balancing octagonal cupolas were placed on the slate roof, providing the structure with a touch of Victorian eclecticism. Every effort, however, was made to blend the new construction with the old. Rufus Sargent (1812–1886) of Newburyport was selected as architect in a design competition with William D. Dennis of Salem, and C.W. Damon, also of Newburyport. The contractors were Joseph Ross of Ipswich, John A. Greeley of Newburyport, and Joseph N. Parsons and Joseph N. Peterson of Salem.

The hipped-roof, three-story brick Federal jailer's (sheriff's) house just to the east was built in 1813 in conjunction with the jail. This handsome dwelling possesses a shaped, brick dentil cornice, splayed and reeded window lintels, and an inviting front entrance (with a fanlight and sidelights) protected by a square porch supported by two slender Doric columns. It has been speculated that the house was built by Samuel Field McIntire (1780–1819), but no supportive evidence has ever surfaced. Labor receipts do show, however, that Joseph Edwards directed construction, John Page supplied the bricks, David Robbins did the masonry work, Abraham Edwards was the glazier, plasterer, and painter, and Micaiah Johnson fabricated the wooden architectural details. Adjacent to the house are several wooden outbuildings of historic interest.

C-39

C-39 FIRST UNIVERSALIST MEETINGHOUSE
6 Rust Street; 9 Ash Street
HABS

1808–1809, etc.

THOMAS PERKINS HOUSE   c. 1811
7 Ash Street
HSI

Built in 1808–1809 from plans by William Putnam, the First
Universalist Meetinghouse (photo, left) is one of the most outstanding Federal-era ecclesiastical structures surviving in Essex County,
Masachusetts. The front projecting gable pavilion, above which rises
a square balustraded bell tower, is particularly noteworthy. This
pavilion also features recessed and arched (round and segmental)
doorways and a delicate Palladian window above. Church records
show that Samuel McIntire was paid $105.85 for interior carving,
and that Charles Nichols, John Woodbury, Robert Clonstone,
Enoch Manning, and Perley Putnam did carpentry work. The
meetinghouse has been modified on several occasions—in 1826 and
1839, when the basement was enlarged and finished; in 1842, when
the gallery was remodeled; in 1855, when the old square pews were
replaced; in 1877/78, when, under the direction of Salem architect
William D. Dennis (1847–1913), the interior sanctuary was done
over and the exterior "Victorianized" by the addition of a patterned pyramidal tower roof, triple-arched tower windows, trapezoidal window and door lintels, and expanded pavilion wings; in
1887, when Dennis designed a new brick chapel (now the parish
house) (photo, center) at the southeast corner; and in 1924, when
the building was largely restored (the pavilion wings remain) by the
Boston office of R. Clipston Sturgis (S. Winthrop St. Clair, architect in charge) by sandblasting the brick, removing the tower cap,
reinstalling the original windows and doors, remodeling the interior,
and furnishing other conjectural elements consistent with Federal
architecture.

Directly in front of the parish house is the Thomas Perkins
house (c. 1811) (HSI) (photo, right), a chaste, hipped-roof, two-story,
brick Federal dwelling, the only one of its type extant in Salem.
The Palladian doorway was placed on the house when it was
restored by architect John Emerson c. 1975. This building was saved
from demolition by urban renewal authorities in 1968 when its
owner, Bessie Munroe, refused to vacate the premises.

C-40 FEDERAL STREET CONDOMINIUMS 1978–
20 and 30 Federal Street at Washington

Developed by the Stern-Tise Salem Group, the Federal Street condominiums are one of the city's newest downtown housing projects.
Commenced in 1978, site development and construction is still in
progress. Eight three-story units at number 20 were completed in
1978/79, and ten additional two-story units (including one unit of
offices) at number 30 were readied for occupancy in 1980/81. Ten
more units of similar design will be erected in the near future. Built
of wood with brick ends, the condominium rows are traditional in
their massing, lines, and window configuration, thus blending well
with Salem's older architecture. Collaborating on the project are
Stephen Tise Associates, architects, of Brookline, Massachusetts,
and the Rostanzo and Lavoie Construction Company of Watertown,
Massachusetts.

C-41

C-41   TABERNACLE CHURCH   1923/24
(United Church of Christ)
58 Washington Street at Federal

Constructed from designs submitted by the Boston firm of Philip
Horton Smith and Edgar Walker, this dignified and graceful Colonial Revival church building (with parish house) is the third
ecclesiastical structure to stand on this site. It replaced a large
wooden Italian Revival church which the parish occupied from
1854 until it was torn down in 1922. Its predecessor, which stood
from 1776 to 1854, possessed an elegant three-stage tower which
Samuel McIntire added in 1805.

The present stone-masonry-and-wood edifice incorporates many of
the best and most distinctive traits of late 18th- and early 19th-
century Salem architecture. Screening the front arched entrance is a
nicely proportioned Roman Doric portico of four columns supporting a fully developed Doric entablature with triglyphs, metopes, and
mutules, under a closed-gable pediment. The tower above is topped
by a pilastered open octagonal belfry with a bellcast dome, set on a
second stage that bears a striking resemblance to that present in the
1805 McIntire tower. The original McIntire drawing for the tower,
as well as the Smith and Walker plans, specifications, and model
for the current church are at the Essex Institute.

C-42 ESSEX COUNTY COURTHOUSES

32-36-42 Federal Street

NR

1839–1841; 1861/62;
1887–1889; 1908–1909;
1979–1981

Aligned in a row on the north side of Federal Street, the three Essex County courthouse buildings form a visually exciting as well as historically significant streetscape. Individually they are noteworthy examples of architectural styles commonly employed in public building design from the mid-19th to the mid-20th century.

The superb two-story, temple-like granite edifice (photo, right) on the corner of Washington Street was erected in 1839–1841 from designs drafted by Richard Bond (1797–1861) of Boston, also the architect of the nearby City Hall (1836–37) (see C-31). It is one of the most outstanding Greek Revival-style civic buildings surviving in New England. On each gabled end two tall Corinthian columns comprise a portico in antis between square Doric corner pilasters. A bold, plain entablature encircles the entire building and helps to unify the whole architectural composition. The structure was remodeled on the interior in 1889, 1910, and 1982/83. Samuel S. Standley and Henry Russell, Jr. of Salem were the original contractors.

In 1861/62 a large brick and brownstone courthouse (photo, center) was erected on adjoining land with Enoch Fuller (1828–1861) as architect, and Simeon Flint and Abraham Towle the contractors. Initially an Italian Revival-style structure, it was altered greatly between 1887 and 1889 by the addition of a towered ell to the rear, and a three-story, pitched-roof pavilion on the front, thereby giving the building an unmistakenly Richardsonian Romanesque appearance. These renovations were carried out by contractors Parsons and Peterson from plans submitted by architects Holman K. Wheeler and W.W. Northend of Lynn. Today it houses the Superior Court.

The newest building (photo, left) in the row was built in 1908–1909 from the plans of architect Clarence H. Blackall (1857–1942) of Boston. The Woodbury and Leighton Company, also of Boston, did the construction work. Accommodating the registry of deeds, the probate court, and related administrative offices, this monumental granite edifice is one of the finest Neoclassical Revival buildings in the Boston area. The six-column Greek Ionic portico in front is particularly eye-catching. Appended to the rear is a modern reinforced concrete and plate-glass extension (1979–1981) designed by Phineas Alpers, Architects of Boston, and built by contractor James J. Welch of Salem.

C-43

C-43 FIRST BAPTIST CHURCH
56 Federal Street

1805–1806; 1827; c. 1850, etc.

The present First Baptist Church has evolved over 175 years and scarcely resembles the building as it looked early in its history. The oldest portion of this structure (it is Salem's earliest extant ecclesiastical building) was erected in 1805–1806 after a smaller building constructed the year before on the same site proved inadequate for the growing congregation. In 1827 the church was enlarged to its present size, and fitted out with a lovely three-stage Federal tower topped by an octagonal dome. Around 1850 a chapel was added, and the brick outer walls were rebuilt in the Italianate vein, with corner quoins, semicircular window hoods, and rusticated stone doorway surrounds. Local architects George C. Lord and George A. Fuller were entrusted in 1868/69 with extensive interior and exterior tower modifications, which were damaged by fire in 1877 and restored the next year. The additional interior remodelings were undertaken in 1909, 1926, and since. The tower, due to the cost of repairs, was removed in 1926. By virtue of this loss, the building was deprived of its original scale and much of its aesthetic merit.

Opposite the First Baptist Church on Federal Street are three other buildings with interesting architectural histories: at number 47, the Capt. John Felt house (1757) (HSI), a representative mid-18th-century, plain, gambrel-roof dwelling of which there are many in Salem; at number 55-57, the Joshua Loring double house (1836) (HSI), a brick-ended, wood-frame structure possessing a fine recessed trabeated Greek Revival double doorway; and, at number 63, the Nathaniel R. Treadwell house (1875), an attractive Victorian eclectic residence resembling several on upper Federal and Essex streets.

C-44

C-44 WESLEY UNITED METHODIST CHURCH   1888/89
8-10 North Street

The Wesley United Methodist Church was planned by a relatively unknown architect, Lawrence B. Valk of New York City. His de-

sign, however, is of high quality. Asymmetrical in plan, with arcades, round-arched window and door apertures, concave pyramidal-
roof nave and corner spires, and slightly projecting wall buttresses,
the building possesses a distinctly Romanesque Revival flavor. The
northwest square corner tower, however, is awkwardly truncated, as
a tall open-belfry, ogee-curve-roof upper stage was never completed.
The cruciform floor plan is unusual for its day, with seating arranged in a semicircle focusing on and sloping down to a raised
pulpit. This seating space may be enlarged to the rear by the use of
a multipurpose apse area which is illuminated by lovely tall stained-
glass windows. The contractors were J.F. Farrin, and Joseph N.
Parsons and Joseph N. Peterson of Salem.

Around the corner (to the north) at 25 Lynde Street is the
Capt. James Barr house (HSI), a small gambrel-roof dwelling with ell
that is typical of the city's pre-Revolutionary War vernacular residential architecture. It was raised sometime after 1753, but before
1760.

C-45

C-45　BOWDITCH-OSGOOD HOUSE　　　c. 1805
9 North Street
NHL; NR

This three-story, low-hipped-roof, clapboard house appears to have
been built c. 1805, based on structural evidence. Some printed
sources indicate an earlier date, but this is unlikely. It is documented, however, that William Ward sold the building to the

famed mathematician and astronomer Nathaniel Bowditch in 1811 and that he and his family lived here until their removal to Boston in 1823. That same year the property was conveyed to the family physician, Dr. John Treadwell, who retained some of the land for a garden, and sold the house to William Proctor. Later in the century the house was owned by Judge Joseph B.F. Osgood who made certain Victorian alterations, including the installation of 2/2 window sashes.

In 1944, when proposed street widenings threatened the house (it was originally situated at 312 Essex Street), Historic Salem, Incorporated was established to save it and the adjacent Corwin house (see D-49) from demolition. As a consequence of HSI fund-raising efforts, the structure was moved to its present site, restored, and turned over to the City of Salem which for many years used it as the headquarters for the Park Department. Despite the fact that its roof balustrade has never been reintroduced, the Bowditch-Osgood house remains a good example of restrained Federal-era residential architecture, highlighted by its lovely recessed front doorway (added c. 1825) set between graceful fluted Ionic pilasters.

SPRAGUE-WAITE house (c. 1796, etc.; demolished, c. 1893) formerly at 376 Essex Street. Photograph, 1891, by Frank Cousins.

D

UPPER FEDERAL
AND
UPPER ESSEX STREETS

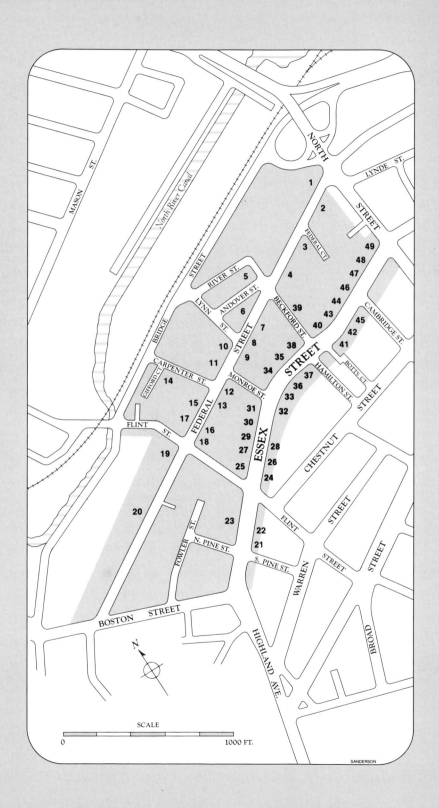

SCALE

0   1000 FT.

N

SANDERSON

INTRODUCTION

Most of Salem's streets to the west of Washington Street are newer than those located to the east in the city center and in the Common and Derby Street areas. While the east end of Salem was traditionally both home and business locale for people of all socioeconomic levels, the western neighborhoods were inhabited by families of high socioeconomic status and hence lacked the same diversity in building types. By the end of the 18th century, many Salemites found it economically possible to separate their place of residency from their place of business. As a result, the upper Federal and upper Essex streets area is almost exclusively residential, with some churches, schools, and social facilities, but no commercial and industrial buildings and only a few shops. The entire area is a marvelously representative collection of high-style and vernacular architecture dating form the late 17th to the early 20th century. In recent years much important restoration work has been completed by private property owners.

According to Joseph Felt's *Annals of Salem* (1827), Federal Street was laid out in 1766 where an old public right of way existed along the south bank of the North River. In its early years this artery was also called "New Street," the "Bank Street," or the "new North Street." The upper end of Federal Street (between North and Boston streets) was officially linked with the present middle and eastern portions in 1853, at which time the entire street assumed its current name of "Federal." Narrow and tree-shaded, the upper section (including the River Street area) contains an unusually fine group of Georgian Colonial and Federal-style dwellings, but also features excellent examples of Greek Revival, Italian Revival, mid-Victorian eclectic, French Academic (Second Empire), late Gothic Revival, and Colonial Revival architecture. There are four houses here with which Samuel McIntire (1757–1811) is believed to have been associated, and two of these, the Peirce-Nichols and the Assembly (owned and maintained by the Essex Institute), are open to the public.

One of Salem's two oldest main thoroughfares (the other is Washington Street), Essex Street (formerly known as the "Great Street," the "main street," the "Queen's Highway," and "Bow Street"), ran from Lynn road and the pasture lands through the center of town and out to the Neck. The name "Essex Street" came into common use by 1796, though the route had existed for over a century before. The meandering western or upper end (between North Street and the junction of Highland Avenue and Boston Street) has always been largely residential, possessing houses dating from the late 17th century. Many of the dwellings on the north side occupy plots of land whose original boundaries ran east 127

to the North River. Upper Essex Street and its side streets have long
been recognized for their outstanding Georgian Colonial and Federal
houses, but not to be overlooked are their unusually fine and varied Victorian eclectic and Colonial Revival residences. Buildings by architects
Gridley J.F. Bryant (1816–1899), the partnership of William H. Emmerton (1828–1873) and Joseph C. Foster (1829–1906), Ernest M.A.
Machado (1868–1907), Clarence H. Blackall (1857–1942), William G.
Rantoul (1867–1948), and Philip Horton Smith (1890–1960) may be seen
throughout the area.

D-1

D-1 PEIRCE-NICHOLS HOUSE   c. 1782, 1801, etc.
80 Federal Street
NHL; HABS; NR; MHD

Nationally renowned for its tasteful elegance, beautiful proportions,
and bold classical details, the Peirce-Nichols house is recognized
as one of the finest three-story wooden residences built in early
Federal-era America. Based on oral tradition and consistency of
style with other documented works, this highly significant building
has long been attributed to Salem's Samuel McIntire (1757–1811),

and is believed to be his first major commission. Although the bulk of the house dates from c. 1782, certain interior areas were remodeled by McIntire in 1801, thereby "combining under one roof superb examples of his Georgian and Adamesque [Federal] styles" (Gerald W.R. Ward, *The Peirce-Nichols House*, p. 5).

The first owner of the house was Jerathmiel Peirce, a leather-dresser turned successful merchant, who with Aaron Waitt, developed the firm of Peirce and Waitt, one of the largest India traders in the United States. During the first phase of construction, the exterior was completed as well as the side stairs and very likely the rear stable, with its distinctive heavy arches. According to Fiske Kimball (*Mr. Samuel McIntire, Carver . . .*, p. 58), McIntire's major source of inspiration for his details was Batty Langley's volume, *City and Country Builder's and Workman's Treasury of Designs . . .*, first published in England in 1740. As we may witness today, the house is sheathed with clapboards and stands three stories high, with a low-pitched roof encircled and obscured by a balustrade above the main cornice and crowned by a second balustrade around a small roof deck above. The third story is effectively foreshortened. Monumental fluted Doric corner pilasters are the major exterior surface ornamentation. The first- and second-story window openings are capped with simple molded flat hoods, positioned above plain entablatures. The front open and side enclosed porches closely follow the principles of the Roman Doric order, with pediments and fully articulated entablatures. The round-arched window in the back wall is an unusual McIntire feature.

The marriage of Sally Peirce to George Nichols in 1801 provided the occasion for the remodeling of the Peirce-Nichols house hallway, east parlor, and chamber in McIntire's later Adamesque style. These alterations have been credited to him by Kimball, and coupled with his earlier work in other rooms, make the house "a veritable textbook of the evolution of McIntire's architectural career and the changing taste of the period" (*The Peirce-Nichols House*, p. 12). Later construction facing the stable court (the one-story ell), as well as the marvelous front fence with urns (restored by architect William G. Rantoul in 1924/25), also date from this time. The property passed to George S. Johonnot in 1827, but was returned to the original owning family in 1840 when Jerathmiel's son-in-law, George Nichols, inherited it. The Peirce-Nichols house remained in the Nichols family until the Essex Institute purchased it by subscription in 1917, but it was not opened for regular public visitation until the late 1930s.

D-2

D-2   ALBERT P. GOODHUE HOUSE   1893
87 Federal Street
NR; MHD

Salem atlas maps and tax records show another house on this site
prior to 1893, with Albert P. Goodhue, employed variously as a
ship chandler, grocer, and commission merchant, as the owner as
early as 1876. It is apparent from other records and structural
evidence, however, that Goodhue had this building demolished to
make way for a replacement. City building permits indicate that in
June 1893, Hamilton and Balcomb, local contractors, erected a new
house for Goodhue and his wife, Sarah, on this land. After her husband's death in 1915, Mrs. Goodhue continued to live in the house
for another three years.

The Goodhue house is a conspicuously fine example of the Colonial Revival style, combining elements from the Georgian Colonial
and Federal vernaculars. It is larger than its average historic coun-
terpart, and some of the individual details (e.g., window frames,
dormer pediments, front entrance porch, cornice console brackets,
etc.) are purposely exaggerated, a practice that is evident in several
other Salem houses of the same period. With one gambrel-roof
gable end facing the street, the building exhibits a number of
historic details, such as corner quoins, an end Palladian window,
window bay and porch balustrades (only remnants remain), cornice
dentil molding, and pedimented and broken round-arched dormers.
Other Colonial Revival features include molded and paneled brick
chimneys and the end bay window.

D-3 MASON-ROBERTS-COLBY HOUSE   1768, etc.
91-93 Federal Street at Federal Court
NR; MHD

A good local example of a late Georgian Colonial residence, this three-story, hipped-roof wooden building displays many features characteristic of its period—corner quoins, a modillioned cornice, molded window caps and sills, and a front central entrance set between square Doric pilasters that support a flat dentiled entablature with molded overhanging cap. A wing and an ell, including a "Beverly jog" on Federal Court, are attached to the house.

Based on entries in Rev. William Bentley's diary, it is believed that the house was originally built in 1768 for Jonathan Mason, a merchant and sea captain, on the present site of the Forrester-Peabody house (see A-9) at 29 Washington Square North. The Mason house was moved to its present location in 1818 when the Forresters decided to replace it with a larger brick dwelling. William Roberts, a masonry contractor who built St. Peter's Church (see C-37), East India Marine Hall (see C-3) and the Bowker block (see C-4), superintended this delicate project, and his descendants owned the property into this century.

D-4

D-4 GLOVER-COOK-CHAPMAN HOUSE

Before 1799

101-103 Federal Street
NR; MHD

Based on research in deeds and tax records, it is known that this
three-story, two-family Federal house dates from at least 1799 and
possibly as early as the 1770s, when the first owner, mariner
Ichabod Glover, acquired the land on which it stands from Samuel
Punchard. Merchant Samuel Cook purchased the property in 1822
and stayed there until 1833. John Jewett, a cabinetmaker, then
bought the dwelling, kept it for three years, and sold it to Rebecca
Thayer, a widowed schoolteacher, and John C. Chapman, a local
printer and the publisher of the *Salem Register*. Benjamin Shreve
and his heirs were the owners from 1874 into the early part of this
century.

Situated flush with a sidewalk on a low granite foundation, the
house presents a plain five-bay clapboarded front facade bounded by
narrow corner boards. The front central doorway is flanked by lights
set inside reeded Doric pilasters, which support a plain entablature
under a dentiled flat cornice. The foreshortened 3/6 third-story windows possess delicately molded sills.

Opposite the Glover-Cook-Chapman house at number 104 is a
two-story, pitched-roof wooden house (NR; HSI; MHD) erected for
upholsterer Asa Lamson in 1814. The front central trabeated doorway, though it is wider and recessed, is the same general type as
that of its neighbor.

D-5 BECKFORD-WHIPPLE HOUSE

c. 1739; after 1788

2 Andover Street at Beckford and Federal
NR; HSI; MHD

This square, three-story, hipped-roof wooden house appears to have been built during the Federal period, but a major portion of the structural framing may well date from as early as 1739. In that year a deed of property transfer from John and Rebecca Beckford to their son, John, Jr., first makes reference to a house on the site. When John, Jr. died in 1788, the house passed to his son, Ebenezer, who retained title until 1816. It is highly probable that early in his period of ownership, the building was enlarged, taking its present form. The Whipple family bought the property in 1826 and held it for well over a century. Virtually all the decorative features of the side porch (square columns, modillioned cornice, etc.) and the asymmetrical front facade (enclosed balustraded and pilastered entrance porch, Palladian window) are Colonial Revival (c. 1885 to c. 1925) refinements. The Beckford Street side door, however, dates from the Federal-era modifications.

Opposite (south of) the Beckford-Whipple house, across Federal Street on the southeast corner of Beckford (number 22), is the irregular-plan Punchard-Chamberlain house (NR; HSI; MHD), which is believed to date from c. 1765, and may have developed from an older building moved to the site. The Chamberlains, who purchased the house in 1777 and kept it until 1834, were responsible for the Federal embellishments (cornice, window heads, closed entrance porch, etc.) on the exterior.

D-6

D-6 ORNE-PRINCE HOUSE

c. 1788

108-110 Federal Street
NR; MHD

PAGE-LAWRENCE-FARRINGTON HOUSE

c. 1786

112-114 Federal Street
NR; MHD

LEACH-NICHOLS HOUSE

c. 1782

116-118 Federal Street
NR; MHD

The trio of early Federal-style, three-story wooden dwellings situated in the block between Beckford and Lynn streets (facing south) form Salem's most impressive immediate post-Revolutionary War streetscape. The house at number 108-110, though it looks to be of a later vintage, was built by sailmaker John Orne c. 1788, but was sold to Rev. John Prince in 1793. The Prince family held title to the property until 1859, after which it was owned by the Parsons and the Moores. It was David Moore who raised the building onto a high foundation and had it remodeled and expanded to the rear. Protected by a hipped roof, the house has retained such clearly Federal features as a molded classical cornice and molded window frames. The recessed trabeated doorway also dates from the time when the house was constructed.

The house numbered 112-114 is unusual in that it has a pitched instead of a hipped roof (see also A-31). Erected by distiller John Page c. 1786, it was acquired by the Lawrence sisters in 1823, before passing in 1845 to druggist George P. Farrington, who owned it until c. 1900. It was probably Farrington who added the Victorian bracketed window hoods and a heavy doorway surround, recently replaced by a pedimented and pilastered surround more appropriate to the period of the structure. Supposedly the famous lawyer Rufus Choate also resided here for a time.

The facade of the house situated at numbers 116-118 bears some resemblance to that of the Joseph Felt house (1794/95) (see D-7) across the street, but lacks the crisply molded window caps and precise friezes of its neighbor. The boldly pedimented and pilastered Palladian doorway is a typical feature of early Federal domestic architecture. This building was erected c. 1782 by mariner John Leach on land purchased from Ebenezer Beckford. Ichabod Nichols bought the property in 1803 and sold it in 1805 to his son George, who lived there with his bride Sally (Peirce) until 1811. From 1831 until the 1860s the Punchard and Chamberlain families shared the house.

D-7

D-7 JOSEPH FELT HOUSE
113 Federal Street
NR; HSI; MHD

1794/95

Set within a few feet of the street, this square, symmetrical hipped-roof, three-story wooden house is a nicely proportioned and handsomely detailed example of early Salem Federal domestic architecture. A legacy from the pre-Revolutionary era is the front central Palladian doorway, featuring fluted Doric pilasters and a closed, molded triangular pediment set on an entablature decorated with triglyphs and metopes. This same entablature treatment is effectively repeated in the first-story window headings of the five-bay facade. The window heights are graduated in size from the first to the third stories. Research in Salem tax records has disclosed that the house was erected in 1794/95 for Joseph Felt, who is listed as a "housewright" and is also known to have been a farmer. It is conceivable, therefore, that Felt himself was the builder, but this has not been documented. The building was originally planned as a double house, but was apparently occupied in entirety by the Felt family for many years.

D-8

D-8 NANCY CURTIS HOUSE
117-119 Federal Street
NR; MHD

1846/47

This outstanding Greek Revival double house was built in 1846/47 for Miss Nancy Curtis, who occupied one of the halves until the seventies. Two stories with a medium pitched roof and paired brick chimneys at each gable end, this building possesses a symmetrical matched-board facade with incised corner boards, a characteristically wide entablature, trapezoidal window lintels, and a recessed double entrance shielded by a beautifully proportioned classical porch supported by fluted Greek Doric columns and square pilasters. Virtually all decorative detail has been concentrated on this facade in an effort to maximize the aesthetic impact.

D-9   JOSEPH WINN, JR. HOUSE   1843
121 Federal Street
NR; HSI; MHD

SAUNDERS-WARD HOUSE   1843
123 Federal Street
NR; HSI; MHD

Paired together on the south side of Federal Street, the Winn and Ward-Saunders houses are the finest local examples of vernacular Greek Revival domestic architecture. Both were erected in the same year, 1843, on land purchased from David Pingree. They are strikingly similar in appearance, with only slight variations in exterior details and interior floor plans.

The house on the east (left) at number 121 was built for Joseph Winn, Jr., a wholesale shoe businessman and the former captain of the *St. Paul*, the largest Salem trading vessel of its era. Two stories with attic under a pitched roof, the Winn residence, in the manner of a Greek temple, presents one of its gable ends as the main street facade. Sheathed with matched boards, this facade is crowned by a closed pediment atop a wide, plain entablature, which encircles the house. Wide boards (mimicking pilasters) accent the corners. The facade window frames are molded, with decorative cornerblocks. In typical Greek Revival fashion the front entrance, which is recessed with a trabeated surround, is placed off center (the left of three bays).

The dwelling on the west (right) at number 123 was erected for Robert S. Saunders, a Salem shoe merchant, by housewright and real estate developer Jonathan F. Carlton (who may also have built the Winn house). After Saunders's premature death in 1846, Andrew Ward, a former sea captain and merchant, bought the property, and he, his wife, and their descendants resided there until 1916. Unlike the Winn house, the Saunders-Ward house possesses a cross-gable roof, full Doric corner pilasters, and narrow window frame moldings.

D-10

D-10 ROPES-WALDO HOUSE
124 Federal Street at Lynn
NR; MHD

c. 1768, etc.

This square, three-story, hipped-roof wooden residence possesses the form of a Federal-era house with porch details (Greek Revival and Italianate) from the early Victorian period, yet it may date from prior to the Revolutionary War. Based on research in deeds and probate records it is known that John Ropes bequeathed the land and a house on it to his son Jonathan when he died in 1754. Local historian Edward S. Waters (*Essex Institute Historical Collections* 16 (1879): 48) wrote that Jonathan lived in the old house for a time, but eventually erected another "mansion-house" on his new land which after his death in 1799, went to his only grandchild, Jonathan Waldo, Jr. The oldest part of the building, therefore, may be securely dated after 1754 and most certainly after 1766, the year that Federal street was laid out. The Waldo family retained ownership until 1818, after which the house passed to John Holman, a mariner, to Rev. John Brazer of the North Church, and to Capt. Thomas Perkins, a shipmaster and merchant. During the 19th century the house was expanded by the addition of the large wing in the west yard and the brick ell in the rear.

To the west (left) of the Ropes house at numbers 120-122 is a rectangular three-story, hipped-roof wooden double house (NR; MHD) built c. 1783 by Jacob and Elijah Sanderson, carpenters and cabinetmakers. The building possesses two entrances, one in each side yard. The western half still displays an early Federal-era pedimented and pilastered doorway surround, and molded window caps and sills, while the eastern half exhibits Victorian trim and bay windows.

D-11

D-11   EBENEZER SHILLABER HOUSE   1800–1801, etc.
128-130 Federal Street at Monroe
NR; MHD

According to Fiske Kimball (who based his conclusions on local tax records), this large three-story wooden double house was erected in

1800–1801 with interior details by Samuel Field McIntire (1780–1819), the famous builder's son, after 1811. Some of these details (split dentils, fluted vases in sunken ovals) are identical to those present in other local houses of the same period where McIntire also executed carving. Unfortunately, much of the original interior finish of the house has been removed and the exterior considerably altered. The Doric double porch, matching front doorways and corner pilasters, which are Greek Revival and date from c. 1830, are by no means a detriment to the house, however, and give it proper scale and excellent proportions. After 1865 the house was owned by members of the Shreve family.

D-12

D-12   IRELAND-EMERY HOUSE   c. 1797
131 Federal Street at Monroe
NR; MHD

This unostentatious three-story, hipped-roof wooden house (photo, center and right) with one end facing Federal Street is believed to have been erected for Jonathan Ireland, a blacksmith, c. 1797, four years before Monroe (originally Ropes) Street was laid out behind it. Except for the presence of a bay window above the main doorway (facing the west side yard), the house appears pretty much as it was built. This doorway is incorporated into a closed porch with sidelights, reeded Doric corner pilasters, and a plain entablature. Otherwise the house is a conventional Federal-period building. In 1828, when he acquired the house, Samuel Emery, a nautical instrument maker, commenced a residency here that lasted half a century.

The two-story, pitched-roof, early Federal house (NR; HSI; MHD) (photo, left) with central chimney at 10 Monroe Street (corner of Federal) was built c. 1782 for the widow Rebecca and the children of Nathaniel Gould, who had died the year before. A dwelling of similarly modest pretensions, it possesses little architectural detail but for a front central enclosed porch with sidelights and square reeded Doric pilasters under a dentiled entablature. A small two-stage wing of undetermined date is appended to the south side.

D-13

D-13 BENJAMIN CARPENTER HOUSE   c. 1801, etc.
135 Federal Street opposite Carpenter
NR; MHD

The evidence that Samuel McIntire (1757–1811) designed this residence is contained in the McIntire papers at the Essex Institute. Bearing in his handwriting the legend, "Sketch of ye plan of Capt. Carpenter's House," is a document providing first-floor details. From tax records it is further known that Carpenter, a sea captain and Revolutionary War soldier, acquired the land on which the house stands in 1801, and presumably had McIntire build for him immediately. After 1828 the house was occupied for many years by Michael Shepard, and later in the century was owned by the Bertrams and Robsons.

Three stories high with a hipped roof pierced by several brick chimneys, the Carpenter house was greatly modified during the Victorian era, and it is thus impossible to illustrate McIntire's work here, of which little has survived. The matched-board front facade displays open triangular, flat, and segmental-arch window hoods and corner quoins, all Italian Revival style. The enclosed front entrance porch, like the front fence and much of the interior, reflects 20th-century efforts in the direction of restoration.

Across Federal Street (north) at number 134 (also 2 Carpenter Street) is the Benjamin Blanchard house (NR; MHD), a plain, rambling, three-story, wooden Federal-era dwelling erected c. 1800. It is interesting for its enclosed pedimented porch laurel wreath and Doric pilasters, and for certain of its interior woodwork details which were carved by McIntire. These were removed from the Enoch Dow House (1807–1809), formerly on Lafayette Street, when this building was torn down c. 1910, and were then reinstalled in the Blanchard house by the owner, architect Philip Horton Smith (1890–1960).

D-14

D-14 JOSEPH EDWARDS'S HOUSE   1807
5 Carpenter Street
NR; HSI; MHD

This three-story, low-hipped-roof brick Federal dwelling was erected by housewright Joseph Edwards in 1807. Traditionally it has been associated with him, although it is believed he never actually re-sided there. Edwards was one of Salem's most active early 19th-century builders, supervising the construction of the Salem Jail and jailer's house (see C-28), and working on the Custom House (see

B-8) and Samuel McIntire's Registry of Deeds building (1807, demolished 1854), formerly at the corner of Summer and Broad streets. Edwards also built his own gambrel-roof house (HSI; MHD) directly opposite at number 8 Carpenter in 1808–1809, but sold it to Joshua Beckford the next year.

With its end toward the street and a yard reached through a handsome Federal wooden fence, the house at number 5 presents an attractive picture to the onlooker. The side yard entrance is capped by a semicircular fanlight set within a modillioned pediment, supported by fluted Doric pilasters. A two-stage ell (c. 1860; c. 1930) extends into the garden at the rear.

D-15

D-15 ASSEMBLY HOUSE
138 Federal Street
NR; MHD

1782; c. 1797/98

Erected in 1782 as a "Federalist Clubhouse," the Assembly House is a rare specimen of early Salem architecture whose history has been divided into two distinct functional phases. Funded by means of a joint stock venture, the building initially served as an assembly hall where balls, concerts, lectures, theatricals, oratorios, and other social and cultural events were held. Its early history is distinguished by the fact that the Marquis de LaFayette was entertained there in 1784, and President George Washington dined and danced there in 1789. Owing to the lack of documentation the precise appearance of the 1782 structure is unlikely ever to be known, and the name of the architect or master builder is thus far undiscovered. It is believed, however, that the ballroom may have been two stories and extended across the back width of the building, while the front half, as today, contained first-floor drawing rooms on either side of an entry hall with chambers above. Gerald W.R. Ward believes that the house "both inside and out was probably very plain and functional" (*The Assembly House*, p. 10), and there is no current reason to doubt this assertion.

Upon the opening of Washington Hall in the new Stearns block (see C-18) in 1792, the Assembly House was rendered obsolete. Jonathan Waldo, one of its developers, then systematically acquired the outstanding shares in the older building and assumed full ownership in 1796. Two years later he sold out to Samuel Putnam. It was either Waldo or Putnam who engaged Samuel McIntire (1757–1811) to remodel the structure, "turning it from a plain public meeting hall into an elaborate and fashionable dwelling" (*The Assembly House*, p. 19). McIntire's association with the house is documented by two front elevation drawings at the Essex Institute, one in his own hand, and the other, a working plan, probably by his assistant Daniel Bancroft (1746–1818).

A fine interpretation of the Adamesque Federal style, the McIntire scheme greatly enriched the front of the Assembly House by adding four pairs of Ionic pilasters (above a belt course) to the second story of the matched-board facade. A broad pediment, enclosing a traceried semicircular lunette, was centered above the facade. The hipped roof was furnished with a deck balustrade and the front doorway was adorned with rosettes and bellflowers. On the interior the ballroom was divided into several rooms on two floors, and the stairway and other decorative features were added in the stairwell and east front parlor. The ornate front porch, with its unusual carved grapevine frieze and Ionic columns, is believed to have been added by the house's second owner, Benjamin Chamberlain, between 1833 and 1856. The house was presented to the Essex Institute in 1965 by Miss Mary Silver Smith in memory of her parents, Mr. and Mrs. Joseph Newton Smith, who had acquired it in 1919. The front half has been open to the public since 1972.

D-16

D-16   RICHARD HARRINGTON HOUSE   c. 1871/72
141 Federal Street
NR; MHD

In 1871 Richard Harrington acquired a portion of the Wait estate, which extended due north from Essex Street, and immediately built this square, symmetrical, two-story wooden residence on his new land. Protected by a concave slate mansard roof, a product of the French Academic influence, the building illustrates well the potential of wooden ornamentation when fabricated by machined tools. Particularly intriguing are the open pediment dormers with gable spade motifs and paneled pilasters terminating in square Egyptianate capitals. Paired corner brackets, ogee-curve modillions, molded window surrounds, square molded porch columns and pilasters, and many other small decorative elements illustrate further the impact of Victorian eclecticism and the technology of the American industrial revolution.

To the east (left) of the Harrington house at number 139 is a simple two-story, hipped-roof wooden house which displays a recessed classical front doorway of c. 1830, but was probably built c. 1800. Those who have researched this area of the city believe that prior to 1875 this dwelling belonged to the Chipman and Cutts-Frye families.

D-17

D-17   COOK-OLIVER HOUSE

142 Federal Street
HABS; NR; MHD

1802–1803; 1808

The Cook-Oliver house is Salem's most notable and innovative Adamesque Federal-style wooden residence and one of the gems of New England architecture. Erected in 1803–1804 for Capt. Samuel Cook, it was designed by Samuel McIntire (1757–1811) when he was at the creative peak of his career. Documents indicate that in 1808, McIntire, influenced by the work of Asher Benjamin and Daniel Raynerd, further embellished the interior of the house. A kitchen extension to the rear ell was built some forty years later. After 1859 Cook's son-in-law, Henry K. Oliver, the former mayor of Lawrence and later mayor of Salem, lived in the house with his family. It was here that Oliver, an amateur musicologist, composed the well-known hymn, "Federal Street."

This three-story, hip-roof dwelling possesses an astounding array of delicate Federal details applied principally to the clapboarded, symmetrical front facade. Featured here are a modillioned cornice, molded window frames, a second-story belt course, and a central doorway flanked by rectangular sidelights and topped by a semi-elliptical fanlight. Shielding this doorway is a graceful flat-roofed porch with a strongly classical dentiled entablature supported by smooth, round Doric columns and attached half columns. Carved wooden swags, bellflowers, and rosettes are applied to the surfaces around the doorway, the belt course, and the panels above the second-story windows. The east end of the house is an unbroken brick wall. At one time an eaves balustrade, now removed, encircled the building.

In front of the Cook-Oliver house is McIntire's finest surviving wooden fence, the four posts of which are decorated with urns, patera, gougework, and beribboned bellflowers resembling the treatment around the front doorway. An elevation drawing (along with a floor plan for the house) of this lovely fence is at the Essex Institute. For many years and in numerous sources the legend persisted that the fence as well as some interior woodwork of the house were among materials taken from Elias Hasket Derby's mansion (1795–99; demolished, 1815) (see C-12), formerly on Essex Street, by Bulfinch and McIntire. It is evident that McIntire imitated certain features of the Derby residence for Captain Cook, but Fiske Kimball's research has convincingly disproved any other connection. The Cook-Oliver house is McIntire's original and complete accomplishment as it stands.

Information gleaned from deeds and tax records indicates that the two-story, gambrel-roof wooden house (NR; MHD) to the right (east) at 140 Federal Street was erected by housewright John Warden for his own use in 1794/95. Warden acquired the land from the proprietors of the Assembly House (see D-15) in 1794. For most of the 1800s this residence was owned by Archelaus Rea and Capt. Jeremiah Page and his heirs. Topped by a simple, fragile balustrade, the house has a matched-board gable end and side walls, unusual for a dwelling of its period. A side yard porch supported by slender, round Doric columns protects the entrance.

D-18

D-18 JOHN CULLITON HOUSE   1859
145 Federal Street at Flint
NR; HSI; MHD

This substantial three-story-plus-hipped-roof house was erected in 1859 on land formerly part of the Stearns estate for John Culliton, a successful tanner and currier in Salem and Boston. Culliton's descendants occupied this residence until 1915, when the Ronan family commenced a forty-year period of ownership. The Culliton house possesses many Italian Revival features which were popular at the time that it was constructed—a low-hipped roof; open-pediment dormers with molded window surrounds; carved, paired corner brackets; flat, broken, and segmental-arch window hoods with supporting brackets; and a front central entrance porch embellished with cornice brackets, molded square columns and pilasters, and round-arch side windows.

Directly opposite the Culliton house at numbers 144-146 is a three-story, hipped-roof Federal-style house (NR; MHD) built about 1802 for Thomas Whittredge, a shipmaster who traded in the Middle Atlantic states. The front doorway surround is particularly lovely with its dentiled broken pediment (enclosing a semicircular fanlight) supported by half-round and fluted Doric pilasters. Fiske Kimball wrote that "the house and stable . . . show close relationships with McIntire's work" (*Mr. Samuel McIntire, Carver . . .*, p. 51), but he was never able to prove an association.

D-19

D-19　ST. JAMES CHURCH (Roman Catholic)　　1891–1900
152 Federal Street at Flint
MHD

Erected over several years as parish funds became available, St. James Church reflects well the principles of the late Gothic

Revival style as applied to ecclesiastical architecture. Situated near the site of the parish's first wooden church (c. 1850; demolished, 1892), this massive brick and stone-trim edifice is 178 feet in length, with a steep-pitched roof nave 98 feet tall. A corner (southwest) tower with spire roof, which more than doubled the height of the church (it was once Salem's tallest building), was reduced to the ridgepole level in 1972 due to the expense of maintenance. Everywhere the Gothic pointed-arch motif is present—in the three recessed front entrance portals; the front gable relieving arch; trefoil apertures; and all window openings in the front facade, side aisles, clerestory, and apse. Built to accommodate 1,300 people, the building was constructed by local contractors (and parishioners) John J. and Thomas F. Mack from plans drafted by architect Thomas F. Houghton of Brooklyn, New York.

With its front Palladian doorway and gambrel roof, the William Orne, Jr., house (c. 1808) (NR; HSI; MHD), across the street at number 151, is a good example of a mid-Federal-era dwelling, with a form and decorative features carried over from the 18th century. It is possible that Orne himself was the builder, in that his trade was that of housewright.

D-20

D-20 JAMES BRADEN HOUSE

c. 1868

170 Federal Street
MHD

Erected c. 1868 for James Braden, a Boston Street currier and tanner, this square, two-story, hipped-roof wooden dwelling is one of

Salem's best Victorian Italianate buildings. A combination of bold
and subtle detail was realized by the builder. Decorating the cornice
are paired curvilinear brackets and modillions interspersed with
linked inverted horseshoe motifs. The molded window hoods are
characteristically flat or segmental-arch with support brackets. Corner quoins define the wall surfaces. The symmetrical matched-board
facade is highlighted by a central entrance that is protected by a
canopy adorned with small, evenly spaced brackets and held in
place by large side brackets with pendants. Above the canopy is a
bay window, so often seen in houses of this type. The bay is illuminated by round-arched windows and is embellished by additional
small brackets and paneled classical pilasters set on square bases.

Providing an interesting contrast with the Braden house is an
earlier, more refined Italian Revival house (HSI; MHD) across the
street at number 171. Erected in 1850 for John Huse, a currier and
tanner, this symmetrical, rectangular-plan, pitched-roof building
features paired eaves brackets, corner quoins, flat window hoods
with brackets, and a trabeated recessed front entrance. Further
down the street at number 177-79 is a three-story brick Federal
mansion (HSI; MHD) erected for Essex Bank cashier William Shepard
Gray by 1809. Recent research suggests that Samuel McIntire
(1757–1811) very likely designed the house and executed carvings
on the interior.

D-21

D-21   JABEZ SMITH HOUSE   c. 1806
397 Essex Street at South Pine
MHD

Jabez Smith, a housewright by trade, is believed to have built this, his own wooden house, c. 1806 and later did work on Chestnut Street. Three stories high with a hipped roof pierced by tall brick chimneys, this interesting structure exhibits an unusual belt course between the first and second stories. Features typical of the Federal style include the cornice with modillions, the applied boards above the third-story windows, and the front doorway crowned by a semi-circular fanlight and flanked by Doric pilasters. Originally the house was L-shaped before additions were made to the rear. Later Victorian bracketed canopy roofs were superimposed over the front and west side entrances, and a bay window was installed over the latter. Capt. John Silver also once lived here.

To the west (right) of the Smith house, across South Pine Street at number 401 Federal, is the Capt. Nathaniel Osgood house (HSI; MHD), a rather conventional, somewhat-altered, but still-command-ing three-story brick Federal dwelling erected c. 1815. A front door-way of the period, with sidelights and a traceried semielliptical fanlight, is hidden under a more recent Victorian porch.

D-22

D-22 LINDALL-BARNARD-ANDREWS HOUSE c. 1740
393 Essex Street
HABS; NR; MHD

Like the Cabot-Endicott-Low house (see D-32) at 365 Essex Street, this two-and-one-half-story, wood-frame and clapboard house is one of Salem's most outstanding large gambrel-roof Georgian Colonial dwellings. Local historian Oliver Thayer believed that it was erected for Judge James Lindall c. 1740 (*Essex Institute Historical Collections* 21 (1884): 222), and this date seems reasonable based on available evidence. Save for the attractive pedimented and pilastered front doorway with transom light, the house is very plain, with a central hallway plan and five-bay facade appropriate for the period. During the Revolution the house was owned by Rev. Thomas Barnard, the pastor of the old North Church, who played a significant role in the "Leslie's Retreat" episode of 1775 at the North Bridge in Salem. Fiske Kimball conjectured that during Barnard's years of occupancy several mantels were introduced on the interior, including one which he attributed to Samuel McIntire. William P. Andrews bought the property in 1816, and the Andrews family owned it for almost a century.

The L-shaped, two-story vernacular brick building (NR; HSI; MHD) to the east (left) at 391-391½ Essex Street at Flint was built for grocer Stephen Fogg in two sections. The brick store on the corner was raised in 1826, replacing a wooden commercial/residential block previously occupied by John Kimball and John N. Sleeper. The simple dwelling facing Essex Street was connected to the store in 1840 and was first lived in by Fogg's step-daughter, Lucinda, and her husband, Brackley Peabody.

D-23

D-23   IVES-PUTNAM HOUSE   1850/51
392 Essex Street
MHD

Erected in 1850/51 for printer William Ives, owner of the house at number 390, this unusually fine cubic-block, three-story, low-hipped-roof wooden dwelling is one of the best examples of the Italian Revival style surviving locally. Present on the symmetrical front facade are wide eaves supported by large brackets, a string course, and windows (graduated down in size from the first to third stories) capped by segmental-arch, broken-pediment, and flat hoods with side brackets. The main entrance, with its segmental-arch heading and flanking pilasters, is protected by a square-columned open porch, above which is an ample bay window at the second-story level, topped by a triple round-arch window in the third story. The formal balance and distinct lines of the house are accentuated by these carefully selected and arranged elements, set off against plain, expansive wall surfaces. George F. Putnam, a Boston Street currier and tanner, bought the property from Ives in 1859, and held it until 1874.

Two doors to the east (right) of the Ives-Putnam house at number 386 (corner of Flint Street) is a rectangular Victorian eclectic residence (MHD) built in 1868 for a successful local carpet retailer, Willard Goldthwait. Covered by a flat, slated French mansard roof, this substantial, symmetrical building displays many features (e.g. eaves brackets, pedimented window hoods, bay windows, front central porch) associated with the Italian Revival style.

D-24

D-24 LEMUEL HIGBEE HOUSE   1858
387 Essex Street
NR; HSI; MHD

DAVID KILEY HOUSE   1881/82
389 Essex Street at Flint
NR; MHD

In 1858 Lemuel Higbee financed the construction of his new,
spacious, square, two-story wooden Victorian eclectic residence at
387 Essex Street. Resembling several Lafayette Street dwellings of
the same period and later (see F-9), the Higbee house (photo, left)
exhibits on its symmetrical front facade numerous features traditionally associated with the Italian Revival style—matched-board
sheathing; corner quoins; a wide cornice with molded brackets;
thick molded window frames and flat bracketed window hoods; an
open porch with square support columns, pilasters, and eaves
brackets; a balustraded bay window above the porch; and open pediment dormers on a truncated hipped roof. The house is a monument to Higbee's rise from leather currier to successful manufacturer
of shoes during the Civil War.

The ornately detailed wooden structure to the west (right) at
number 389 (photo, right) was built almost a quarter of a century
after the Higbee house and is a fine example of a Victorian eclectic
dwelling of its time, differing markedly from its neighbor. Erected in
1881/82 for liquor dealer David Kiley, it occupies the site of an
older house lived in by ship captain Henry F. King and his family
from c. 1820 until c. 1880. Capped by a truncated, patterned-slate
mansard roof, the Kiley house shows the hybrid influence of the
High Victorian Gothic (chevron window hoods and porch gable),
High Victorian Italianate (bay windows, eaves and dormer brackets,
flat window hoods, classical pilasters and porch columns) and Stick
(horizontal, vertical, and diagonal wall boarding, exposed framing)
styles of residential architecture.

D-25 DEAN-SPRAGUE-STEARNS HOUSE   c. 1706; before 1793
384 Essex Street at Flint
NR; HSI; MHD

Recent research into probate records, deeds, and family papers indicates that this large, three-story, medium-pitched-roof wooden residence dates from c. 1706 and the ownership of Capt. Joseph Dean. The house remained in the Dean family until 1774/75 when Joseph's sons, John and Joseph, sold their half shares to Col. Joseph Sprague, a prominent ship owner and merchant who had moved from Newburyport to Salem. When Colonel Sprague passed away in 1808, his daughter, Mrs. William Sprague, and her physician husband moved in, and they and their descendants owned the property until 1930. During the thirties the building was used as an inn and tea room, and acquired the name of "The East India House," by which it is still popularly known.

The Dean-Sprague-Stearns house is noted primarily for its handsome front entrance porch. In *Mr. Samuel McIntire, Carver . . .*, Fiske Kimball observed that "among all the numerous tabernacle doorways and porches which adorn surviving Salem houses before 1793, the only one which we may confidently attribute to McIntire is that . . . at 384 Essex Street" (p. 70). Kimball founded his attribution on McIntire's ties with Dr. William Stearns, one of his clients in the construction of the Stearns block (see C-18), and on the "unusual elaboration of . . . [the] doorway with its flanking pilasters and perfect academic correctness of its Doric detail . . ." (p. 70). An unusual feature of the porch is the addition of fluted pilasters at either side of the main projection.

D-26 GRACE CHURCH (Episcopal)   1926/27
NR; MHD
BURRILL HOUSE (Parish House)   c. 1806
385 Essex Street
MHD

Grace Church was organized in 1858 by a group of parishioners
from St. Peter's Church (see C-37) on St. Peter Street. The first
church, a wooden Gothic Revival structure, was erected the same
year on the site of the present building from plans by the local
architectural firm of William H. Emmerton (1828–1873) and Joseph
C. Foster (1829–1906). When in 1926 this structure was no longer
able to meet parish needs, it was demolished and replaced by the
present stone masonry English late Gothic Revival edifice (photo,
left). Serving as architects for this project were Philip Horton Smith
and Edgar Walker of Salem and Boston, whose initial Georgian
Colonial Revival plans were rejected in favor of the final design.
Four of the pointed-arch, stained-glass windows, two of which are
by Tiffany, were transferred from the earlier building.

To the west (right) of Grace Church is the former Ebenezer
Smith (now Burrill) house (photo, right), constructed c. 1806. Three
stories high, with a low-hipped roof, it exhibits molded window
frames and a fine Palladian doorway on its front clapboarded facade.
The end walls are brick, unusual for a Salem residence of this
period and type. Grace Church acquired the property in 1926.
Three years later the house was remodeled, enlarged, and connected
by a cloistered wing to the church building under the direction of
architect Woldemar H. Ritter.

D-27   SPRAGUE-PEABODY-SILSBEE HOUSE   c. 1807, etc.
380 Essex Street
NR; HSI; MHD

Although it has been enlarged and remodeled since it was built
c. 1807, the Sprague-Peabody-Silsbee house remains the most impressive example of a three-story, square brick Federal mansion on
upper Essex Street. The construction of this building was financed
by Joseph Sprague, Jr., on land owned by his father Colonel Joseph
Sprague, who lived next door at number 384 (see D-25) until his
death in 1808. The name of the designer/builder of the house has
not been discovered, but Fiske Kimball attributed certain of the interior woodwork details to Samuel McIntire (1757–1811) because of
similarities to McIntire's other documented work. Only one original
McIntire mantel, alas, survived Victorian alterations.

Kimball also observed that "both the main cornice of the house
and that of the portico have forms derived from the *American
Builder's Companion* by [Asher] Benjamin and [Daniel] Raynerd,
published in 1806" (*Mr. Samuel McIntire, Carver . . .*, p. 121). Apparently McIntire used plates from the book as inspiration for the
interior embellishments, but did not adopt any forms from these
plates for exterior work. Hence, currently available evidence indicates that such features as the roof balustrade, splayed window
lintels with keystones, traceried front doorway lights, Ionic columned porch, and wrought-iron porch balustrade should not be
credited to him. The brick stable behind the house, though it also
has been altered, is the central-arch type which McIntire introduced
to Salem.

In 1822 the house was sold to Joseph Peabody, whose son Francis lived in it for many years, constructing a new brick addition on the northeast corner in 1833/34. From 1840 to 1901 the Silsbee family owned the property.

D-28   FORD-EMERSON-IVES-GIFFORD HOUSE   1764; 1893
377 Essex Street
NR; MHD

At first glance this outstanding Colonial Revival wooden dwelling would appear to date from the turn of the century, and indeed most of it does. In 1892 a building permit was issued to the recent purchaser of the property, Nathan Gifford, a dealer in lumber. This permit specified that Gifford and builder George F. Woodbury were authorized to complete "general repairs and alterations." Local tax records for the following year mention a "house unfinished" at the above address. This evidence, combined with the presence of old hand-hewn timbers in the structural frame, suggests that when Gifford made his modifications in 1893, he incorporated an older dwelling into the remodeled building. The timbers were probably from the James Lord house, erected on the same site in 1764. Earlier in the 19th century this house had been owned by the Reverend Brown Emerson and fancy goods dealer David P. Ives, who sold it to Gifford.

The imposing two-story, truncated, hipped-roof building that one may see today presents a symmetrical street facade, with two-story rounded window bays on either side of the principal entrance, which is shielded by a flat-roofed porch supported by Ionic columns. Tall Ionic pilasters, a legacy from Georgian Colonial architecture, appear at the front corners, while small Ionic pilasters may be observed in the front window bays and roof dormers. A broad cornice, decorated with Adamesque Federal modillions and swags, encircles the building. The resulting profusion of heavy and delicate elements is almost overwhelming. Because of the close similarity in massing and certain details, this dwelling may be compared with the Clark house (see below), directly across Essex Street.

D-29

D-29   CLARENCE S. CLARK HOUSE
376 Essex Street
NR; MHD

c. 1894

This large rectangular, two-story, wood-frame and clapboard residence was built c. 1894 for businessman Clarence S. Clark on the site of the Sprague-Waite house (c. 1796). Fiske Kimball believed that the Sprague house "[was] conceivably . . . a work of [Samuel] McIntire, but its plan, as revealed by the fenestration and chimneys, . . . [did] not conform with any of his plans which survive" (see photo, p. 125) (*Mr. Samuel McIntire, Carver . . .*, p. 91). Apparently it had been altered at an early date; hence, little original detail on which an attribution could rest existed at the time it was torn down. The original Federal-style stable in the back yard has survived, and displays a semicircular arch with keystone over the former front entrance.

The Clark house is a fine example of the Colonial Revival style, exhibiting many of its most pronounced traits. Covering the structure is a hipped roof broken by paired brick chimneys and closed pediment gable dormers, with a flat roof deck surrounded by a lightly constructed balustrade. A wide, plain cornice punctuated by modillions encircles the entire house. Characteristically, the front facade is perfectly symmetrical, with two-story rounded window bays balancing each other on either side of a semicircular, balustraded open entrance porch, which is topped by a modified Palladian window.

D-30

D-30   BUFFINGTON-GOODHUE-WHEATLAND HOUSE   By 1785; 1832

374 Essex Street
NR; HSI; MHD

This substantial two-story, gambrel-roof wooden residence has long posed a problem to researchers, and no one has yet been able to establish a definite date for its construction. Recent investigation, however, strongly suggests a building date of c. 1785, or possibly before, for Capt. Nehemiah Buffington on land previously owned by the Ruck, Burns, and Hicks families. It is conceivable that materials from an older building were incorporated into the present house, but this has yet to be documented through manuscript records or structural analysis. When Captain Buffington died in 1832 the property passed to his wife, and ultimately to Benjamin Goodhue, "a yeoman," who immediately moved the house forward to the

street and carried out extensive renovations. The heavy Doric
Greek Revival front entrance and much of the interior finishing
date from this remodeling. Otherwise, the house gives the appearance of being Georgian Colonial in vintage. In 1849 Benjamin and
George Wheatland purchased the house and it remained under
Wheatland family ownership until after World War I.

D-31

D-31 BERTRAM-WATERS HOUSE
(Salem Public Library)
370 Essex Street at Monroe
HABS; NR; MHD

1855; 1888/89; 1911/12

This imposing High Renaissance Italianate building was erected in
1855 as a residence for Capt. John Bertram from designs drafted by
Salem architects William H. Emmerton (1828–1873) and Joseph C.
Foster (1829–1906), the latter a resident of Essex Street. Their
drawings are at the Essex Institute. In 1887 Bertram's heirs donated
the building to the city for use as a public library, a purpose which
it still serves. Almost immediately it was completely remodeled on
the interior, with the Boston firm of Robert D. Andrews (1857–
1928) and Herbert Jacques (1857–1916) serving as principal architects and Hamilton and Balcomb of Salem as contractors. The
refurbished facility contained a main hall, public reading room,
trustees' room, reference room, storerooms, and bookstacks. In
1911/12, under the direction of Boston architect Clarence H.
Blackall (1857–1942), contractors Joseph N. and V.S. Peterson appended a four-story fireproof bookstack ell, a one-story reference

room wing, and a corresponding office and cataloguing wing to the original structure. Additional expansion is contemplated for the 1980s.

Three stories high with a balustraded hipped roof, the Bertram-Waters house, though not as ornate as the John Tucker Daland house (see A-1) at number 132, is still a superb example of its style and shows the same studied formalism. Constructed of brick with brownstone trim, it possesses numerous elements customarily found in High Renaissance Italianate buildings—a heavy bracketed cornice; corner quoins; a plain belt course; segmental arch and flat window hoods; tall first-story windows; and a front balustraded porch canopy held up by round Corinthian columns. The front elevation is characteristically symmetrical and the wall surfaces smooth and plain.

On the east (right) side of the building is a landscaped and fenced yard extending to Monroe Street. Behind this yard at number 5 is the Chaplin-Bowditch-Williams house (MHD), built in c. 1809 and expanded in 1884. This rectangular, three-story, wooden structure possesses an unusually deep enclosed entrance porch (with fluted Doric pilasters) on its front facade. It is very likely that the first owner, Solomon Chaplin, a housewright by profession, was the builder. For most of the 19th century the property was owned by the Bowditch and Williams families.

D-32

D-32 CABOT-ENDICOTT-LOW HOUSE   c. 1744–1748, etc.
365 Essex Street
NR; HSI; MHD

This large, two-story, gambrel-roof, Georgian Colonial residence was built for merchant Joseph Cabot on land acquired by Joseph and his brother Francis from Samuel Sibley in 1744. The house has not been definitely dated, but published sources suggest that it was constructed between 1744 and 1748. It is Salem's finest mid-18th-century work of "high style" domestic architecture. Some sources state that it was designed by an English architect, but this has not been documented.

After Joseph Cabot's death in 1767 the house remained in his family for over a century until 1870 when William C. Endicott purchased the estate. Endicott served as a justice of the Massachusetts Supreme Court and secretary of war in the administration of Grover Cleveland, and he hosted many famous visitors here, including Prime Minister Joseph Chamberlain of England, who married Endicott's daughter. Retail merchant Daniel Low and his wife, friends of the Endicotts, bought the house in 1894 and remained there until 1919.

Although the Cabot-Endicott-Low house has been subjected to some restoration work (e.g. the front doorway surround), most features are original. Piercing the front roof plane over a modillioned cornice are five dormers, the central one of the "bonnet-top" type and the others pedimented. The corners of the building are adorned with quoins and the first-floor windows are capped with molded hoods. The lot to the west (right), in front of the garage, is now open space, but once accommodated the Jeffrey Lang house (c. 1740), a gambrel-roof, two-family dwelling removed by the Lows.

The two-story, pitched-roof, wooden house (NR; HSI; MHD) to the west (right) at 373 Essex Street was built for Mary Ann Ropes (later Mrs. John Bertram) and her two maiden sisters by their parents c. 1843/44. Typical of the uncomplicated vernacular Greek Revival style, the principal matched-board gable end faces the street, with a closed-pediment gable and an off-center recessed and trabeated doorway. Another fine Greek Revival house (c. 1845) (see D-43) of the same type but with richer decoration, exists at number 330.

D-33   SMITH-CROSBY-ENDICOTT HOUSE   1789
359 Essex Street
NR; HSI; MHD
CAPTAIN NICHOLAS CROSBY HOUSE   1800
361 Essex Street
NR; HSI; MHD

These two Federal-period houses are closely linked historically as
well as stylistically. In 1788 Benjamin Smith and Nicholas Crosby
purchased the property which is today 359 and 361 Essex Street.
Local tax records suggest that Smith and Crosby probably erected
the house, now number 359, in 1789. Ten years later the entire
property was divided, with Smith obtaining the eastern half including a "dwelling house." Master mariners William Lander and
Robert Emery lived there in the early 1800s, and were followed by
Capt. Samuel Endicott and his heirs, the owners from 1815 to after
1885.

When Smith and Crosby divided their land, Crosby became the
owner of the western half, which contained a store and outbuildings
but no house. Tax and probate records indicate that the residence
at number 361 displaced these buildings in 1800, but quickly passed
to Crosby's wife upon his death in late 1800. Oliver Thayer wrote
that grocer Michael Webb lived there in 1804, and that later the
house became the home of Capt. Benjamin Creamer, remaining in
his family until late in the century.

The Smith-Crosby-Endicott and Capt. Nicholas Crosby houses
are each covered by low hipped roofs penetrated by tall paired interior brick chimneys and are three stories in height with central

hall floor plans. Both possess simple molded cornices, narrow corner boards and 6/6 double sash windows. The entrance of number 359, however, appears to date from c. 1830, as suggested by its wide transom and side lights, Ionic pilasters, and flat entablature porch canopy supported by fluted Ionic columns. In contrast, number 361 exhibits a plain Federal-style trabeated front doorway surround, a delicate latticework roof balustrade, and a west side enclosed porch with fluted Doric pilasters, an entablature, and a pedimented gable.

D-34

D-34 EMERY S. JOHNSON HOUSE
1853
360 Essex Street
NR; MHD

The Emery S. Johnson house is situated above the level of Essex Street on sloping terrain and is one of Salem's finest and most imposing Italian Revival-style residences. Erected in 1853 for Johnson, a local merchant and shipmaster, this square, two-story wooden structure with ell occupies a site formerly part of the Jonathan Ropes estate. Like the later Rogers/Russell double house (see D-38) at number 350-352, the front facade is symmetrical, with foundation-to-cornice bows on either side of an open entrance porch. Familiar Italian Revival features include corner quoins, rusticated facade boarding, carved and paired cornice brackets and modillions, segmental-arch dormers, thin modeled chimneys, a front window bay (second story), heavy molded window frames, and flat molded window hoods supported by side brackets. An original Victorian wrought-iron fence extends along the sidewalk. The architects for the house were William H. Emmerton (1828–1873) and Joseph C. Foster (1829–1906) of Salem. The floor plans and building agreement are at the Essex Institute.

D-35

D-35 CLARK-MORGAN-BENSON HOUSE   c. 1729, etc.
358-358½ Essex Street
NR; MHD

One of the oldest surviving buildings on Essex Street, the Clark-Morgan-Benson house has puzzled researchers over the years. We do know, however, that Richard Croade purchased the land on which the present dwelling stands in 1664 and that there was a house on it before that date. This house remained in the Croade family until 1729, when it burned. Apparently it was rebuilt c. 1729 by the new owner, Joseph Neal, and some of the timbers from the first house were reused. The name of the house is derived from the ownership of the western half of the structure by the Clarks and their heirs from 1787 to 1896, the eastern half by the Morgans from before 1836 to 1900, and the entire building by the Bensons from 1904 to 1981.

U-shaped with two large ells (the western is gambrel-roofed), the Clark-Morgan-Benson house, both in massing and detailing, is a representative early 18th-century, central-chimney-plan residence. Penetrating the front lower roof plane are three evenly spaced open pediment dormers. Echoing the dormer roof lines are closed pediment caps above the first floor windows, which, judging by old photographs, appear to have been 20th-century additions. The front and west-side Palladian doorways, which are very similar, are certainly mid-18th century at the latest. The house has been enlarged at least twice since it was first built.

D-36

D-36 Z. AUGUSTUS GALLUP HOUSE

1889/90

357 Essex Street

NR; MHD

Another of Essex Street's superb Colonial Revival style houses (see D-28 and D-29), this commodious two-story wooden residence was built in 1889/90 for Z. Augustus Gallup, the manager of the Naumkeag Clothing Company. It is located on the site of banker William H. Foster's house, which was demolished c. 1889. Breaking with the customary Colonial Revival pattern of front facade symmetry, the Gallup house possesses a two-story oblong bay to the left of the central entrance, balanced by a square, balustraded one-story bay to the right. Other features associated with the style are the truncated hipped roof, the pilastered and modeled brick chimneys, the large Doric corner pilasters, the broad cornice decorated with dentil molding, the eaves modillions, the modified front Palladian window, the pilastered closed pediment dormers, and the front porch canopy supported by classical columns. Recalling the McIntire version of the Adamesque Federal mode, once so dominant in Salem, are the delicately constructed balustrades with miniature urns, and the swags, festoons, and laurel wreath motifs above the windows. Typical of the Colonial Revival, certain elements are out of proportion with other parts of the building.

D-37

D-37   JOSEPH H. HANSON HOUSE
355 Essex Street at Hamilton
NR; MHD

c. 1865

In the residence (c. 1865) of merchant Joseph H. Hanson, the traditional three-story, low-hipped-roof, cubical massing characteristic of Salem Federal-style townhouse architecture is updated, with exterior decorative elements from the Italian Renaissance Revival mode. The thick eaves cornice is fitted out with carved, paired brackets. Quoins are present at the front corners. The rusticated board facade and clapboarded side walls display windows graduated in size and topped with bracketed flat, broken-arch, and segmental-arch hoods. The recessed front central doorway is sandwiched between incised Doric pilasters, which support a bracketed, flat, molded cornice. This embellishment provides the building with a chaste, formal, uncluttered classical dignity that is also achieved in brick and brownstone in the John Tucker Daland house (see A-1) at 132 Essex Street.

D-38 ROGERS/RUSSELL DOUBLE HOUSE 1875
350-352 Essex Street
NR; MHD

Erected in 1875, the Rogers/Russell double house is an excellent example of the late Italian Revival style as expressed in urban townhouse architecture. From listings in city directories it is apparent that the building was jointly financed by Arthur S. Rogers, the treasurer of the Atlantic Car Company, who resided at number 352, and Benjamin W. Russell, a teller at the Salem National Bank, who lived at number 350. Three stories high with a low hipped roof penetrated by four thin brick chimneys, this interesting wooden structure possesses rounded bows on its matched-board symmetrical front facade, both with tall double windows on each floor that are topped by broken-arch and semicircular hoods with ornate keystones. The curvature of the bows is repeated in a central segmental-arch pediment, enclosing paired semicircular attic lights. The cornice is adorned with delicately carved brackets with drops. Reached by a flight of granite steps, the double front entrance is both formal and inviting—it is sheltered by a lightly constructed porch canopy, set on attenuated round columns with high bases. The combined visual emphasis of all these elements is on verticality.

The Samuel C. Oliver house (NR; MHD) to the east (right) at number 348 (corner of Beckford Street) is another of Salem's several outstanding Victorian eclectic residences. Built c. 1872, it illustrates the impact of the French Academic influence in its concave mansard roof and its dormer and window ornamentation. Italian Revival details (corner quoins, cornice brackets, classical pilasters, round hoods, square porch columns, etc.) are also very much in evidence.

D-39 COOK-DALAND HOUSE   Between 1706 and 1720; c. 1733, etc.
14 Beckford Street
NR; HSI; MHD

What limited knowledge we have about this intriguing early Georgian Colonial house is the product of research conducted by Historic Salem and an on-site inspection made by architectural historian Abbott Lowell Cummings. The first house on the site was built for Abraham Cole c. 1675. In 1706 this small building passed to John Cook, a mariner, who either tore it down soon after acquiring it or replaced it after it had burned. Whatever its fate, Cummings has concluded that based on the structural evidence (summer beams; floor-to-ceiling measurements), the east end of the present house was raised soon after 1706 and assuredly before 1720. John Cook died in 1721 and ten years later his property was divided, his son Joseph Cook receiving the house. In 1732 he purchased additional land and had the western portion of the house erected. The leanto on the north side was probably added after 1750. The Palladian doorway surround, which may be a restoration, could date from before 1800. For most of the 19th century the house was owned by the Daland family and was moved back from the street c. 1915, at which time the brick chimney was probably rebuilt.

Behind (north of) the Cook-Daland house at number 16, and

also facing south, is a large, distinguished gambrel-roof Colonial Revival residence (MHD) erected in 1905–1906 for William M. Jelley, teller at the Salem Five Cents Savings Bank. According to tradition, local architect Ernest M.A. Machado (1868–1907) prepared the plans.

D-40

D-40 HENRY L. WILLIAMS HOUSE
342 Essex Street opposite Botts Court
NR; MHD

1846

Located on the site of the former Punchard residence, this comfortable but unostentatious mid-Victorian eclectic wooden house was built in 1846 for Henry Williams, who was a partner in the Boston merchant firm of Williams and Daland, the president of the Salem Five Cents Savings Bank, and the mayor of Salem in 1875/76. From the original plans deposited at the Essex Institute, we know that the designer was Boston's notable architect Gridley J.F. Bryant (1816–1899). The supervising carpenter was Aaron Kehew, Jr., and the mason was Aaron Russell, both of Salem. The building which they produced combines Greek Revival characteristics (wide corner pilasters and window frame moldings, off-center and recessed front doorway with thick molded surround and lights) and Italian Revival elements (bracketed porch canopy, bay window, modillioned cornice, flat modillioned window hoods, molded brick chimneys) in an innovative manner that sets it apart from other Salem houses of the same era.

Directly across the street at number 343 (corner of Botts Court) is a plain but charming small gambrel-roof house (NR; HSI; MHD) built for a member of the Pickering family before 1736 and later owned by the Botts. Anchored by a large central brick chimney, it possesses a trabeated doorway on the Botts Court facade. It is one of the oldest dwellings of its kind in Salem.

D-41

D-41 SALEM ATHENAEUM (Plummer Hall) 1906–1907
337 Essex Street
NR; MHD

In 1907 the Salem Athenaeum (incorporated, 1810), a private proprietary library, was moved to this new brick facility from its former quarters in old Plummer Hall (see A-1) at 132 Essex Street. Designed by the Boston and North Shore architect William G. Rantoul (1867–1949), the building (also known as Plummer Hall) was executed in the Colonial Revival style, and closely resembles "Homewood" (minus its wings), a well-known Neoclassical residence (1801–1803) on the campus of Johns Hopkins University in Baltimore. One story with a hipped roof, the Athenaeum building has a symmetrical front facade highlighted by a Doric portico of four columns shielding a tall pilastered doorway and reached by a broad flight of granite steps. On the interior are a large reading room, three levels of book stacks, and special collections rooms. The construction project was financed by the sale of old Plummer Hall to the Essex Institute in 1906.

D-42   CURWEN/GILLIS DOUBLE HOUSE   c. 1854
331-333 Essex Street
NR; MHD

In 1851 the Curwen family purchased the Thomas Maule house and
promptly had it demolished for the construction of the handsome
Italian Revival double house now located at 331-333 Essex Street.
Erected c. 1854, this three-story, square, hipped-roof building
reflects the mid-Victorian interest in the architecture of the Italian
Renaissance. In imitation of stone on the symmetrical front facade
are rusticated wooden wall boarding and corner quoining. Further
typical of the style are the paired cornice brackets and dentil
molding and the segmental-arch, flat, and pedimented window
hoods supported by brackets. Protecting the front double doorway is
a flat-roof classical porch canopy held up by tapered, fluted Corinthian columns—this porch, though of wood, is similar in scale and
proportions to the front brownstone porch of the John Tucker
Daland house (see A-1) at 132 Essex Street. The Curwen/Gillis
double house is one of a half-dozen outstanding Italian Revival
dwellings on Essex Street, between North and Boston.

  Between the Curwen/Gillis double house and the Salem
Athenaeum (see D-41) at 335 Essex Street is a modest two-story,
gambrel-roof wooden residence (NR; HSI; MHD) built for Col. John
Page c. 1793 or possibly before. With one gable end facing the
street, it possesses a simple pedimented enclosed entrance porch.
Later it was the home of Capt. Thomas Holmes and of Frank
Cousins, a professional photographer known for his marvelous views
of Salem life and architecture.

D-43 HOLMAN-PRICE HOUSE

1845/46, etc.

330 Essex Street

NR; MHD

In 1845 Jonathan Holman, a hatmaker, acquired land on the north
side of Essex Street and had this modest Greek Revival house constructed on it. Merchant Joshua Phippen was a tenant here until
1863, when the property passed from Holman's estate to Richard
Price, a Boston ice company executive; it remained in his family
into the 20th century.

Two stories with a pitched roof, the Holman-Price house has
many of the hallmarks of a simple but architecturally correct Greek
Revival dwelling. On its principal street-facing gable end are a
closed-boxed gable pediment above a molded entablature and wide
corner boards. Set in the matched-board facade are an off-center
recessed and trabeated doorway and 6/6 double sash windows with
trapezoidal and flat molded (with corner blocks) lintels. These
elements are effectively combined to make a unified visual statement. The ell to the rear consists of two parts, the first of three
stories added about 1865 and the second of one story appended
later in the century.

D-44 LORING-EMMERTON HOUSE 1818; 1885
328 Essex Street
HABS; NR; MHD

Despite extensive remodeling in the Colonial Revival vein, the Loring-Emmerton house remains one of Salem's loveliest brick Federal-style dwellings. Erected in 1818, it gained its historic name from the residencies of statesman and diplomat George B. Loring and of philanthropist and historic preservationist Caroline O. Emmerton, under whose leadership the House of Seven Gables Settlement Association was formed (see B-13, B-14, B-15, and B-16). Three stories high with a low-hipped roof and tall brick end chimneys, the building has the same basic form, facade symmetry, and rectangular central-hall floor plan as Chestnut Street and Washington Square houses of the same period.

In 1885, under Miss Emmerton's ownership, architect Arthur Little (1852–1925) of Boston expanded the structure and transformed it into a close twin of the Dodge-Shreve house (see E-18) at 29 Chestnut Street. Nearly identical window lintels, modified Palladian windows, traceried front doorway lights, balustraded front entrance porches (the column orders differ), and narrow cornices with beaded molding are present in each building. Little also added a fine porte-cochere (with cantilevered balcony and rusticated window frame above) on the west side, a lavish carriagehouse, and a rear balustraded ell with a polygonal corner bay and a portico of four free-standing columns, doubtless inspired by those of the Andrew-Safford house (see A-4) at 13 Washington Square. Little's interiors, particularly the two rear bedrooms, the entrance hall, and the dining room, are spectacular exhibitions of Colonial Revival ornamentation and illustrate the ambitious tastes of Gilded Age America.

D-45

D-45   PUTNAM-BALCH HOUSE ("Greymoor")   1871/72
329 Essex Street at Cambridge
NR; MHD

This majestic Victorian eclectic mansion was the former headquarters of Post 23 of the American Legion and was painstakingly restored by Donald Costin in 1979/81. It is now open to the public. The most ambitious and outstanding residence of its era in Salem, it was erected for James S. Putnam in 1871/72 on the site of the Benjamin Marston house, which Putnam had demolished. Frank Balch acquired the property in 1881 and held it until 1921 when it was purchased by the Legion.

Two stories high with a truncated hipped roof, the Putnam-Balch house illustrates dramatically the possibilities of wooden ornamentation in the immediate post-Civil War period. Reflecting the French Academic as well as the High Victorian Italianate styles are a wide variety of decorative details which predominate on the front rusticated board facade but are also present on the other elevations. Tall molded window frames are capped by heavy segmental-arch and flat hoods with carved support brackets. The facade entrance porch is supported by eight square modeled columns (two of which are attached) and is embellished by a bracketed cornice. Paired square pilasters set atop paneled bases are present at the front corners. A rounded facade gable and a heavy bracketed cornice, surely Salem's most elaborate, complete the ornamentation.

Providing a stark contrast with the Putnam-Balch house to the east (left) at 1 Cambridge Street is the Capt. Thomas Mason house, a modified but still-interesting Georgian Colonial dwelling erected c. 1750. Two stories high and irregular in shape to conform to its lot, this building displays closed pediment dormers, a modillioned cornice, a gambrel roof (which may not be original), and a recessed front entrance set between Doric pilasters and topped by a molded, dentiled pediment characteristic of the times.

D-46

D-46 ROPES MANSION (Ropes Memorial) Late 1720s, etc.
318 Essex Street opposite Cambridge
HABS, NR; MHD

Built in the late 1720s for merchant Samuel Barnard, a native of Deerfield, and later owned by the Ropes family, this lovely gambrel-roof Georgian Colonial mansion is one of New England's most significant and thoroughly documented historic house properties. This building is owned by the Trustees of the Ropes Memorial and has been opened to the public since 1912; it is presently under the curatorial management of the Essex Institute. Behind the house is a spacious, meticulously groomed formal garden laid out in 1912 and nationally renowned for the beauty and variety of its plants and shrubs.

In 1768 Judge Nathaniel Ropes, II, purchased the property from Samuel Barnard's nephew Joseph and his son Ebenezer and commenced a period of Ropes family ownership which extended until 1907. In that year, upon the death of the last two unmarried Ropes sisters, Mary and Eliza, the house and grounds were bequeathed to the public as an educational memorial. The house, however, had previously undergone sweeping changes at the direction of the Ropes. In 1807 the structure was extensively renovated on its interior. In the mid 1830s, five interior rooms and the central hall were remodeled, and a new recessed Ionic-pilastered doorway was installed, the details of which were inspired by a plate in Asher Benjamin's *American Builder's Companion . . .* (1827). Finally, in 1894, under the supervision of architects Stone, Carpenter, and Willson of Providence, Rhode Island, the Misses Ropes moved the house back from the street, installed central heat, plumbing, and electricity, added the large two-and-one-half-story kitchen and service ell, and made several interior modifications (dining room, hallway, double parlors, etc.) in the Colonial Revival vein. Despite all these changes, the house has not lost its stately 18th-century character, as evidenced by its traditional exterior form, fragile roof balustrade, pedimented dormers, and modillioned cornice. Decorated with pilastered posts crowned by carved urns, the handsome front fence is a conjectural copy of a McIntire Federal type, and was erected in 1894, also from plans by Stone, Carpenter, and Willson.

D-47

D-47   FIRST (North) CHURCH (Unitarian)   1835/36, etc.
316 Essex Street
NR; MHD

The home of the oldest continuous Protestant congregation (established 1629) gathered in North America, the First Church edifice is considered by architectural historians to rank with St. Peter's Church (see C-37) as one of the most outstanding stone masonry Gothic Revival ecclesiastical structures in the United States. The late Talbot F. Hamlin praised this building for its "simple, dignified charm" and "homely simplicity" which is "more akin to the true Gothic spirit than other richer and more pretentious works" (*The American Spirit in Architecture*, p. 138). Constructed of cut and regularly coursed Quincy granite and covered by a low-hipped slate roof, the building possesses a symmetrical front facade on which is centered a square, crenelated attached bell tower. Although this tower, like that of St. Peter's, features quatrefoil openings on each wall face and a front Tudor-arch doorway with a large traceried pointed-arch window above, it has a more finished appearance, perhaps because of the first-story belt course, the recessed panels, and the smoother and more even stonework. Additional pointed-arch windows, all with basic tracery and diamond-shaped panes, are positioned on either side of the tower and on each side wall. There are stained-glass windows by Tiffany, LaFarge, and Reynolds. The architect was Gridley J.F. Bryant (1816–1899) of Boston, but the choice of the Gothic Revival style is said to have resulted from the persuasions of parishioner Francis Peabody, who oversaw the construction. Interior ornamentation was added in 1848, and the addition to the rear was built in 1927 from plans by the firm of Little and Brown of Boston.

D-48 LINDALL-GIBBS-OSGOOD HOUSE   1755
314 Essex Street
NR; HSI; MHD

According to Samuel Curwen's list of Salem houses (see bibliography), this virtually unchanged wooden Georgian Colonial dwelling was erected in 1755 for spinster Mary Lindall, who lived here until 1776. The property then passed to the Gibbs family, and ultimately to the Appletons and Nicholses before acquisition by Capt. William Osgood in 1825. For the next 125 years the house remained in the Osgood family. Then in 1947 it was acquired by the Salem chapter of the American Red Cross, the present owner. In recent years the building has been painted red with white trim, most appropriate colors considering its current occupant.

Covered by a gambrel roof with three pedimented dormers and a modillioned and dentiled cornice, the Lindall-Gibbs-Osgood house possesses a perfectly balanced front facade with a recessed central entrance framed by rusticated boarding. Superimposed on this boarding are fluted Doric pilasters, above which are a dentiled entablature and molded pediment. A small pitched-roof ell extends to the rear. A coherent and discreetly detailed work of architecture, the house is a fine representative example of a building of its period, size, and type.

D-49 JONATHAN CORWIN HOUSE   c. 1675
("Witch House")
310½ Essex Street at North
HABS; NR; MHD

One of Salem's oldest and most historic buildings, this 17th-century, wood-frame-and-clapboard dwelling was acquired in an in-completed state in February 1675 by Jonathan Corwin, a merchant, from Capt. Nathaniel Davenport of Boston. Corwin then contracted with mason Daniel Andrew for the finishing of the structure. It is in connection with Corwin's period of ownership that its more popular name, the "Witch House," derives, for during the infamous 1692 Salem witch trials, he served as a magistrate and justice and many of those suspected of practicing witchcraft were brought to the house for pretrial examinations. As completed, the house possessed a central-chimney floor plan, a projecting two-story porch with flanking peaked gables on the front facade, and a rear leanto. On the facade the entire second story overhung the first with decorative drop pendants at the porch and end corners. A clustered pilaster brick chimney, which has been restored, anchored the house at its center.

When Jonathan Corwin's grandson George died in 1746, the house was nearly in its original form, but c. 1746/47 his widow Sarah apparently "enlarged the house according to a well-substanti-ated word of mouth tradition of the family, at which time facade gables were removed, two chambers built over the leanto and a gambrel roof constructed which covered the entire frame" (Abbott Lowell Cummings, "Massachusetts Bay First Period Houses," *Architecture in Colonial Massachusetts* . . ., p. 171). The Corwin house underwent additional changes between 1856 and 1885 when owner George P. Farrington attached a drugstore to the east side front. In 1945, when demolition threatened (see C-45), Historic Salem bought the property and had it moved back and restored by Boston architect Gordon Robb, with consulting assistance from the well-known author and architect Frank Chouteau Brown (1876–1947), also of Boston. The City of Salem took title to the building in 1948 and has since maintained it as a furnished historic site open to the public.

SOUTH CHURCH (1803/1804; destroyed by fire, 1903) by Samuel McIntire (1757–1811) and formerly at Chestnut and Cambridge streets. Photograph, c. 1890.

E

CHESTNUT
AND
BROAD STREETS

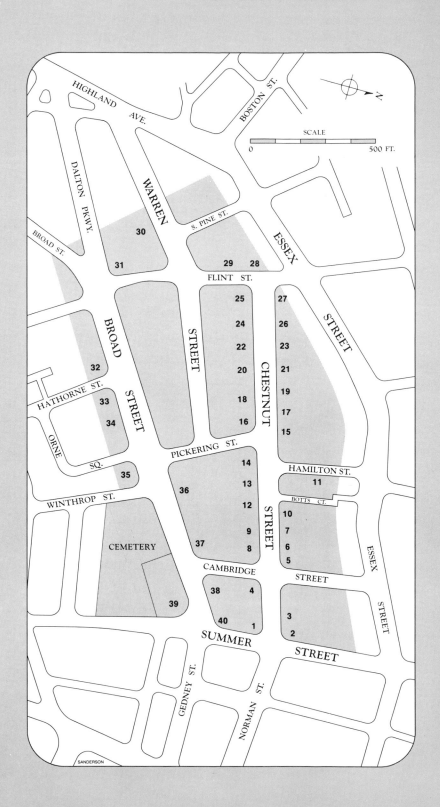

Most who have commented in print about Chestnut Street (MHL), whether they are serious scholars or more casual writers, consider it to be one of the most outstanding streets architecturally in the United States. Samuel Chamberlain, the compiler of three photographic works on Salem, referred to the street as "the finest, best preserved and most aristocratic thoroughfare in America" (*A Stroll Through Historic Salem*, p. 103). Surely, as a collection of Adamesque Federal buildings (all but one residential and dating from c. 1800 to c. 1830) it has no equal anywhere in the country. A physical monument to Salem's most prosperous years as a world leader in maritime trade, Chestnut Street has been a peaceful and beautiful home to merchants, sea captains, diplomats, statesmen, politicians, artists, and literary men, who have all contributed to the establishment of the city's rich historic legacy. The street's designation for virtually every kind of official landmark status is a proper outgrowth of its broad and distinguished reputation.

Chestnut Street was first laid out in 1796 by the town of Salem and is a superb example of urban planning. Initially it was forty feet wide, but in 1804, at the urging of John Pickering and Pickering Dodge, it was doubled in width. The reasons for the name "Chestnut Street" have never been clear—the first trees on either side were poplars and elms, and a few elms still stand. The combination of these stately trees and the tall brick chimneys of the houses creates a delightful sense of vertical rhythm, as well as grace and elegance. In addition, the repetitive three-story house forms, with their Federal or later Greek Revival porches, offer an equally pleasing uniformity to the architecture of the street.

Contrary to popular myth, Samuel McIntire (1757–1811) did not design most of the houses on Chestnut Street—in fact, only one (Jonathan Hodges house, see E-6) is definitely his, though two of his public buildings, Hamilton Hall (see E-4) and the South Church (see E-3), were built in the same neighborhood. The other grand and expertly crafted houses on the street are proof that Salem had numerous talented master builders and skilled artisans during the early 1800s—the work of William Lummus, John Nichols, Perley Putnam, William Roberts, Jabez Smith, Sims Brothers, and David Lord is well represented on Chestnut Street as it was in other sections of the city at that time.

Running parallel to Chestnut Street to the south are Warren and Broad streets, where one may find excellent examples of architectural styles from the pre-Federal era to the late Victorian period. Along the south side of upper Warren Street are a half dozen outstanding architect-designed Colonial Revival one, two, and three-family residences which 185 replaced older structures destroyed by the 1914 Salem fire. On Broad Street, one of the city's oldest highways (it was referred to by its current name by 1799), is a representative collection of Georgian Colonial, Federal, Greek Revival, Gothic Revival, and Victorian eclectic buildings, highlighted by the imaginatively "Gothicized" Pickering house (see E-36) and the Federal and mid-Victorian eclectic complex (see E-39) of former educational buildings at the corner of Broad and Summer streets. Running from the west end of Chestnut Street east to Broad is Flint Street, on the west side of which is a row of three pleasantly embellished mid-Victorian eclectic dwellings.

E-1

E-1   FRANCIS COX HOUSE
1 Chestnut Street at Summer
NR; MHD

c. 1846

Prominently situated at the corner of Chestnut and Summer streets is the Francis Cox house, erected c. 1846 on land acquired by Benjamin Cox from Deacon John Stone (see E-2) in 1837. The Cox house is an outstanding Italian Villa building; although it lacks the customary ornate corner tower, it does possess many of the other features normally associated with this style—asymmetrical principal wall elevations, smooth and uniform (matched-board) wall surfaces, medium-pitched intersecting roofs, projecting cornices with brackets, bay windows, cutout balustraded balconies, and flat and round-headed (in two instances they are paired) windows. The Cox house is one of Salem's earliest Italianate buildings and represents a departure from the balanced formal facades of the Federal era that line both sides of Chestnut Street.

To the west (right) at numbers 5 and 7 is a two-story, pitched-roof, wooden double house (NR; MHD) built in 1826/27 as an investment property by carpenter William Lummus for Deacon John Stone. A plain and unimposing structure, it displays recessed and trabeated paired doorways on its front facade, with a later round bay window over the westernmost of the two. Richard Wiswall's list of Chestnut Street houses (see bibliography) states that the first occupant of number 5 was Samuel Hodges, and of number 7, the Reverend W.R. Babcock.

E-2

E-2 "THE STUDIO" DOUBLE HOUSE
(Robinson Block)
2-4 Chestnut Street at Summer
NR; MHD

c. 1826/27

Another of Salem's fine brick row houses, this solid three-story, pitched-roof brick building was built about 1826/27 by Deacon John Stone on the site of Mrs. Dowst's one-story wooden candy shop (c. 1800). Until 1839 Stone lived in the western of the two residential units. The block acquired its familiar name, "The Studio" after 1869 when it was rented as studio space to such distinguished Salem artists as Frank Benson and Phillip Little (see E-5). It is also known as the Robinson block owing to the long presence of the Robinson family in the eastern half after 1839.

Architecturally "The Studio" is a particular interest because of the presence, adjacent to each other, of two large, deeply recessed entrances, connected in a neighborly way by a small door portal that is unique locally. Under the roof eaves is a beaded wooden cornice similar to those on other Chestnut Street houses built at the same time. According to Lee family correspondence (Essex Institute), "Clark and Pike, and perhaps Whitaker [were the] carpenters," and James Stone was the mason.

Until 1853 the lot to the west (left) of "The Studio" at number 6 was occupied by the plain wooden house and shop (c. 1800) of carpenter Joseph McIntire, the brother of Samuel. In this year Charles S. Nichols had the present two-story wooden Italian Revival dwelling (NR; HSI; MHD) erected in its place. Features typical of the style include the segmental-arch dormers, flat balustraded window hoods, corner quoins, cornice dentils and paired brackets, matched board facade sheathing, bracketed porch canopy, and central bay window above (added in 1874).

E-3

E-3 GREGG-STONE HOUSE   1805; c. 1829
8 Chestnut Street
NR; MHD

The only Chestnut Street house with its main facade at right angles to the sidewalk, this simple but attractive hipped-roof brick residence had its origins in a one-story store built on the site in 1805 by Daniel Gregg. In 1825 Deacon John Stone acquired most of the land between Summer Street and the South Church (see E-1 and E-2), and c. 1829 he added two additional stories to the store building of a different brick bond than that (Flemish) used by Gregg. At some later time the gambrel and pitched-roof wooden ells were appended to the rear. A lovely semielliptical fanlight tops the front central doorway with sidelights. The windows lack lintels, and the 6/6 sashes are set in so-called molded "plank-frames" which do not appear in Salem after c. 1810. The house was owned by Stone and his heirs until 1850, and later was occupied by Capt. Daniel H. Mansfield, Rev. Edwin C. Bolles, and architect William G. Rantoul.

Next to number 8 is a large vacant lot, now a garden, which once accommodated the majestic South Church (see p. 183), Samuel McIntire's masterpiece in ecclesiastical architecture, built in 1803–1804 and destroyed by fire in 1903. Some surviving architectural fragments are at the Essex Institute. This building was succeeded c. 1904 by a stone Gothic Revival church that was used by the South congregation until 1927 and then by the Calvary Baptist Society until 1950, soon after which it was razed by the Chestnut Street Associates.

E-4

E-4 HAMILTON HALL   1805–1807
9 Chestnut Street; 7 Cambridge Street
NHL; HABS; NR; MHD

Named in honor of Alexander Hamilton, the first secretary of the treasury, this magnificent Adamesque Federal brick building was erected between 1805 and 1807 at a cost of $22,000 as a social gathering place for Salem's Federalist merchant families. For many years it was suspected that Samuel McIntire (1757–1811), because of his close connection with the Derbys, was the designer, but firm documentation did not appear until the discovery and identification of his first- and second-floor plans at the Essex Institute in 1954. Because the records of the owners, the "proprietors of the South Buildings," begin only in 1820, it has long been a challenge to reconstruct the early history of this edifice.

Hamilton Hall, three stories high with a pitched roof broken by tall brick chimneys, is considered one of the most outstanding Federal-era public buildings in the United States. Its north-facing side wall (with its McIntire-carved eagle and swags in panel inserts, and its five recessed Palladian windows) is refined, but at the same time spectacular. The first-floor windows under the belt course are set in "plank frames" with no lintels. The west-facing gable end exhibits a closed gable pediment containing a segmental-arch window and splayed window lintels with keystones (second story). The proprietors' records indicate that this western end was not completed until 1824 and that the western doorway, with its Doric Greek Revival portico, was not installed until 1845. Traditionally the ground floor has accommodated shops and caterers, while the ballroom, with its unusual curved musicians' balcony and "spring" dance floor, takes up most of the space on the second and third floors. Even today, Hamilton Hall remains a major center of social and cultural activity on the North Shore.

On the opposite side of Cambridge Street at number 14 is a three-story, end-to-the-street wooden house (NR; HSI; MHD) built for Thomas Butman by Samuel McIntire in 1806–1807. The plan for this rather plain building is preserved at the Essex Institute. All exterior architectural details are intact, and fine McIntire wood-carving (fireplace surrounds and a spiral staircase) remains on the interior. The north facade enclosed porch and the two extensions to the rear ell were not part of the initial plan, but were almost assuredly added before the Civil War. The Waters family owned the property from 1834 to 1962.

E-5 ROBINSON-LITTLE HOUSE c. 1808–1809
10 Chestnut Street at Cambridge
NR; MHD

About 1808, a local mason, James Nichols (1770–1828), built this fine square, three-story brick (Flemish bond) Federal residence for Nathan Robinson, a Salem merchant, who lived there until the mid 1830s. After lengthy periods of ownership by the Choate, Neal, and Fabens families, the artist Phillip Little bought the property in 1890 and lived there until 1939. The house commands immediate attention for its inordinately tall brick chimneys with wide, black-painted bands and its magnificent Greek Revival front entrance porch (added c. 1835) with its thick dentiled entablature and nicely proportioned Ionic columns. The stone window lintels, which are both splayed and reeded, are original, but the 2/2 Victorian windows replaced 6/6 Federal-era predecessors. When Little owned the house, he rearranged the interior and installed the large multipaned window on the east side.

Facing the Robinson-Little house at number 13 (also at the corner of Cambridge Street) is a plain two-story, pitched-roof wooden dwelling (NR; MHD) erected by carpenter William Lummus for Miss Elizabeth King c. 1832. From 1884 to 1923 Dr. Thomas Kittredge, the surgeon general of the Commonwealth, lived here. Penetrating the matched-board facade is a recessed and trabeated Greek Revival doorway above which is a later bay window.

E-6

E-6   JONATHAN HODGES HOUSE

1805; after 1845

12 Chestnut Street

NR; HSI; MHD

Despite some assertions to the contrary, the Jonathan Hodges house is the only dwelling on Chestnut Street whose design and construction can be securely credited to Samuel McIntire (1757–1811). His original first-floor plan is in the Essex Institute archives. Erected in 1805 for Hodges, a sea captain, on land acquired from Samuel Holman, the elegant but severe three-story, hipped-roof brick (Flemish bond) structure was originally laid out as a double house with three stairs and doors on the southeast and north. Fiske Kimball believed (*Mr. Samuel McIntire, Carver . . .*, p. 112) that the building was altered to a single house after 1845 by a new owner, J. Willard Peele, a merchant, with "the west door and stairway being removed, and the arrangement of the northeastern quarter being modified." During this same period the old woodwork was largely taken out and was "replaced by black walnut and marble, removed in turn by Arthur Webster West who bought the house in 1888." The strikingly handsome Greek Revival doorway and boldly detailed Corinthian entrance porch, conceived in "a sort of tight-laced austerity" (Talbot Hamlin, *The American Spirit in Architecture*, p. 128), also date from around 1845. The rectangular stone window lintels are similar to those used in early 19th-century commercial blocks and lack the ornateness of other Chestnut Street examples. The original masonry work has been attributed to James Nichols (1770–1828), who also built the Robinson-Little house (see E-5) next door at number 10.

Northeast of the house is a Federal-era wooden carriage house which was partially destroyed by fire in the 1960s and was then rebuilt. The arched entrance portal resembles those of other Salem carriagehouses (see D-1 and D-29) with which McIntire is believed to have been associated.

E-7

E-7 LEE-BENSON HOUSE 1834/35
14 Chestnut Street
NR; HSI; MHD

Built in 1834/35 for Boston banker John C. Lee, cofounder with George Higginson of Lee-Higginson Company, this ample two-story wooden residence is by far the grandest and also one of the earliest examples of Greek Revival architecture in Salem. For the next century and a quarter, the property was owned by just two families—Lee and his heirs until 1924, and then the celebrated portrait painter and etcher Frank W. Benson and his heirs from 1925 to 1957.

With its principal gable end facing the street in characteristic Greek fashion, the house is L-shaped with a large wing to the east and an open entrance porch (with a dentiled entablature and Ionic columns and engaged pilasters) set in the angle formed by the L. The matched-board end facade exhibits a closed pediment (containing a segmental-arch louvred aperture with attic window insert) above a plain entablature supported by four broad Ionic pilasters. The first-story windows are suitably capped by molded cornices above plain friezes. Balanced and stiffly formal, this facade harmonizes well with those of the older brick and wooden Neoclassical houses which line both sides of Chestnut Street.

E-8

E-8   AMOS AND SOLOMON TOWN HOUSE   c. 1804
15 Chestnut Street
NR; HSI; MHD

One of the oldest of Chestnut Street's Federal-style wooden mansions, this rectangular, three-story, hipped-roof residence was built c. 1804 for brothers Amos Towne, a schoolmaster, and Solomon Towne, a shipmaster, both originally from nearby Boxford. For a brief time the brothers and their families appear to have shared the house; then in 1807 Amos and his wife Rebecca removed to New Hampshire, selling their interest in the property to Solomon. He in turn sold to merchant James King in 1821 and it remained in his family until c. 1855, during which time it was rented to a succession of tenants. More recent owners include the Goss, Osgood, and Parker families.

The Towne house is embellished with strongly stated, well-proportioned architectural details. Commanding foremost attention is the beautifully scaled, pedimented (displaying mutules) Doric entrance porch with its triglyph frieze, and its full and three-quarter attached support columns. As Fiske Kimball has correctly observed (*Mr. Samuel McIntire, Carver . . .*, pp. 49–50), several of McIntire's early houses, particularly the Peirce-Nichols (see D-1), possessed entrance porches similar to the one on the Towne house—whether or not McIntire was responsible for this masterpiece is unknown, however. Complementing the details of the porch are the front facade window caps, which on the first story are positioned above reeded friezes. The original house was expanded to the southeast by the Kings, to the east (rear) by the Gosses, and to the southwest by the Osgoods (number 15½).

E-9

E-9 CAPTAIN STEPHEN PHILLIPS HOUSE   1804–1805
17 Chestnut Street
NR; MHD

The list of brick houses in Salem printed in the 1806 *Salem Gazette* includes this three-story, hipped-roof dwelling with brick ends, built for Capt. Stephen Phillips in 1804–1805. Entries in William Bentley's diary and Phillips family manuscripts prove without doubt that Perley Putnam (1778–1864), the presumed builder of the Williams-Rantoul-Peabody house (see E-12) at number 19, supervised the construction, and was assisted by David Newhall (stone), Loami Coburn and William Roberts (masonry), William Luscomb (painting and wallpaper), Abner Goodhue (hardware), and others. The house was later occupied by Stephen C. Phillips, the mayor of Salem (1838–1842), and remained in the Phillips family until 1883, when it was sold to Benjamin D. Shreve and converted into a two-family residence. His descendants still live there today.

The front facade is covered by matched boards and is penetrated by a central doorway (with a semielliptical fanlight and sidelights) that is protected by a semicircular porch with smooth, slender Doric columns. This porch bears a close resemblance to that of the

Gardner-Pingree house (see A-2) at 128 Essex Street, built under Samuel McIntire's direction at the same time. The three-sided bay window above, rather an abrupt intrusion on the facade, may date from the 1883 remodeling. The 6/6 double sash windows are set in molded "plank-frames" with sills but no lintels. A wooden service ell extends to the rear, and a two-story, hipped-roof, wooden barn is attached to the west side of the house by a one-story shed.

E-10

E-10 BOTT-FABENS HOUSE
18 Chestnut Street at Botts Court
NR; MHD

Before 1800

Although it has not been firmly documented, the Bott-Fabens house is considered to be the oldest residence on Chestnut Street, and supposedly dates from before 1800. In fact, this three-story, hipped-roof building may have been built before Chestnut Street was laid out in 1796, with access to it from Essex Street (north) through surrounding marshy land. The first owner was James B. Bott, who maintained a saddle shop. In 1847 the famed author Nathaniel Hawthorne lived here with his family for a brief time. After a succession of owners, Augustus J. and Benjamin H. Fabens purchased the building in 1888 and converted it to a single-family house, moving the principal entrance from the west side to the south end. This entrance features fine geometric tracery, in the doorway fanlight and sidelights, and an unusual Doric porch. The porch consists of a flat roof with a thin projecting cornice and mutules (no entablature is present) set on reeded side timbers supported by round columns and square attached pilasters. The bay window above was added by the Fabens.

Standing on the west side of Botts Court (and the east corner of Hamilton Street) at numbers 20-22 is a three-story, hipped-roof, wooden double house (NR; MHD) erected for Rev. James Thompson (eastern half) and William Rea (western half) in c. 1836. Highlighting its front matched-board facade is a double Roman Doric entrance porch protecting identical doorways with paneled transoms and full-length sidelights.

E-11

E-11 HENRY P. BENSON HOUSE
7 Hamilton Street
NR; MHD

c. 1898

One of Salem's finest Colonial Revival wooden residences, the Henry P. Benson house has had a most interesting history. From the time that it was built c. 1898 until 1957, it was owned by Mr. Benson and his wife, Rebecca. After his death in that year, Mrs. Benson lived here until 1960. Henry P. Benson was the mayor of Salem in 1916/17, and a director of the Naumkeag Steam Cotton Company. For a designer the Bensons selected Henry's brother, John P. Benson (1865–1947), a New York-area architect and later an accomplished marine scene painter, who also prepared the plans for the Wheatland-Phillips house (see E-19) at 30 Chestnut Street.

Like many other buildings of its style and type, the Benson house possesses the traditional symmetry and gambrel-roof massing of a pre-Revolutionary War residence, but the proportions are purposely exaggerated. The major elements, however, are beautifully scaled, particularly the dormers and the recessed front entrance. This entrance is enframed by a handsome surround made up of a broken dentiled pediment positioned above a plain entablature supported by fluted Ionic pilasters. In the facade the architect was notably successful in his attempt to achieve historical accuracy.

E-12

E-12 WILLIAMS-PEABODY-RANTOUL HOUSE   1805–1806
19 Chestnut Street
NR; MHD

In 1805 the Reverend Charles Cleveland, a deputy collector of the port of Salem, sold this wood-frame and clapboard residence, then in an unfinished state, to Israel Williams, a shipmaster and merchant, who proceeded to finish it while also building the two-story, L-shaped carriagehouse in the yard. Capt. Williams and his family remained in the house until 1857 when it was bought by merchant Henry W. Peabody, who retained ownership until 1905. Boston and North Shore architect William G. Rantoul (see D-41) owned the dwelling from 1907 to 1939.

Strikingly similar to the Towne house at number 15, the Williams-Peabody-Rantoul residence possesses a front Roman Doric entrance porch (c. 1905) that Rantoul, an imaginative Colonial Revivalist, copied directly from Towne porch for his own house. Frank

Cousins and Phil M. Riley claimed (*The Colonial Architecture of Salem*, p. 68) that Rantoul also added a delicate stickwork balustrade (since removed) at the roof eaves, as well as new window frames, those on the first story possessing architrave casings. Covered by a hipped roof and one room deep, the house depends on a three-story ell for sufficient living and service space. It has been conjectured that the master builder may have been Perley Putnam (1778–1864), who supervised the construction of the Stephen Phillips house (see E-9) at number 17.

E-13

E-13 PICKERING-MACK-STONE DOUBLE HOUSE   1814/15
21-23 Chestnut Street
NR; MHD

This substantial three-story rectangular brick (Flemish bond) double house was erected in 1814/15 by master builder Jabez Smith for brothers John and Henry Pickering. It is believed that William Roberts did the masonry work. Henry Pickering, who made the construction and furnishing arrangements, first occupied the smaller eastern half, while John, the linguist and lexicographer, moved into the western half. From 1837 to 1896 Judge Elisha Mack and his son Dr. William Mack owned the eastern half. In 1820 Pickering Dodge acquired the western half and lived there until his house at number 29 (see E-18) was completed, then selling in 1822 to the Stone family, who remained here until 1898. When Andrew Jackson paid a visit to Salem in 1833 he was entertained at the house.

The Pickering-Mack-Stone double house possesses a symmetrical front facade with matching doorways screened by identical semicircular Ionic porticos, similar to but heavier than the one at number 29. All of the windows are capped by splayed lintels with beaded keystones. Above the modillioned cornice of number 21 is a ribbon of iron cresting to hold back snow in winter. The front cast-iron fence and stair railings are among the best on Chestnut Street. Behind number 23 is an outstanding two-story Federal-style brick carriagehouse with a brick dentiled cornice.

E-14

E-14   DODGE-BARSTOW-WEST HOUSE   c. 1802
25 Chestnut Street at Pickering
NR; MHD

According to Richard Wiswall (see bibliography), Pickering Dodge had this house constructed c. 1802 on a tract purchased from John Pickering. It has been owned by very few families, the Barstows occupying it from c. 1837 to the 1890s and George S. West and his heirs residing here from 1895 to 1939. A conventional three-story, hipped-roof, wooden Federal residence, one room deep with a large three-story ell, this building features a handsome fanlighted doorway shielded by a chaste and simple semicircular porch set on a semicircular granite base with delicate ironwork rails. The porch, with its balustrade, modillioned cornice, and smooth Tuscan Doric columns, resembles several of the same type gracing Salem brick mansions of the next decade. The window frames are the molded "plank" type (see E-3) without lintels. With its balanced front facade and sparse detail, the Dodge-Barstow-West house is both formal and academically correct, as well as refined and unostentatious.

E-15

E-15 DEVEREUX-HOFFMAN-SIMPSON HOUSE   1826/27
26 Chestnut Street
NR; MHD

The last of the pretentious one-family brick mansions to be built on Chestnut Street, this late Federal-era residence was first occupied by Humphrey Devereux. From 1842 to 1878 it was the home of Charles Hoffman, a merchant in the African trade and a noted horticulturalist. After his death his widow resided here until 1904. Hoffman maintained a greenhouse, large gardens, and an innovative brick barn "cold storage" facility on the property. From 1906 to 1939 the house was in the possession of Dr. James E. Simpson and his wife.

The Devereux-Hoffman-Simpson house is three stories high with tall brick paired end chimneys and a medium-hipped roof, and it is the only residence of its period and type on Chestnut Street which is not symmetrical—curiously, the front entrance porch is slightly off-center. Particularly lovely are the traceried transom and sidelights of the doorway, and the attenuated and fluted porch columns with their hand-carved Ionic capitals. The bay window above and a side office door are modifications carried out by the Simpsons. The house displays a beaded cornice similar to those of several other dwellings in the neighborhood.

To the east (right) at number 24 (corner of Hamilton Street) is a small wooden Greek Revival house (NR; MHD) built for the Misses Peele c. 1833, and later occupied by members of the Safford and Gardner families. On its front gable-end, matched-board facade is a recessed entrance screened by columns, unusual for Salem.

E-16

E-16   PICKMAN-SHREVE-LITTLE HOUSE   c. 1819
27 Chestnut Street at Pickering
NR; MHD

This richly detailed, three-story brick residence is one of Salem's finest Federal-style mansions. The city possesses no better proportioned or more discreetly adorned house of its type and period. Designed and erected by the master-builder Jabez Smith, the building accommodated Dudley L. Pickman (of the merchant firm of Pickman, Stone, and Silsbee), his family, and subsequent generations until 1865. The Shreve family owned the property from 1872 until 1898, after which naval architect David Mason Little and his wife occupied it for nearly twenty-five years.

The Pickman-Shreve-Little house demonstrates the use of special window motifs (a lunette and a recessed modified Palladian) in an unbroken front facade. These effectively repeat the visual effect produced by the arched central doorway below. Also noteworthy is the raised entrance porch, the flat top of which is supported by slender, precisely carved Corinthian columns. The doorway, sidelights, and semielliptical fanlight illustrate in their tracery the delicacy and beauty of detail for which Chestnut Street's Neoclassical houses are justly renowned. Splayed granite lintels with beaded and molded keystones are set above each front window aperture.

E-17

E-17   ICHABOD TUCKER HOUSE   1800; 1846
28 Chestnut Street
NR; MHD

This three-story, hipped-roof, L-shaped wooden mansion is deceiving in appearance. Although it possesses the form of a late Georgian Colonial or Federal Neoclassical house, the architectural ornamentation on its front facade is clearly Greek Revival. Believed to be the second oldest dwelling (see E-10) on Chestnut Street, it was built in 1800 by carpenter Sims Brothers for Ichabod Tucker, the clerk of courts in Salem. Originally it had an altogether different facade, the exact composition of which will likely never be known. In 1846, when the house was enlarged and remodeled, this facade was completely rebuilt and furnished with matched-board siding, thick molded window frames, trapezoidal window caps (first story), and a wide central doorway shielded by a boldly embellished pedimented Doric porch. For many years it was thought that the original facade had been moved and attached to a house (since demolished) on lower Warren (Green) Street near Flint, but this theory was disproved by Elizabeth Orne Sturgis in her c. 1900 story of the house (*Essex Institute Historical Collections* 74 (1938): 109–141). For much of the 19th century the house was occupied by Tucker, his wife, and their family.

E-18   DODGE-SHREVE HOUSE   1822–1825
29 Chestnut Street
HABS; NR; MHD

Chestnut Street's most extravagantly decorated three-story Federal
brick mansion is the Dodge-Shreve house, erected on a double lot
between 1822 and 1825 for merchant Pickering Dodge. The building was planned by and built under the supervision of master
builder David Lord (1783–1845), with assistance from several artisans, including local carpenter V.G. Spofford, and carver Joseph
McIntire, Jr., the nephew of Samuel. During the era when the
Colonial Revival style was popular in Salem, numerous of this
dwelling's exterior details were copied and introduced in other local
buildings (see D-44 and F-4). Over the years the house has been
owned by several distinguished Salemites, including members of the
Phillips, Peirce, Allen, Cabot, and Shreve families.

Though it is comparable in size, grandeur, and floor plan to the
Pickman-Shreve-Little house (see E-16) next door at number 27, the
Dodge-Shreve house possesses a greater variety of architectural
detail, representing the last gasp of the highly developed Federal
vernacular in Salem. This is expressed principally in the window
lintels with their Greek fret motifs, the balustraded Corinthian entrance porch, and the second-story modified Palladian window, a
virtual twin to that of the Andrew-Safford house (see A-4), the construction of which Lord helped direct at 13 Washington Square.
The Dodge-Shreve house is further noted for its unusually thick
bearing walls, interior Italian marble mantels, and an imported
marble basement bathtub, reputed to be Salem's first! It is a build-

ing of exceptional beauty worthy of the regional and national notice which it commands.

E-19 WHEATLAND-PHILLIPS HOUSE 1896
30 Chestnut Street
HABS; NR; MHD

A spectacular, flamboyant example of the Colonial Revival style, this large square wooden mansion was erected in 1896 by Mrs. Stephen G. Wheatland on a tract formerly part of the garden of the Cabot-Endicott-Low house (see D-32) at 365 Essex Street. It has since been owned by the Pickering and Phillips families. One of the newest houses on Chestnut Street, it was designed by John P. Benson (1865–1947), who also drew up the plans for the nearby Henry P. Benson house (see E-11) at 7 Hamilton Street. In an innovative, almost whimsical manner, the architect employed a variety of Colonial Revival idioms, including the ornate cornice (with dentils and pendants in relief), the wide fluted Corinthian pilasters (reminiscent of the work of McIntire), the narrow roof balustrade, the flat window caps, the second-story Palladian window with miniature pilasters, the broad doorway with semielliptical fanlight, and the overly large flat-roofed porch with Corinthian columns. The facade is executed with such well-proportioned historical accuracy that the house gives the impression of being an original late 18th-century building.

E-20   ALLEN-OSGOOD-HUNTINGTON   c. 1828/29, etc.
TRIPLE HOUSE
31-33-35 Chestnut Street
NR; MHD

The only triple house on Chestnut Street and one of just two surviving in Salem (see also C-26) is this rectangular pitched-roof brick
structure, an excellent example of early 19th-century urban row
housing. Built c. 1828/29 and later by Pickering Dodge (see E-18),
supposedly for his daughters, it was not completed until after 1833
by Dodge's son-in-law, John Fiske Allen, a horticulturalist, who
resided in number 31 for many years. The middle residential unit
was lived in by Charles M. and Nathan Endicott, Pickering Dodge,
Jr., and William E. Greeley until 1864 when George P. Osgood and
his family bought it, remaining here until the 1940s. The western
end has the unique distinction of having been home to three of
Salem's mayors—the Reverend Charles W. Upham, Asahel
Huntington, and his son Arthur.

The tallest of Chestnut Street's many Federal-era buildings, the
Allen-Osgood-Huntington triple house features firewall construction
(between the units), six tall brick chimneys, a beaded wooden cornice, reeded rectangular window lintels, and heavy single and
double entrance porches with flat roofs, plain entablatures, and
fluted Ionic columns. The middle bay window is a late Victorian
addition. Behind number 35 is a small pitched-roof wooden carriagehouse, converted c. 1912 to a residence, inheriting its interior
woodwork and pedimented surround from the Chase house (c.
1790), formerly at 21 Federal Street.

E-21

E-21 STEPHEN PHILLIPS MEMORIAL TRUST HOUSE
Early 19th c.; 1824, etc.

(West-Phillips House)
34 Chestnut Street
HABS; NR; MHD

This historic residence is the most ornate Federal-period wooden house on Chestnut Street and the only house there which was not erected in its present location. Originally this building was part of an early 19th-century house on the West family farm at Oak Hill in South Danvers (now Peabody), and was moved on wheels to its present site in two sections by Capt. Nathaniel West in 1824. John H. Nichols, writing in 1884, states that the two sections were placed so that there was room left between them for the construction of a wide stair hall. Supposedly, on its South Danvers site the house was two stories high with a pitched roof and a gable end forward which incorporated the present third-story central window. On its new Chestnut Street foundations a third story was added, eliminating the roof peak and creating the rectangular, hipped-roof dwelling that we may see today. Old photographs show that the original entrance was approached by a double flight of granite steps.

The Stephen Phillips Memorial Trust House has accommodated many important Salem people during its history. Before 1837 it was occupied by Mr. and Mrs. Nathaniel West and a number of tenants. From 1837 to 1874 Mrs. M. Tabitha Ward kept an aristocratic boarding house and school here—while she owned the property, the original steps were removed and a dining room ell added. Over the period 1874 to 1896, William G. Webb owned the property before it passed to David M. Little and the Misses King. In

1913 it was acquired by Stephen W. Phillips, and he hired architect William G. Rantoul (1867–1949) to design the handsome front Ionic entrance porch and the McIntiresque wooden fence. The oval, Palladian, and bay windows on the east and west sides, and certain interior modifications were probably made under Rantoul's direction; thus, many of them have a distinct Colonial Revival flavor. The corner quoining, cornice with modillions and linked-arch molding, central doorway, and molded window caps with friezes on the front facade all appear to date from 1824 or before. In the rear yard is a two-story, Federal-era, brick carriagehouse with round-arched doorways.

After the death of Mr. Phillips' son Stephen in 1971, the Stephen Phillips Memorial Trust was established. Under its auspices the house is open to the public today, displaying fascinating family furniture, memorabilia, and decorative and fine arts objects.

E-22

E-22 GEORGE NICHOLS HOUSE   1816/17
37 Chestnut Street
NR; HSI; MHD

This beautifully proportioned brick townhouse was erected in 1816/17 by local master builder Jabez Smith for George Nichols, a successful sea captain and merchant, and his bride Sally Peirce. For much of the next century it was lived in by members of the Nichols family, except for the period from 1827 to 1845 when it was owned by merchant David Pingree and William A. Landers. While Landers occupied the house, he made several alterations and improvements, putting up the delicate iron front fence and adding on to the rear. In 1872 owner Charles Nichols removed a handsome brick stable, formerly to the west of the house.

Despite these changes, the Nichols house has retained its dignified charm and is an uncommonly fine example of a three-story, hipped-roof, L-shaped brick (Flemish bond) Federal Neoclassical residence. Its basic architectural trim consists of a roof-top balustrade, a molded cornice with modillions, splayed and reeded window lintels, and a heavy but nicely scaled raised and flat-roofed front entrance porch with a plain entablature and smooth Ionic columns.

E-23

E-23 THOMPSON/WEST DOUBLE HOUSE   c. 1845/46
38-40 Chestnut Street
NR; MHD

This late example of a pitched-roof brick double house was built c. 1845/46 for the Reverend James W. Thompson (see E-10) and Nathaniel West, Sr. Thompson lived in the western half until 1859, while Joseph B. Andrews, the mayor of Salem in 1854/55, resided in the eastern half at the same time. Although this building possesses the mass and certain of the features (paired parapet end chimneys, brick dentiled cornice, rectangular stone window lintels, matching doorways with traceried semielliptical fanlights and sidelights) of many Federal-era housing blocks, it also displays certain hallmarks (floor-to-ceiling first-floor windows, heavy double Ionic porch) of the Greek Revival style. The bay window on the west (left) side was probably added around World War I when the Colonial Revival style was in fashion and so greatly influenced Salem's architectural development. Some alterations are known to have been made at the direction of William B. Cowen between 1914 and 1920.

E-24

E-24   CAPTAIN THOMAS SAUNDERS HOUSE   1805; 1893
39 Chestnut Street
NR; MHD

This substantial, hipped-roof brick Federal mansion was constructed in 1805 for Capt. Thomas Saunders and was the first house of its size and type on Chestnut Street. It is the only residence in the neighborhood in which splayed, rusticated lintels with keystones are combined with "plank-frame" windows. Much of the architectural ornamentation, however, appears to date from 1893, when the distinguished Boston architect Arthur Little (1852–1925) made extensive modifications in the Colonial Revival vein for a new owner, William G. Barker. At this time the roof balustrade was rebuilt, the two-story bay attached to the west side, and the balustraded semielliptical bay window added above the central Ionic entrance porch. This porch, which appears to be original, protects a doorway with an unusually fine patterned semielliptical fanlight and rectangular sidelights. The house has also been owned by the Saltonstall and

Ives families. There is a superb one-story, wooden Colonial Revival carriagehouse in the back yard that may have been designed by Little.

E-25 SAUNDERS-SALTONSTALL-TUCKERMAN DOUBLE HOUSE
1810/11

41-43 Chestnut Street at Flint
HABS; NR; MHD

Thomas Saunders, who lived next door at number 39 (see E-24), had this large, three-story, rectangular brick double house erected in 1810/11 as a gift for his two daughters, Caroline and Mary Elizabeth, when they were married to the Saltonstall brothers, Nathaniel and Leverett (later the first mayor of Salem). Leverett and his family occupied the eastern end until 1851, after which it was occupied by the Tuckermans until the end of the century. The western end was the home of Nathaniel and his family until 1880, and then was owned by Charles Saunders until after World War I.

Unlike other Federal-era brick double houses in the city, this building is asymmetrical, with dissimilar entrance porches at opposite ends. The balustraded, flat-roofed porch facing Flint Street is probably original, while the deep, six-columned Ionic porch on Chestnut Street is believed to date from 1838, when a two-story wing was appended to the east end. The long north side is discreetly embellished with molded brick cornice modillions, white-painted sandstone window sills, and reeded splayed lintels. Both residential units possess graceful suspended spiral staircases.

E-26

E-26   MARIA ROPES HOUSE   1858
42 Chestnut Street
NR; MHD

In 1858 the architectural team of William H. Emmerton (1828–1873) and Joseph C. Foster (1829–1906) designed this modest two-story wooden Italian Revival dwelling for Miss Maria Ropes. She resided here until 1878, when the property was sold to Tobias A. Hanson and his family. The front facade with medium-pitched gable exhibits numerous features associated with Italian Revival domestic architecture—rusticated matched-board siding, incised corner boards, paired cornice brackets, a three-sided, flat-roofed bay window, molded flat window caps, "Siamese-twin" windows with semicircular headings, and an off-center, flat-roofed porch with square support columns. In terms of scale and style, the Ropes house is a marked contrast to the more grandiose Federal residences and row houses of Chestnut Street.

Complementing the Ropes house to the west (left) at numbers 44-46 is a large wooden Italian Revival double house (NR; MHD) constructed c. 1869/70 for James B. Curwen and William G. Webb. Protected by a concave mansard roof, this building has rusticated matched boards, paired cornice brackets, window caps, and a bay window similar to those of the Ropes house. The major visual focal point, however, is a central double porch with ornate Corinthian columns, set on a high granite stairway base.

E-27

E-27 FRANCIS A. SEAMANS HOUSE

1909

48 Chestnut Street at Flint
NR; MHD

At a glance, the last house on the north side of Chestnut Street would seem to date from before 1796, when this artery was first laid out. In fact, it is the newest residence on the street, and an excellent Colonial Revival adaptation of the Richard Derby house (1761/62) (see B-10) located at 168 Derby Street. Planned and executed in 1909 by Boston and North Shore architect William G. Rantoul (1867–1949) for philanthropist Caroline O. Emmerton (see B-13 and D-44), this two-story, gambrel-roof, brick dwelling was promptly sold to Francis A. Seamans, who lived there with his wife until after 1930.

The Seamans house lacks the double parapet end chimneys, wide 12/12 double sash windows, boldly defined dormer pediments, and Palladian doorway surround of the Derby house, but in most other respects it is similar. The brickwork, as is evident in the molded water table, string courses, and dentiled cornice, is as fine in the newer building as in its 18th-century predecessor. The Roman Doric entrance porch of the Seamans house was most likely copied from the McIntire entrance porches of the Peirce-Nichols house (see D-1) at 80 Federal Street.

E-28 KIMBALL-FOGG HOUSE

c. 1807; 1818

25 Flint Street
NR; MHD

Conspicuously situated at the western end of Chestnut Street, this simple wood-frame and clapboard residence is actually two buildings joined together. Salem historian Sidney Perley (*The History of Salem, Massachusetts*) wrote that the original part (north section, facing the street) was built c. 1807 for John Kimball. In 1818 he sold to Stephen Fogg (see D-22), the owner of the brick store to the north, and c. 1825 he added a shop (the section with gable end forward), moved from another site nearby, to the southern end. George L. Peabody owned the property for a time after buying it in 1859. The oldest wooden dwelling in the immediate neighborhood, the Kimball-Fogg house lacks exterior architectural detail, save for the superb off-center, closed entrance porch with its pedimented gable, dentiled cornice, and reeded Doric pilasters. Three tall brick chimneys rise high above the house, creating an impression of reduced scale.

E-29   LEONARD HARRINGTON HOUSE   1871/72
19 Flint Street
NR; MHD

This monumental, square, eclectic Victorian wooden mansion is the most outstanding example in the Chestnut Street area of a residence conceived in the French Academic (Second Empire) vein. Erected for Boston leather dealer Leonard Harrington in 1871/72, it is covered by a characteristic patterned-slate, hip-on-concave-mansard roof, penetrated by boldly detailed dormers with pedimented roofs. Encircling the two-storied building is a sharply projecting cornice embellished with carved modillions and heavy paired brackets. On the symmetrical front facade is a recessed central doorway shielded by an ornate open porch, above which is a three-sided bay with semicircular topped windows. The matched-board facade is plain except for the pronounced baroque (first story) and segmental-arch (second story) window caps. The house was built on land acquired from Samuel P. Andrews.

To the south (left) at number 17 is Andrews's own residence (NR; HSI; MHD) (photo, left), erected in 1856. Reflective of the Italian Revival style of which it is a fine example are a bracketed projecting cornice, paired round-arched gable windows, rusticated matched-board siding, corner quoins, and flat window hoods, all concentrated on its gable-end facade. The floor plan is appropriately irregular.

On the other side (north) of the Harrington house at number 21 is another eclectic Victorian wooden dwelling (NR; MHD) constructed in 1871/72 for George W. Brown, also on land purchased from Andrews. Though less ambitious in scale and detail than its neighbor, it has a similar irregular floor plan, a hip-on-concave-mansard roof, ornate dormers, a bracketed cornice, and bay windows. The fancy cut-out fence in front is an attractive surviving relic of the era.

E-30

E-30   ROBERT M. MAHONEY HOUSE   c. 1916/17
39 Warren Street
MHD

When the great Salem fire of 1914 swept from Boston Street, where it started, towards Salem Harbor, it cut a patch across the west end of Warren Street, destroying all the buildings on the south side between Flint Street and Highland Avenue. In their place were constructed a half dozen substantial Colonial Revival houses, the most interesting for lawyer Robert M. Mahoney from designs by architect A.G. Richardson of Salem and Boston. Like the B. Parker Babbidge house at 12 Fairfield Street (see F-3), which Richardson also planned, this handsome brick dwelling borrows extensively for its adornment (cornice, window lintels, front modified Palladian window) from the Dodge-Shreve house (see E-18) at 29 Chestnut Street. The front Ionic entrance porch with iron balustrade is a close reproduction of the porch (now at the Essex Institute) of the former Joseph Peabody house (see C-1), which once stood at 136 Essex Street. The double parapet end chimneys and the pedimented dormers were in all likelihood inspired by those of the Richard Derby house (see B-10) at 168 Derby Street. Like most Colonial

Revival architects, Richardson depended greatly on the forms and features of Georgian Colonial and Federal building in developing his own design concepts. For the two-story, semicircular porch (west end) of the Mahoney house, however, he must be given credit for an innovative Neoclassical planning solution.

Two doors to the east at 31-33-35 Warren Street at Flint is a two-story, gambrel-roof, brick triple house (c. 1914/15) (MHD) that replaced the famed Tontine block (1806), leveled by the Salem fire. Developed under the guidance of owner Stephen W. Phillips, and designed by architect William G. Rantoul (1867–1949), this long gambrel-roof brick structure repeats the multifamily planning idea embodied in its predecessor. Through the use of fine brickwork and historic details, it harmonizes well with its older neighbors on Chestnut Street.

E-31

E-31 DR. FRED G. ROBBINS HOUSE
c. 1917/18
50 Dalton Parkway at Flint Street
MHD

Erected c. 1917/18 for Dr. Fred G. Robbins, a Boston physician, this two-story brick dwelling is another of architect A.G. Richardson's fine Colonial Revival residences in Salem. It owes its existence, along with many other houses in the Warren and Lafayette streets areas, to the disastrous 1914 Salem fire which destroyed scores of old buildings, offering opportunities for new construction. Characteristically, the Robbins house is a successful amalgamation of Georgian Colonial and Federal architectural features, with the latter predominating. Embellishing the typically Georgian Colonial, gambrel-roof form are Federal elements copied from nearby Chestnut Street houses—a cornice with linked-arch molding (West-Phillips house, see E-21); splayed, rusticated lintels with keystones (Capt. Thomas Saunders house, see E-24); and a heavy Doric entrance porch with full frieze (Amos and Solomon Towne House, see E-8). The attractive open-pediment dormers with their traceried round-arch windows have no surviving historic model locally, but are appropriate for a house of this period and type.

E-32

E-32   CHARLES M. RICHARDSON HOUSE   1845/46
31 Broad Street at Hathorne
HSI; MHD

According to Salem tax records, this unusual mid-Victorian eclectic house was constructed in 1845/46 for Charles M. Richardson. The Richardsons remained here until 1884 when the property was purchased by the Haywards, who held title until 1913. Since then it has been owned by members of the Cass, Strongman, and Davis families, and by the Roman Catholic Archdiocese of Boston.

Two stories with a medium-pitched roof, the Richardson house defies normal stylistic classification. The front central entrance porch, with its plain entablature and tapered Ionic columns, is reminiscent of the Federal vein, while the rusticated (first story) and matched-board (second story) front facade with its tall windows reflects the influence of the Greek and Italian Revival modes. The most outstanding features of the building are the festoon contained within the shallow front gable, and the bowed and curved ironwork balconies of the three second-story windows. The other clapboarded walls of the house are free of decoration.

Next door to the west (right) at 35 Broad Street is a simple but pleasantly proportioned Greek Revival house (c. 1845) (MHD) with an asymmetrical, matched-board, gable-end front facade. Attracting primary visual notice on this facade are trapezoidal window lintels and an off-center Doric entrance porch with an unusually thick cornice and dentiled entablature.

E-33

E-33   EZEKIEL SAVAGE HOUSE   c. 1808
29 Broad Street at Hathorne
MHD

In an 1884 article on recollections of upper Essex Street (*Essex Institute Historical Collections* 21 (1884): 217), Oliver Thayer makes reference to Ezekiel Savage's "new house on Broad, corner of Hathorne," erected c. 1808. The three-story, hipped-roof, wooden Federal dwelling that we may observe there today is without question this buildling. The only surviving house of its period and type south of Chestnut Street, it possesses a distinctive matched-board, symmetrical front facade like that of the Capt. Stephen Phillips house (see E-9) at number 17 Chestnut. The other walls are clapboarded, as is the rear ell. Highlighting the facade is a wide fan-lighted central doorway protected by a porch with a modillioned but otherwise plain entablature and Doric support columns. An old latticework balustrade was removed from the roof some years ago. To the east of the house is a small wooden barn of the same era.

E-34

E-34 DRIVER-MANSFIELD-NICHOLS HOUSE   c. 1830
27 Broad Street
MHD

Erected c. 1830 for Capt. Stephen Driver, this small but imposing wood-frame and clapboard house is unique in Salem's surviving architecture. Though it is just one-and-one-half stories high, the building appears to be larger by virtue of the vertical emphasis provided by the tall brick chimneys, the steep-pitched roof with flared eaves, the narrow closed-pediment dormers with steep-pitched roofs, the triple-sash floor-to-ceiling windows, and the raised terrace siting, well above street level. Elements of the Greek Revival style, as expressed in domestic architecture, may be seen in the molded frames (with their ornate corner blocks) of the first-story and dormer windows, and in the wide recessed front entrance, with a typically wide transom light and sidelights. The rear kitchen ell was added before 1900. The small building in the side yard, presently used for storage, was formerly situated at the old Mill Hill railroad crossing where it served as a gate-tender's shelter.

E-35

E-35 WILLIAM BROWN COTTAGE   1847
19 Broad Street at Winthrop
HSI; MHD

This deceptively small one-and-one-half-story, steep-pitched-roof
building is Salem's most outstanding example of a wooden vernacular Gothic Revival cottage. It was erected in 1847 for William
Brown, a printer and clerk at the State House in Boston, on land
acquired from the Pickerings. Brown's widow sold to the Bartletts in
1865, and they retained ownership until 1919.

Typically Gothic are the pierced bargeboards of the gable eaves,
and the front central steep-pitched dormer, also with pierced bargeboards and a cut-out pendant. The front facade is sheathed with
matched boards, and is highlighted by tall French windows and a
heavily molded central doorway with a transom light and sidelights
reflecting the eclectic influence of the Greek Revival.

A few blocks to the south of the Brown cottage at 112 Margin
Street at Summer is another cottage (c. 1850) of similar size and
scale that also illustrates well the impact of the Gothic Revival
style. Grouped on the front plane of its steep-pitched roof are three
steep-pitched dormers, the left and right of which contain pointed-
arch windows with pendants. Gothic-derived incised pointed-arch
panels decorate the closed front entrance porch.

E-36 PICKERING HOUSE
18 Broad Street at Pickering
HABS; NR; MHD

c. 1651, etc.

Both historically and architecturally this fascinating wooden dwelling is one of this country's most important surviving 17th-century buildings. Since c. 1651 when the first section was constructed, it has been owned and lived in by ten successive generations of Pickerings, making it the oldest house in the United States to have been continuously occupied by one family. There is no known older building extant in Salem. The most famous family member to reside here was Col. Timothy Pickering, an aide to Gen. George Washington during the Revolution and later a cabinet member in the Washington and John Adams administrations. Today the house, with its furnishings and memorabilia, is open to the public under the auspices of the Pickering Foundation, a charitable organization established in 1951.

Like the few remaining Elizabethan houses of its period and region, the Pickering house has evolved physically over many years. Using a statement by Col. Pickering as the basis for dating, architectural historial Abbott Lowell Cummings (*Architecture in Colonial Massachusetts* . . ., pp. 178–79) concluded that the original right-hand (eastern) portion of the two-story, single-room plan with entry bay was probably erected by John Pickering, Sr., a carpenter, before his death in 1657. The house was then expanded to the west (left) at the instigation of the second John Pickering c. 1671. The next major changes took place during the ownership of Deacon Timothy Pickering when the house (which at one point had acquired a lean-to) was in 1751 raised to a full two stories in the rear, as it exists today.

The front facade was "Gothicized" in 1841, with the peaked "facade gables, hitherto thought to be original, . . . [forming] a part of this transformation" (Cummings, p. 179). The roof finials, gable round windows and modillions, matched-board siding, cornice brackets, and extended entrance porch all date from this year. Family records further suggest that at the same time a passageway was cut through the chimney stack on the first and second floors and that this stack above the roof received its clustered column configuration. In 1904 a two-story clapboarded ell was added to the rear, and in 1948, under the aegis of Boston architect Gordon Robb, interior restoration work was carried out. The marvelous Gothic cut-out fence with finial-capped posts, and the wooden barn to the northeast were built when the 1841 modifications were made.

To the west (left) of the Pickering house across Pickering Street is a relatively recent (c. 1902–1903) two-story, wooden Colonial Revival residence (NR; MHD) erected for Harlan P. Kelsey, a Boston landscape architect. Particularly striking is the central balustraded pavilion with its Corinthian corner pilasters, deep and open entrance porch, and Palladian window above. Salem architect Ernest M.A. Machado (1868–1907) is supposed to have designed the house.

E-37

E-37 JONATHAN NEAL HOUSE   1767
12 Broad Street at Cambridge
NR; HSI; MHD
WILLIAM STEVENS HOUSE   1836
14 Broad Street
NR; HSI; MHD

The Neal and Stevens houses are integral members of the historic streetscape on the north side of Broad Street between Pickering and

Summer. Here is located a random sampling of Salem domestic architecture (see also E-36, E-38, and E-40) dating from the late 17th to the early 19th centuries.

The house (photo, right) at number 12 was erected in 1767 for Jonathan Neal, a local dock laborer, on land owned by his father, Jonathan. Descendants of the first owner retained an interest in the house until after the Civil War. A two-story, gambrel-roof, wooden building with a symmetrical front facade, the Neal house is representative of the high level of craftsmanship exhibited in pre-Revolutionary War Salem. Most of the interior detail is intact; however, the first-story triple windows and closed entrance porch on the facade appear to be alterations. The house is rooted to its site by a massive central brick chimney.

Although it gives the impression of being an older building, the symmetrical wood-frame and clapboard house (photo, left) at number 14 was not built until 1836, evidently for William Stevens, a local grocer. The land on which the house stands was acquired in that year by James Stevens for his brother William from the Pickerings (see E-36). It has been conjectured that James, a Boston planemaker and carpenter, may have erected the dwelling. In 1864 William sold to Augustus Blake, who in 1908 sold to Anna D. Pickering, thus returning the property to the earlier owning family. Devoid of excessive architectural detail, the house does possess an uncommon shallow center gable with dentil molding, and a recessed, trabeated front central doorway, a product of the Greek Revival influence.

E-38

E-38 JOSIAH WOODBURY HOUSE
6 Broad Street
NR; HSI; MHD

c. 1774

Situated on the north side of Broad Street is this small, aesthetically appealing, two-story, gambrel-roofed wooden house raised for Josiah Woodbury, a mason, c. 1774, on land purchased from Jonathan Neal (see E-37). Josiah's heirs retained title to the property until 1815, after which it passed to a long series of owners, including members of the Orne and Morse families. The trabeated front doorway surround with its boldly defined cornice is typical of pre-Federal houses in Salem. An ell attached to the rear forms a "Beverly jog" with a separate entrance. With successful scale and inherent charm, the Woodbury house is a noteworthy local example of the vernacular domestic architecture of its period.

E-39

E-39 STATE NORMAL SCHOOL   1853/54; 1870/71
1 Broad Street at Summer
NR; MHD
LATIN GRAMMAR AND ENGLISH   1818/19, etc.
HIGH SCHOOL
(Broad Street School; Olivery Primary School)
3 Broad Street opposite Cambridge
HABS; NR; MHD
CLASSICAL AND HIGH SCHOOL   1855/56
5 Broad Street
NR; MHD

The triangle containing these three fine educational structures was once completely surrounded by streets, the southerly of which bordered on the historic Broad Street Cemetery and ran directly into High Street. A traditional center of public affairs (it formerly accommodated an almshouse, a haymarket, and public scales, etc.), this district became the locus of educational activity in Salem in the 19th century. The buildings serve varying purposes today.

The oldest of the buildings, the Latin Grammar and English High School or Broad Street School (later the Oliver Primary School) (photo, center) was erected in 1818/19 from plans drawn by an unknown disciple of the famed Charles Bulfinch, master builder John Milligan of Boston. Other artisans who worked on the construction were Loami Coburn (masonry), John Warden and Daniel Bancroft (carpentry), Robert Peele (hardware), and Joseph Newhall (metalwork). This two-story, hipped-roof brick structure exhibits many features associated with New England Federal public building architecture—these include a wooden cornice trimmed with modillions, a brownstone belt course between the two stories, applied wooden Ionic pilasters and balusters (west end), and double-sash windows with rectangular brownstone lintels set in blind arcades (a typically Bulfinchian touch). The original roof balustrade is gone. Initially rectangular, the school was remodeled on the interior and enlarged to its present size in 1842. Additional interior modifications were made in 1868/69 from plans by George C. Lord and George A. Fuller.

In 1855/56 a new building (photo, right) was constructed for the new Classical and High School just to the west of the first school. The well-known Salem architect, Enoch Fuller (1828–1861), was selected as designer. Masonry work was assigned to Russell and White, and the carpentry contract was awarded to Theodore Brown, and Stickney and Brown. Despite some exterior alterations and changes in function over the years, this imposing brick structure has retained most of its distinctive Italian Revival elements—an open ornate wooden bell cupola with a bracketed cornice and dome roof; a heavy, wide cornice decorated with brackets and dentil molding; projecting pavilions penetrated by rusticated brownstone entrances; and an intriguing variety (round-arch, segmental-arch, trapezoidal, and flat) of brownstone window hoods.

The third edifice in the group, the State Normal School (photo, left) was constructed in 1853/54 on the site of Samuel McIntire's old Registry of Deeds building (1807), which was razed to make way for it. Designed by Salem architects William H. Emmerton (1828–1873) and Joseph C. Foster (1829–1906) and built by contractor John Kinsman, the Normal School originally was a chaste two-story brick Italian Revival building with a balustraded and hipped roof, a bracketed cornice, and a central recessed and trabeated entrance facing Summer Street. In 1870/71, under the direction of Lord and Fuller (see above), this structure was drastically altered and enlarged. Among the changes made were the addition of a third story under a flat mansard roof with dormers, the placement of a mansard-roofed tower with a new arched entrance on the Broad Street end, and the expansion of the building to the rear. A variety of Italianate hoods were placed above the windows. After 1897, when the City of Salem acquired it, the building served as the community high school for several years.

E-40

E-40 EDEN-BROWNE-SANDERS HOUSE   c. 1762
0 Broad Street; 40 Summer Street
NR; HSI; MHD

This long, gambrel-roof, two-story wooden residence was erected c. 1762 for Capt. Thomas Eden, a mariner and merchant, on land which he had purchased from Jonathan Neal (see E-37). Here he accommodated his family in the eastern end, and a retail shop in the southern end, with a warehouse nearby. After Eden's death in 1768 the house descended to his heirs, and was ultimately acquired in 1810 by Capt. Edward Smith, who partitioned it with the other owner, Salem mariner William Kelly. Benjamin Cox owned the property from 1833 until his death in 1863, and in 1889 it passed from his heirs to the Browne family. The Sanders family purchased the house in 1923 and remained here for the next three decades.

Conspicuously located on the corner of Broad and Summer streets, the Eden-Browne-Sanders house is a fine representative mid-18th-century dwelling of asymmetrical plan, with closed pediment dormers, a modillioned cornice, and an unusual matched-board gable end (facing Broad Street) with an off-center, flat-roofed, closed entrance porch that does not appear to be original. In *Mr. Samuel McIntire, Carver . . .* (p. 131), Fiske Kimball attributed the east side trabeated doorway surround, with its carved rosettes, swags, and reeded pilasters, to either Samuel McIntire or his son Samuel Field McIntire.

Naumkeag Steam Cotton Company complex (1845, etc.; destroyed in the 1914 Salem fire) at Congress Street on Stage Point.

F

SOUTH SALEM

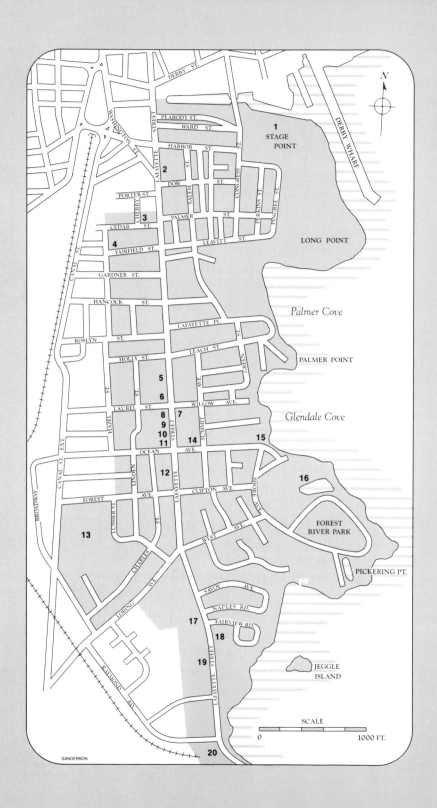

N

DERBY ST.

WASHINGTON ST.

PEABODY ST.
WARD ST.

1
STAGE
POINT

DERBY WHARF

HARBOR ST.

LAFAYETTE STREET

2

DOW SALEM ST.
ST.

CONGRESS

PERKINS ST.
PINGREE ST.

PORTER ST.

CHERRY ST.

3

PALMER ST.

CEDAR ST.

LEAVITT ST.

LONG POINT

4

FAIRFIELD ST.

GARDNER ST.

CANAL ST.

HANCOCK ST.

Palmer Cove

LAFAYETTE PL.

ROSLYN ST.

LEACH ST.

GREEN ST.

PALMER POINT

HOLLY ST.

5

HAZEL ST.

LAUREL ST.

WILLOW AVE.

AVE.

Glendale Cove

6

8
7

9

10

SUMMIT STREET

11

14

15

OCEAN AVE.

CANAL ST. EXT.

LINDEN ST.

12

LAFAYETTE

16

BROADWAY

FOREST AVE.

CLIFTON AVE.

SHORE AVE.

13

TUSSIER ST.

CHARLES ST.

WEST AVE.

FOREST
RIVER PARK

PICKERING PT.

LORING AVE.

SAVOY AVE.

NAPLES RD.

17

FAIRVIEW RD.

18

RAYMOND RD.

LAFAYETTE STREET

19

JEGGLE
ISLAND

SCALE

0   1000 FT.

SANDERSON

20

INTRODUCTION

At one time South Salem (originally known as the "Southfields") was a peninsula of land bounded on the north and west by the South River and on the east by Salem Harbor. The first access to the area from the town center was by the mill dam bridge near the eastern end of present-day Washington Street adjacent to Mill Hill. Soon after the Civil War the bridge was replaced by a road as parts of the South River and the Mill Pond became filled land.

In 1805, to better reach their farms and summer houses in the Southfields, Ezekiel H. Derby and others sponsored the construction of the South Bridge near the present intersection of New Derby and Lafayette streets. Later rebuilt, this bridge was also ultimately replaced by a road. Over the years Lafayette Street, named for the Marquis de Lafayette, was developed into a broad, beautifully landscaped boulevard lined with substantial, stately dwellings representing a mix of architectural styles from the Adamesque Federal to the Queen Anne. So many of the houses showed the influence of the French Academic (Second Empire) vernacular that the street was known locally as the "Champs Elysees of Salem." By the 1870s the land on both sides of Lafayette Street had been divided into building lots serviced by new streets extending out to the east and west. At the south end of the long, straight section of Lafayette Street (before it bends eastward toward Marblehead) is Salem State College (formerly the State Normal School), which was moved from its original site at Broad and Summer streets in the mid 1890s.

The third access route to South Salem was via the Union Bridge, erected in 1847 from the Union Wharf across the South River to "the Point," where the Naumkeag Steam Cotton Mills were located. Established in the mid 1840s, this manufacturing concern, located partially on filled land, became one of the largest and most advanced of its kind in the American textile industry. The area adjacent to the factory complex was developed for workers' housing and was initially inhabited by Salem's largest ethnic group, the French Canadians, who established their own church (St. Joseph's parish), schools, stores, clubs, societies, and newspaper. In recent years this group has been largely displaced in the area by Spanish-speaking Americans.

Disaster struck Salem on 25 June 1914 when the Great Fire cut a swath across the north end of Lafayette Street (reaching south as far as Leach and Holly Streets), destroying everything in its path. The land, however, was quickly cleared and rebuilt, but the complexion of South Salem was forever altered to meet new needs. On lower Lafayette Street, hotels, commercial blocks, and automobile sales outlets were erected and   231 the area became physically linked with the center of Salem. The Naumkeag Mills complex and its associated housing were completely reconstructed, and new single-, double-, and triple-family houses appeared, highlighted by several outstanding architect-designed Colonial Revival residences. Many of the new houses were catalogue (kit-plan) houses of standardized design, examples of which were built throughout the United States during and after World War I. In 1930, at Forest River Park near the college, the city erected Pioneer Village, a replica of Salem's earliest settlement, in commemoration of the Massachusetts Bay Tercentenary.

F-1

F-1   NAUMKEAG STEAM COTTON COMPANY COMPLEX
20 Congress Street at Stage Point, Salem Harbor

1914–1916, etc.

The former Naumkeag Steam Cotton Company (incorporated 1839) complex, the four buildings of which are rented to several businesses today, replaced on the same site a 19th-century brick factory group (see p. 229) that was catastrophically destroyed by the Salem fire of 25 June 1914. Typical of many of the great American textile mills (e.g., American Woolen Company mills, Lawrence and Andover, Massachusetts) of early in this century, the "Pequot Mills," as the new complex was also known, was constructed of "fireproof"

steel structural framing encased in concrete, with reinforced concrete floors, and walls filled in with brick and glass. A tall front
stair tower, with four clock faces, is the principal visual feature of
the main factory. An improvement over the older Naumkeag buildings, the more modern box-like structures allowed for greater un-
obstructed interior space, the installation of heavier and more
sophisticated machinery, and superior natural illumination of manufacturing areas. Until after World War II the saw-tooth-monitor-roof
weave shed, covering ten acres, was considered to be the largest in
the world. In the Naumkeag complex and others like it, function
rather than aesthetic beauty was the dominant design consideration.
It is hardly surprising, then, that an engineering firm (Lockwood
and Greene of Boston) rather than an architectural office planned
the buildings.

Directly in front of the Naumkeag complex, beside the South
River, is "Pequot House," a conjectural reproduction of a 17th-
century Salem dwelling, erected in 1930 for the Massachusetts
Tercentenary celebration. Designed by Boston and North Shore
architect Philip Horton Smith (1890–1960), the building is a free
interpretation of Salem's John Ward house (see A-5), with certain
features borrowed from other 17th-century domestic structures.
Originally employed as a reception and exhibit center, it is now
used for administrative purposes.

F-2

F-2 ST. JOSEPH'S CHURCH (Roman Catholic) 1949/50
135 Lafayette Street at Dow

A prominent landmark in the Lafayette Square area since it was
completed and consecrated, St. Joseph's Church occupies the site

of its immense brick-and-stone, twin-towered, Romanesque Revival predecessor (c. 1910/11), reduced to a hollow shell by the 1914 Salem fire. For years the parish based its activities in the renovated cellar and tower bases of the old edifice, until in 1949, under the direction of architect James J. O'Shawnessey, construction of a new church was commenced.

Following the traditional cruciform plan (with side aisles) of ecclesiastical buildings, St. Joseph's Church illustrates many of the principles of International Style architecture. Mass and weight are minimized in the structure in order to emphasize sheer volume. Horizontality and verticality predominate in the design, the major components of which are box-shaped sections with flat roofs. Ornament is largely absent except for a tall grey Modernistic spire with a gleaming gold cross situated over the point where the wings join the nave. Expansive outer brick walls, smooth and white-colored, are penetrated by flush mosaic vertical strip windows depicting the history of the Roman Catholic church. The street facade, with its three-portal, canopied entrance, displays a massive stone statue of the suffering Christ set against a large patterned rectangular window.

F-3

F-3   GEORGE A. MORRILL HOUSE   1915
2 Cedar Street at Cherry

This simple wood-frame, Colonial Revival house is a good representative example of the kind of domestic architecture that was erected in the area devastated by the great Salem fire of 1914. Pleasantly situated on a moderate hillside site, it features on its front facade classical entablature molding and a recessed central Palladian doorway consisting of a broken triangular pediment supported by Ionic pilasters. It is possible that this doorway was modeled after that of the John Hodges house (1788) (see A-33) at 81 Essex Street. The design was by A.G. Richardson, a Boston architect who resided in Salem.

Directly opposite the Morrill house at 15 Cedar Street is the T. Irving Fenno house (1914/15), erected from plans prepared by Grandagent and Elwell of Boston. With walls of fireproof concrete, this equally modest edifice possesses a nicely articulated Neo-Federal front central porch topped by a Palladian window.

F-4

F-4   B. PARKER BABBIDGE HOUSE   1914/15
12 Fairfield Street

The B. Parker Babbidge house was designed by architect A.G. Richardson of Boston and Salem and is a handsome example in brick of Colonial Revival-style architecture. Constructed in 1914/15, it is one of several Salem residences conceived by a group of Boston-area architects to replace older structures lost in the 1914 Salem fire.

For its ornamental detail, the Babbidge house, like other buildings of its type and era, borrows heavily from Salem's finest Federal architecture. Under the eaves of a hipped roof pierced by tall chimneys and dormers is a cornice with carved modillions and ball molding. The fenestration, especially the fret-decorated lintels and the modified central Palladian window, bears a marked similarity to that of the Dodge-Shreve house (see E-18) at 29 Chestnut Street.

The Ionic order is used to positive advantage in the front entrance pilasters and side porch columns.

Facing the Babbidge house at 11 Fairfield Street is the more chaste George W. Hooper house (1914/15), another of Salem's fine Colonial Revival residences. Designed by architect Robert C. Coit of Boston, it features a semicircular front entrance porch, the shape of which is repeated effectively in the first-floor window headings.

Other notable post-Salem fire Colonial Revival dwellings in the immediate neighborhood are the Henry M. Batchelder house (1914/15; Little and Brown, architects, Boston) at 204 Lafayette Street, and the Walter K. Bigelow house (1914/15; A.G. Richardson, architect) at 220 Lafayette Street.

F-5

F-5   WILLIAM H. GOVE HOUSE

254 Lafayette Street

1888

Built for lawyer William H. Gove in 1888, this spacious, irregularly shaped, and richly textured residence is as forceful a statement of the Queen Anne style as may be found in Salem. Dominating the building at its southeast corner is a grandiose, three-story cylindrical tower capped by a conical roof with finial. Other distinctive Queen Anne features are the pedimented dormers, projecting gabled pavilions, tall step-patterned brick chimneys, multistoried window bays, heavy roof cornices, roof balustrades, and balustraded porch.

The dwelling to the north (right) of the Gove house looks very much today as it did when it was erected for merchant John Clifton in 1848. Perfectly symmetrical, with gable end to the street like many Greek Revival houses in Salem, it also features hallmarks of the Italian Revival style in its roof cornice brackets and horizontal bracketed window hoods. For a period after 1872 this dwelling was owned by Charles Osgood (1809–1890), the portrait painter of many North Shore personages.

F-6

F-6 HENRY M. BROOKS HOUSE   1851
260 Lafayette Street at Laurel

This exquisite, dramatic wooden building is one of New England's most outstanding Gothic Revival houses. It is also one of the gems of Salem's rich domestic building heritage, there being no other examples of its style and type surviving in the city. Erected in 1851 for Timothy Brooks, a grocer, it passed in 1854 to his son Henry M., later president of the Forest River Lead Company and a historical scholar and collector.

It would be difficult to argue that the source for the Brooks house was not Design II of Andrew Jackson Downing's *Cottage Residences . . .* (New York and London, 1842). Preserved today in this perfectly symmetrical house are the same first-floor, pointed-arch, leaded-glass windows, steep front central gable with crocketed finial and "gingerbread" vergeboards, gable trefoil window, second-floor window hood molds (with corbel stops), open porch with Tudor arches and miniature battlements, and other charming features that appear in the Downing plate. Rusticated flat wall boarding and corner quoins are employed to suggest stone construction. The builder, as yet unidentified, made a supreme effort to copy the plate to the last detail, and the results, in terms of academic correctness, are noteworthy.

F-7

F-7   HARRIS/WEBB DOUBLE HOUSE   c. 1872
265-67 Lafayette Street at Willow

This rectangular-shaped, French Academic-style double house was erected c. 1872 for George R. Harris, a Boston bookkeeper, and Joseph H. Webb, a cashier at the National Exchange Bank in Salem. Architecturally it is the most interesting of a group of wooden dwellings of the same period and type that line the east side of Lafayette Street. The building is endowed with a variety of decorative details which are pleasantly light and understated. Among the most prominent of these are the paired curvilinear cornice brackets with pendants, incised corner pilasters, open pediment dormers, thin segmental-arch window caps, and a flat-roofed front entrance porch supported by five fragile-appearing square modeled columns.

F-8 LANGMAID HOUSE   1870
266-268 Lafayette Street

This ornate Victorian eclectic double house was built in 1870 by
lumber dealer Frank Langmaid for his two sons—number 266 for
Frank A., aged twenty-one, and number 268 for John H., aged
twenty-two. The building loosely conforms to the principles of the
French Academic tradition, most often expressed in masonry as op-
posed to wood. Protected by a distinctive concave mansard roof, the
house features a large two-story front entrance bay embellished with
Doric columns and pilasters, windows with bracketed baroque caps,
and a flat roof with paired eaves brackets and a wide architrave
with dentil molding. Varying stylistic treatments are further evident
in the bracket-supported first-floor window hoods, the simple
second-floor window molding, and the highly detailed third-floor
dormers with their segmental-arch lintels, pilasters, and closed flat
triangular gables.

To the south (left) of the Langmaid house at 270 Lafayette Street
is an interesting but plain and somewhat-altered Queen Anne house
built for Francis S. Barrows in 1894. Attracting principal notice are
the southeast octagonal corner tower with its pyramidal roof cap
and the front dormer gable, displaying a carved triangular panel
luxuriantly decorated with leaf and flower patterns.

F-9   EDWARD S. THAYER HOUSE   1871
274 Lafayette Street

Edward S. Thayer, a young Salem oil dealer, commissioned this square wooden Victorian eclectic house in 1871. Like several other French Academic-influenced residences lining Lafayette Street, the Thayer house possesses a heavy cornice broken by closely spaced console modillions and pairs of brackets, elaborate segmental-arch dormers, flat horizontal hoods (supported by brackets) over large window apertures, bay windows, and a sumptuously decorated front entrance porch. The front elevation is symmetrical but for the presence on the south side of a veranda. The truncated, hipped slate roof is crowned by a heavy but successfully proportioned balustrade recalling those of the city's splendid Federal brick mansions.

Across Lafayette Street from the Thayer house are several other Victorian eclectic dwellings (277, 281, and 285, etc.) which, though much plainer in appearance, illustrate many of the same French stylistic characteristics.

F-10 MARY A. DEVINE HOUSE 1892
278 Lafayette Street

This solidly massed, asymmetrical-plan house and adjacent stable
were constructed in 1892 for Mary A. Devine, the wife of liquor
dealer Thomas A. Devine, on land formerly part of the Derby farm.
Although a subdued articulation of the Queen Anne style, the
house is one of Salem's best examples, and has been only slightly
modified over the years. Dormers, multiple intersecting pitched
roofs, bay windows, balustrades, variously sized windows, modeled
chimneys, and a wide entablature (embellished with dentils and
modillions) are all characteristically Queen Anne. The detail is
largely classical and small in scale. Both the front gable pediment
and roof dormer possess intriguingly decorated triangular panels, the
former containing an ellipse and the latter a shield suggesting a
coat of arms. Unlike more fully developed Queen Anne houses in
which several differently textured wall surfaces appear, the Devine
house is sheathed entirely in shingles, suggesting the influence of
the Shingle Style, also in vogue during the late 19th century.

F-11   EPHRAIM A. EMMERTON HOUSE   1879
284 Lafayette Street at Ocean Avenue

This imposing Victorian eclectic residence (today the Coach House
Motor Inn) was erected for Ephraim Augustus Emmerton, one of
the last Salemites to make his livelihood from maritime commerce.
Strongly classical in its adornment, the Emmerton house is an effec-
tive expression of the French Academic vein evident in other
Lafayette Street houses. Essentially symmetrical, this cube-shaped
building is covered by a substantial hip-on-mansard slate roof,
pierced by a tall modeled chimney and dormers topped by closed-
pediment pitched roofs with wide dentiled entablatures. Correspond-
ingly, the first-floor windows feature closed pediment caps, while
the main building mass, bay windows, front pavilion, and porch are
fitted out with identical entablatures. The presence of bay windows,
varied wall surfaces, and random window shapes provides a hint of
the Queen Anne style, yet to make its mark in Salem at that
period.

Behind the house is a superb carriage house that, though of a
different form and scale, bears many of the same stylistic features.
To the south of these two buildings, across Ocean Avenue at
number 47, is the South Branch Library (1912–13), a small, plain
Colonial Revival structure with a fine Roman classical portico
screening its front entrance.

F-12 WILLIAM S. NICHOLS HOUSE   1889
300 Lafayette Street

Conceived in the same restrained Queen Anne vein as the nearby
Gove and Devine houses (see F-5 and F-10), this ample residence
was built for William S. Nichols, a young bank teller at the Salem
Safe Deposit Company. The Nichols house is altered from its original appearance, but remains, nonetheless, an excellent example of
its style. Characteristic features include an irregular floor plan, an
asymmetrical front elevation, intersecting pitched roofs set at right
angles to each other, a round corner tower crowned by a conical
roof with finial, pedimented dormers, bay windows, an encircling
porch (now partially filled with expanded interior space), varied wall
surfaces (shingles and clapboards), a tall molded brick chimney,
thick raking cornices, and a wide entablature with dentil molding.
Additional carved decorative motifs and stickwork adorn the tower
and gable pediments of the front facade. The creator of this eye-
catching visual display is unknown, but considering its similarity to
the Gove and Devine houses, it is possible that the same builder
may have constructed all three.

F-13

F-13　RICHARD B. O'KEEFE PHYSICAL　　1973–1976
EDUCATION/ATHLETIC CENTER,
SALEM STATE COLLEGE
Canal Street, Forest Avenue and Lussier Street

Erected on a large open tract two blocks to the west of the main Salem State College campus, the O'Keefe Center is the city's most monumental example of contemporary architectural design. Planned by Edward J. Tedesco Associates of Winchester, Massachusetts, and built by J.A. Sullivan Corporation of Boston, this sprawling, highly functional complex contains an ice arena, swimming pool, basketball courts, exercise rooms, handball, squash, and racketball courts, locker areas, and coaches' and administrative offices. The center is comprised of variously shaped geometric solids and possesses flat brick wall surfaces which are crisply defined by reinforced vertical concrete buttresses and corner posts, counterbalanced by horizontal concrete bands—thus, the interior steel structural system is candidly expressed on the exterior. Further breaking the monotony of the wall surfaces are projecting concrete window and door bays and oval stair towers strategically positioned to help unify the whole composition.

F-14 ALBERT C. PETTINGILL HOUSE

1887

36 Ocean Avenue at Summit

HSI

Raised for local wholesale fish dealer, Albert C. Pettingill, this modest-sized but well-developed Queen Anne cottage is decoratively rich and varied in composition. There is diversity in form, texture, and color. Irregular in floor plan, with asymmetrical street elevations, the Pettingill house displays a combination of elements from several late-Victorian eclectic vocabularies. Of primary visual interest are a circular corner veranda with nicely turned posts and balustrades, a two-story window bay with bracket-supported pediment, and hand-crafted triangular gable pediment decorations. A symmetrical carriage house (now a garage), surmounted by a square cupola with pyramidal cap, complements the main house just to the rear.

F-15   EDWARD P. BALCOMB COTTAGE   1870
4 Ocean Avenue at Shore

Strategically sited overlooking Salem Harbor, this quaint, visually appealing dwelling exhibits a remarkable collection of mid-Victorian eclectic stylistic features, considering its small size. Evidence of the Italianate and French Academic influences, so forcefully expressed in several larger Lafayette Street houses, is everywhere present. A hip-on-mansard (concave) slate roof, pierced by segmental-arch dormers and capped by a square box cupola, rests atop the cubical building mass. The off-center front doorway is protected by a flat-topped modillioned canopy supported by curvilinear brackets with pendants. This doorway is counterbalanced by a front projecting bay and a lightly constructed side porch leading to a rear ell.

F-16 PIONEER VILLAGE   1930 (Replica)
Forest River Park, accessible from Clifton or West avenues

Under the direction of historian George Francis Dow, Pioneer
Village (c. 1931 photograph) was built in 1930 for the Massachu-
setts Bay Tercentenary and commemorates the arrival of Gov. John
Winthrop, his ship *Arbella,* and the Charles I charter to the New
World. Situated on city park land on Salem Harbor, the village is a
conjectural recreation of the wilderness settlement of Salem during
its first years. At the same time it provides a more general picture
of what architecture and domestic life were like in all of New
England's primitive 17th-century seacoast communities. Only at
Plimouth Plantation (Plymouth, Mass.) is it possible to view similar
replica structures in an appropriate historical setting.

   Contained in the village are representative reconstructions of
dwellings and outbuildings believed to have been erected from c.
1628 to c. 1630. The earliest of these, derived from local Indian
shelters, are three palisaded-log, sod-roofed dugouts, and three
"wigwams" made of bent-pole frames, lashed together and covered
with bark slabs, sailcloth, or thatched mats, but improved with
English-style wooden doors and fireplaces. In his replica village Dow
also included four small one-story cottages, roofed with thatch,
walled with pine weather boarding (with nogging) or wattle and
daub, and equipped with brick or "catted" (log and clay) chimneys.
Dominating this entire group is the two-storied "Governor's Fayre
House," an interpretation of Gov. John Endecott's 1630 dwelling
moved from Cape Ann—roofed with large hand-hewn wood
shingles, it has brick chimney and external walls faced with wide
flush boards and penetrated by diamond-paned casement windows.
Unfortunately, the village has been overgrown and vandalized in recent years, but it remains open to the public in season under the
administration of the Salem Park Department.

F-17 SALEM STATE COLLEGE LIBRARY   1969–1974
352 Lafayette Street opposite Naples Road

This modern six-story yellow-brick-and-concrete complex was constructed between 1969 and 1974 at a cost of $6.2 million. Plans
were prepared by Desmond and Lord, a Boston architectural firm,
with Palandjian and Sons serving as contractors. Contained in the
climate-controlled interior are reading space for 1,500 students and
100 faculty, stacks to accommodate up to 1,000,000 volumes, offices, classrooms, lounges, meeting rooms, gallery displays, and an
auditorium and work areas.

A bold, forthright work of architecture, the library is inspired by
the Brutalist school of modern design (popularized by Le Corbusier,
Paul Rudolph, and Louis I. Kahn) in which mass, weight,
roughness, and solidity are the primary qualities and the interior
structure, customarily concrete and steel frame, is frankly displayed.
Horizontal and vertical lines, accentuated by the exposed structural
support system, intersect and counterbalance each other, bringing
cohesiveness to the whole composition. Broad, inactive wall surfaces
are interrupted by windows and dark penetrations which are treated
as holes or voids, rather than continuations of the outer skin of the
building. Adjacent college buildings, though constructed of similar
materials, lack the innovativeness or excitement of the library
design.

F-18 JAMES F. ALMY HOUSE

c. 1896

395 Lafayette Street

James F. Almy was the founder in 1858 of the firm that subsequently became Almy, Bigelow, and Washburn, the well-known Salem dry goods store. Eleven years later he joined with two other purchasers to acquire the former Derby estate lands in South Salem. In approximately 1896 he had this superb Colonial Revival mansion constructed on the east side of Lafayette Street. Drawing its inspiration from New England Georgian Colonial architecture, the Almy house is rectangular in plan with only one major projection—a two-story open porch on the north side. The front facade is symmetrical and is bounded by beautifully articulated Ionic corner pilasters set on high block bases. The main front entrance, topped by a semielliptical fanlight and flanked by rectangular sidelights, is shielded by a delicate semicircular porch consisting of a flat canopy roof supported by Ionic columns. The truncated hipped roof, formerly embellished by a balustrade, features tall paired brick chimneys as well as dormers covered by truncated pitched roofs, except for the one over the front entrance which possesses a semicircular roof and a carved urn motif. Classical roof cornices are decorated with closely spaced modillions. A large two-story, round-headed window, illuminating an interior stairway, may be seen on the west side.

F-19   MORGAN-METCALF-ATWOOD HOUSE   1762, 1766, etc.
416 Lafayette Street
HSI

In 1753/54 Dixey Morgan, a farmhand at the Pickman farm, acquired sixteen acres of Southfields land at the mouth of the Forest River and began cultivation of this tract. Eight years passed, however, before Morgan was able to take out a mortgage and build his own house. Supposedly, this first building was a basic vernacular pitched-roof structure with one chimney and two rooms on each of two floors. It has been conjectured that in 1766, when Morgan took out a second mortgage, the house was doubled in size, and a second chimney added. This building, the oldest in South Salem, is the central core of the present residence.

The house passed out of the hands of Morgan's heirs in 1824, and eventually was acquired by the Metcalf family under whose ownership it was "Victorianized." After almost a century in possession of the Metcalfs, the house was purchased in 1929 by the Byron T. Atwoods who restored it and improved it, adding a wing and expanding the ell.

F-20 BENJAMIN G. HATHAWAY HOUSE 1874
452 Lafayette Street
HSI

Situated near the Marblehead line on land originally part of the
Pickman farm, this outstanding, aesthetically pleasing Victorian
eclectic house was built in 1874 by Benjamin Hathaway of Marblehead. Elements from several major 19th-century American architectural styles are represented in the building. In the Victorian Gothic
style, one may observe steep-pitched roof gables with king-post
trusses, pointed-arch window caps, and steep-pitched dormer roofs.
The influence of the Italian Revival may be seen in the rusticated
wall boarding, the flat bracketed window hoods, the round-headed
tower and gable pediment windows, and the asymmetrical plan, developed around a central square tower. A touch of the French
Academic (Second Empire) style is provided by the bellcast mansard
tower roof with its iron cresting. Somehow this hodgepodge of stylistic elements speaks as a unified composition.

CHARLES A. ROPES house (later the North Shore Babies' Hospital) (c. 1856; destroyed by fire, 1972) formerly at 75 Dearborn Street on Ropes Point. Photograph, 1885.

G

NORTH SALEM

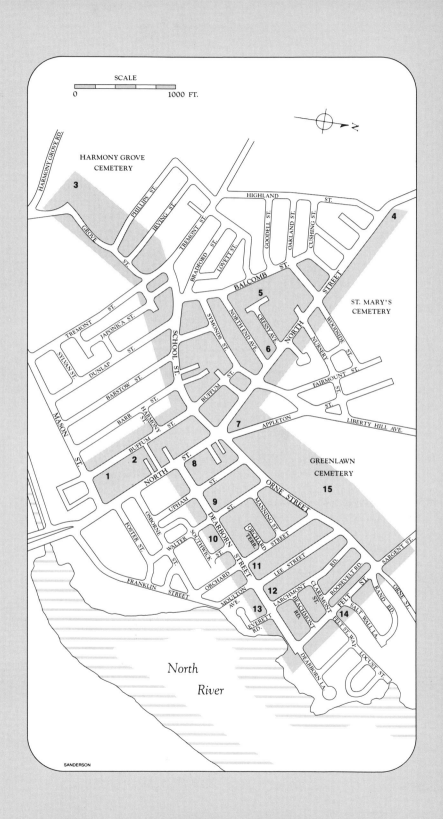

INTRODUCTION

Known as the "Northfields" district to the early residents of the area, North Salem was originally used for farming and animal grazing. It was isolated by water (the North River) from the principal town population of the central peninsula much in the way that the "Southfields" district (see Section F) was also separated off by water (the South River). It was in the Northfields that Salem's first Indian settlements were situated, and that Leslie's Retreat (the first instance of colonial resistance to British authority in the Revolutionary War) took place at the North Bridge on 26 February 1775.

North Salem's residential areas are both contained and broken up by several large cemeteries and public parks. Ledge Hill Park (Mason, Tremont, and Grove streets) overlooks the North River, which, though it was never a major navigable channel, became the locus of much varied industrial activity by the early 19th century. To the west of this park is Harmony Grove Cemetery (Harmony Grove Road; Grove and Tremont streets), a beautifully maintained, garden-like tract which was established in 1840 and is the burial ground for many prominent North Shore citizens. To the east of North Street is Greenlawn Cemetery (Liberty Hill Avenue; Appleton, Orne, and Sargent streets), which was first laid out in 1807 and was formally landscaped during the 1880s. Further out North Street at the Peabody line is St. Mary's Cemetery, the Roman Catholic burial area. To the east (Kernwood Street) on the Danvers River is the former "Kernwood" country estate of the Peabody family, today occupied by the Kernwood Country Club and Kernwood Park, a city recreational tract.

The residential architecture of North Salem broadly ranges from the late 18th- and early 19th-century rural vernacular, to the mid-19th-century Victorian eclectic. Dearborn, Buffum, and North streets contain the richest and most diverse concentrations, with the Greek Revival, Italian Revival, French Academic (Second Empire), and Queen Anne the most prevalent styles. Three provocative variations of the late Gothic Revival in ecclesiastical building may be seen in the chapels of Harmony Grove and Greenlawn cemeteries and in St. Thomas the Apostle Church on North Street.

G-1   CARLTON-WATERS COTTAGE
4 Buffum Street

c. 1852

This appealing and unusual little one-and-one-half-story, mid-Victorian eclectic cottage was constructed for S. Augustus Carlton, a Salem clothier, c. 1852. It passed to William W. Boswell, a wood, coal, and bark dealer at the North Wharf c. 1855. He held title to the house only briefly, however, and c. 1860 it was acquired by Thomas S. Waters, the proprietor of a local machine sewing business. It remained in his family until the end of the century.

In its exterior form and adornment, the Carlton-Waters cottage combines elements of two major mid-19th-century American architectural styles. Reflective of the Greek Revival is the raised front central pavilion with its closed pediment roof, molded entablature, incised corner pilasters, and first-story doorway flanked by square Doric pilasters. Illustrative of the Italian Revival are the matched-board siding (front facade), paired cornice brackets, corner quoins, and flat bracketed window hoods.

G-2 JOB V. HANSON HOUSE 1872–1874
18 Buffum Street

Perhaps North Salem's most outstanding Victorian eclectic residence, this square, two-and-one-half-story wooden house was erected
between 1872 and 1874 for Job V. Hanson of the local grain and
meat business of J.V. and J. Hanson. Not surprisingly it shares certain features with a house at 162 North Street (see G-6) built for
Hanson's brother and business partner John in 1871. The ornamentation of 18 Buffum Street, however, tends to be heavier and more
ornate. Penetrating the low, hip-on-mansard (concave) roof are fine
segmental-arch-roof dormers with modillions and side brackets
which conform to the roof shape. Among the many common Italian
Revival elements are the upper and lower cornice modillions, the
paired lower cornice brackets, the matched-board siding, the
segmental-arch window headings with elaborate keystone motifs
(second story), the broken pediment window hoods with brackets
(first story), and the open, square-columned entrance porch with a
variety of cornice modillions, drop pendants, and curvilinear
brackets.

G-3   BLAKE MEMORIAL CHAPEL   1904–1905
30 Grove Street at the entrance to Harmony Grove Cemetery

Just inside the main entrance to historic Harmony Grove Cemetery
(incorporated 1840) is the Blake Memorial Chapel, an outstanding
late Gothic Revival ecclesiastical structure with seating for 150
people. Erected in 1904–1905 from plans by local architect Ernest
M.A. Machado (1868–1907), it was funded by the estate of Nancy
Cardwell Blake of Salem and Boston in memory of her son George
Harrison Blake, who died in 1869. Built of seam-faced Cape Ann
granite irregularly coursed with trim, the chapel follows traditional
English Perpendicular precepts, with quiet, uncomplicated elevations, harmonious proportions, subtle polychromatic effects, and
beautiful masonry tracery and vaulting. A square, castellated, off-
center bell tower, stepped wall buttresses, and pointed and Tudor-
arch window and door apertures are the dominant architectural
elements. Stained glass memorial windows crafted by Charles J.
Connick, with the assistance of Ralph Adams Cram (both of
Boston), were installed during the 1920s. Attached to the west wall
of the chapel is a porte-cochere. An administrative and service wing
is appended to the east side by means of a covered walkway link.

To the right (east) of the cemetery entrance, before the Blake
Chapel is reached, is the superintendent's house (c. 1840), a fetch-
ing little early Gothic Revival building. Represented here are
several features common to the style, including gable-end bargeboards, flat hood molds with corbel stops, and diamond-pane
windows.

G-4 ST. THOMAS THE APOSTLE CHURCH   1930
(Roman Catholic)
260 North Street

Adjacent to St. Mary's Cemetery, where North Street crosses the
Peabody city line, is St. Thomas the Apostle Church, serving a
parish in the east end of Peabody and part of North Salem. For the
first three years of its existence the parish celebrated masses in a
temporary wooden structure. Then in 1930, after funds had been
raised for a permanent church, work on the present building was
carried out under the supervision of parishioner and architect John
M. Gray (1887–1977), a resident of Salem who based his practice in
Boston.

A late Gothic Revival interpretation of an early English Perpendicular Gothic chapel, St. Thomas the Apostle Church is constructed of light buff-colored brick with limestone trim and a steep-
pitched slate roof broken by dormers. The modified cruciform plan
is L-shaped with a chapel wing and an off-center, three-story bell
tower attached to the southwest side. Unlike early Gothic Revival
or High Victorian Gothic buildings, this structure is plainer and
quieter in design, lacking clashes in scale, complicated silhouettes,
and excessive polychromy. Nevertheless, many of the same elements
(e.g. pointed-arch doors and windows; round, traceried windows;
graduated wall buttresses, etc.) that are present in the older styles
appear here.

G-5   CALEB A. SMITH HOUSE   1860/61
3 Ridgeway Street off Cressy Avenue
HSI

From data gleaned from Salem directories and tax records it is possible to assign a date of c. 1860/61 to this unusual mid-Victorian eclectic house. It was erected for Caleb A. Smith, an executive at the Danvers Iron Works, on an elevated tract of land that he purchased from Pierce L.W. Gardner in 1855. The Cressy family held title to the property from 1867 to 1924. The dominant feature of the building is the two-story front portico with a roof overhang and second-story balustraded balcony supported by four massive Greek Doric columns. The front facade windows are framed by wide curvilinear moldings with labels. A whimsical touch is provided by the latticework strip extending around the top of the portico just under the roof eaves.

G-6 DUNCKLEY-SARGENT HOUSE c. 1802
161 North Street
HSI

The Dunckley-Sargent house is the only surviving local example in wood of a two-story, hipped-roof, rectangular-plan Federal residence. A basic New England rural type, it is, therefore, very appropriate for the Northfields farming district in which it was built. Although Salem tax records are inconclusive as to construction date, there is enough evidence to suggest that the house was erected c. 1802 for John Dunckley, a blacksmith, and that he and his descendants held title to the property until 1874. The Sargent family has owned the house for most of this century. Set back from the street, and almost hidden between the adjacent buildings, it is impressive for its simple lines, successful proportions, and fine fanlighted doorway with broken pediment. The open canopy-type front porch is clearly not original with the house, and was probably added since the late 19th century.

G-7 JOHN HANSON HOUSE   1871
162 North Street at Orne and Appleton

Located at the junction of three streets, this tastefully articulated
two-and-one-half-story wooden residence was built in 1871 for John
Hanson, the coowner of J.V. and J. Hanson, grain and meat dealers
of Salem. It rivals his brother Job's house (1872–1874) (see G-2) at
18 Buffum Street as North Salem's most outstanding Victorian
eclectic dwelling. Like other Salem houses of its period, it is protected by a low, hip-on-mansard (concave) roof, with upper cornice
modillions and boldly decorated dormers topped by closed pediment
roofs. The lower projecting cornice is typically adorned with carved
pairs of brackets and modillions set off against a plain frieze.
Familiar Italian Revival elements on the symmetrical front facade
include incised corner boards, flat and segmental-arch molded window frames, flat, bracketed window hoods, and an open, flat-roofed
raised porch supported by square columns.

G-8 NORTH STREET (Hose Company Number 6)   1881/82
FIREHOUSE
142 North Street

Erected in 1881/82, the North Street (Hose Company Number 6)
firehouse is the oldest structure of its kind in Salem that still serves
its original purposes. A representative late Victorian eclectic structure, it displays outstanding brickwork in its window and door
hoods, cornice corbels, and string courses. Attracting primary notice
on the front facade is a second-story, round-arched window with
flower-petal tracery. The projection on the south side is the truncated base of what was formerly a tall tower capped by an open,
square-columned bell housing with a concave spire roof of patterned
slate. The loss of this tower some years ago deprived the building
of its once logical scale. Almost identical in appearance was the
former Lafayette Street firehouse, erected about the same time, but
subsequently destroyed by fire.

G-9   DEVEREUX DENNIS HOUSE   1843
15 Dearborn Street
HSI

This modest Greek Revival building is one of only a few in Salem
designed and built by a professional housewright as his own place of
residence. Erected in 1843 by carpenter Devereux Dennis on land
acquired from William M. Arrington, it eventually descended to
Dennis' wife, daughter, and granddaughter, remaining in the same
family for over a century. It was here that Dennis' son, William
Devereux Dennis (1847–1913), later the architect of several Salem
buildings (see index), was raised.

With its principal gable end towards the street, the Dennis house
assumes the Greek temple form, though it lacks the pronounced
raking cornice, closed gable pediment, and corner pilasters of many
local Greek Revival residences. The boldly stated, trabeated doorway with narrow sidelights is, however, of unusually high quality.
Apparently Dennis was able to convince other North Salemites as
to the simple beauty, innovativeness, and practicality of the design,
for two other houses on Buffum Street—for Mark Lowd (1851) at
number 9, and for Nathaniel Horton (1850) (HSI) at number 22—
were subsequently built by Dennis and are similar in mass, proportions, and details to his own house.

Two doors to the east (right) at number 19 is a two-story,
wooden, Italian Revival dwelling built in 1855 for Capt. Edward
Pousland. Additions were made in 1884 and 1885 for the next

owner, David P. Carpenter. Familiar Italianate details on the front gable end include matched-boarding, corner quoins, cornice brackets, paired round-headed windows, and a bracketed porch canopy.

G-10 MANNING COTTAGE 1828
26 Dearborn Street

This quaint one-and-one-half-story, wood-frame-and-clapboard dwelling was originally built in 1828 on the site of the former Frank E. Locke house (across the street at number 31) and next to the Manning family home (1824) at number 33. Its construction was financed by Robert Manning for his sister, Elizabeth, the mother of Nathaniel Hawthorne. From 1828 to 1832, just after Nathaniel graduated from Bowdoin College, Mrs. Hawthorne and her son lived here. The house was moved in 1852 by then-owner George Brown, but its original rear ell was left behind and now is a part of number 31. The Ropes family owned the house from c. 1856 to c. 1919 and enlarged it to the rear. Architecturally this building deserves notice for its Dutch-type gambrel roof with flared eaves, and its deep, heavily detailed, closed Doric entrance porch.

Around the corner from the Manning cottage at 26 Walter Street is a small Greek Revival cottage erected in 1849/50 for Nathaniel Heard, a mariner. Until c. 1899 it stood just to the west of the Manning cottage at 24 Dearborn Street, but it was apparently moved at that time to its present site for a new owner, Arthur L. Goss, the proprietor of a local shoe and bicycle repair business. The front matched-board facade displays an unusually fine off-center, recessed doorway with a surround of incised side boards, and a trapezoidal pediment with corniced corner blocks.

G-11

G-11　ALBERT N. LOCKE HOUSE
35 Dearborn Street at Orchard

1896

This asymmetrical wooden residence was constructed in 1896 for Albert N. Locke, the treasurer of the Locke Regulator Company, a North Salem business firm. The site was previously unoccupied, having been owned by the Manning family (see G-10) for many years. The Lockes held title to the property until 1920, in which year it was sold to the Dube family, the owners until 1943. Although it has been modified and expanded in this century, the house is still a provocative late example of the Queen Anne style, and bears a marked similarity to the earlier Gove (see F-5) and Nichols (see F-12) houses on Lafayette Street. All three buildings possess three-story cylindrical corner towers with conical roofs topped by finials. Other features which they have in common are intersecting pitched roofs, irregular floor plans, varied wall surfaces (shingles and clapboards), bay windows, dentiled cornices, molded brick chimneys, closed gable pediments, and off-center front porches with classical column and balustrade details. In the Locke house the latticework pattern of the front gable pediment is effectively repeated in the upper sashes of the tower windows.

G-12

G-12 JAMES DUGAN HOUSE

41 Dearborn Street at Lee

1872

An excellent though understated example of the High Victorian Italianate style, this square, two-story wooden house was erected in 1872 for James Dugan, a prominent leather manufacturer, and was enlarged to the rear in 1881. It once stood at the center of an eight-acre estate on which there were several outbuildings. The Dugan family occupied the house until c. 1918, at which time it was transferred to new ownership. In recent years the house has become crowded by smaller dwellings raised on the former Dugan tract.

It is by the varied treatment of the windows that the Dugan house may be stylistically classified. Present on the front facade are rectangular-arch, segmental-arch, and flat-topped (with side brackets) hoods, all of which are routinely present in High Victorian Italianate architecture. A feeling of verticality is emphasized in all components of the building. All details appear overly stylized for dramatic effect. Included in the standard collection of classical features, especially in the front entrance porch, are several motifs carried forward from the earlier Italian Revival modes—heavy, carved cornice brackets and modillions; square Doric columns on high paneled bases, and molded rails set on fancy turned balusters.

G-13

G-13 DODGE-BERTRAM-WHIPPLE HOUSE   c. 1834 or before
46 Dearborn Street at Everett Road
HABS

The early history of this much-modified and enlarged farmhouse has long mystified historians of Salem. At first glance the building appears to be a product of the Greek Revival period, with later Neoclassical embellishments. Structural and other evidence (the date 1790 is etched in horsehair plaster on an interior wall) suggests, however, that it may possibly date from before 1800, which would make it one of the oldest surviving structures in the Northfields district (see G-14). Until more substantial documentation is uncovered, however, we must rely on deeds, tax records, and family papers which indicate that the house was built c. 1834 for John C. Lee, a resident of 14 Chestnut Street (see E-7), on land formerly owned by James Ropes.

In 1836 Pickering Dodge, Jr., whose father had built the grand brick mansion at 29 Chestnut Street (see E-18), acquired the property to engage in horticultural pursuits, and it is from his period of ownership that the Greek Revival features (end Doric porticos, closed pediment dormers, closed, pilastered side entrance porch, etc.) almost certainly date. Developing its rear gardens, Dodge retained his fine North River estate until 1849, when he sold it to merchant John Bertram (see D-31) of Salem. When Bertram died in 1882, he left the "farm" to his wife, Mary, but during the ensuing fifteen years it was more directly associated with his daughter, Jennie (Mrs. George L.) Emmerton. She and her family used it as summer residence, expanding the garden and making additional alterations to the house. In 1897 the Bertram heirs sold to Everett Whipple, whose descendants lived here until after World War II, adding the east wing c. 1929. In recent years virtually all of the land around the house has been sold off for house lots, and the once lavish gardens have disappeared.

G-14

G-14 BROOKS-BELL HOUSE 1807
40 Felt Street at Claremont
HSI

One of a very few vernacular farmhouses surviving in Salem, this plain, two-story, pitched-roof frame dwelling was built jointly by housewright James Brooks and mariner John Bell in 1807, partly on each other's land. Soon afterwards Benjamin Felt, Jr., the original owner and developer of the land, regained title to it by foreclosure on the mortgages. This residence was for many years the only house on Felt Street, and it has had a complicated history and a long succession of owners, including members of the Dodge, Farrell, Warren, Currier, Gillhooly, Lee, and Ropes families. A dignified and restrained structure (the front Palladian doorway with fanlight is the only embellishment), the Brooks-Bell house is one of the oldest documented buildings in North Salem, with only the houses at Cabot Farm on Upham Street and the Harris house (near the corner of Walter and Dearborn streets) considered to be older (see also G-13).

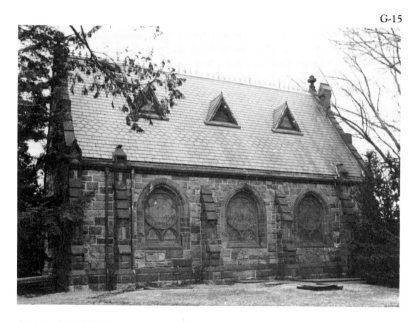

G-15

G-15 DICKSON MEMORIAL CHAPEL AND CONSERVATORY
Greenlawn Cemetery off Orne Street

1892–1894

Salem's only High Victorian Gothic work of architecture, the Dickson Chapel was donated to the city in 1894 by Walter Scott Dickson in memory of his wife, Georgia. Standing on a slight rise near the east end of the Greenlawn Cemetery, it is the visual ordering point for the entire landscape plan and road system. The chapel was built by the well-known Salem contracting firm of Hamilton, Balcomb, and Peterson, with Phipps and Slocum of Boston supplying the stained glass. Plans for both the chapel and the attached conservatory were drafted by George F. Meacham, a rather obscure architect from Newton, Massachusetts. The highly specialized iron-frame and glass construction of the conservatory was the work of Thomas W. Weathered and Sons of New York City, with assistance from Henry Ross of Newton.

Of modest scale and pretentions, the Dickson Chapel is constructed of seam-faced, light-brown granite, with trim of olive stone and Cleveland cream-colored sandstone—this polychromatic combination of differing stone types is a major characteristic of the High Victorian Gothic style. Also typical is the heaviness of such details as the pointed-arch door and window frames, wall buttresses, window tracery, finials, and other carved ornament. Unlike the more fragile details of earlier Gothic Revival buildings, those of the Dickson Chapel tend toward coarseness. The patterned-slate roof planes are broken by triangular dormers, and culminate in fanciful iron cresting at the ridgepole intersection. The oakwood-finished interior of the chapel connects by three doors to the hipped-roof conservatory, which also exhibits Gothic motifs (cresting, pointed-arch roof profiles, trefoil-arch and traceried windows). For the indefinite future the city has closed the complex, and its condition is deteriorating.

SALEM ALMSHOUSE (1815/16 and 1884, etc.; demolished, 1954) by
Charles Bulfinch (1763–1844), etc., and formerly on Salem Neck.
Photograph, 1876.

H

OUTLYING BUILDINGS

INTRODUCTION

This section consists of six entries for local architecture geographically removed from the preceding seven tour districts. These buildings may be best reached by automobile (see general Salem map on inside back cover). Four of the entries describe educational and health facilities which illustrate important design developments in 20th-century American architecture. The entries for Juniper Point and the Baker's Island lighthouse treat two older and larger summer recreational/residential areas of Salem in which buildings dating largely from the late 19th and early 20th centuries were conceived for seasonal use.

H-1 OLD SALEM HIGH SCHOOL
1908–1909; 1927/28

29 Highland Avenue at Jackson Street

The old Salem High School is embellished with Colonial Revival
details recalling Salem's Federal-era architectural heritage. It was
constructed in two major stages approximately twenty years apart.
Drafted by the Boston partnership of Walter H. Kilham (1868–
1948) and James C. Hopkins (1873–1938), the first-stage plan
(published in *The American Architect*, 9 March 1910) called for a
square-shaped, three-story, brick-and-terra cotta building with a symmetrical front facade. This facade consisted of a central entrance
pavilion and flanking projections skilfully tied together by a continuous, pronounced cornice, belt courses, and repetitive fenestration. Reflecting Kilham and Hopkins's extensive experience in
school design was the interior plan in which the classrooms, offices,
laboratories, and technical training areas were conveniently arranged around a spacious two-story auditorium. When student en-
rollment increased from about 700 to over 1,300 after World War I,
the complex was enlarged in 1927/28 by the addition of east and
west wings and an ell containing a gymnasium, kitchen, domestic
science and manual training rooms, additional classrooms, and other
facilities. For this expansion local architects John M. Gray (1887–
1977) and Philip Horton Smith (1890–1960) worked in collaboration. Since January 1976, when the new Salem High School (see
H-3) on Willson Street was opened, the city has used the complex
for a variety of educational and administrative purposes.

H-2 SALEM HOSPITAL

81 Highland Avenue

The Salem Hospital was established in 1873/74, largely through the initiative of Capt. John Bertram (see D-31). For the first four decades of its existence it occupied the enlarged brick Nathan Peirce mansion (1804–1805), formerly at 31 Charter Street. In 1915, prompted by damage wrought by the 1914 Salem fire and the desire for a rural location with room for expansion, the hospital trustees announced plans to build a new medical complex on a twenty-five acre parcel of rocky and hilly land originally part of the Ware estate south of Highland Avenue. In 1916/17, on the highest elevation, a new Colonial Revival-style, H-shaped brick structure (see photo H-21) was erected, along with separate emergency, domestic, and boiler room outbuildings. Supposedly the layout of the main building with its south porch bays was unique for its time. The planners of this complex were the architectural partnership of Parkman B. Haven (1858–1943) and Edward A. Hoyt (1868–1936) of Boston. This firm also designed the former School of Nursing building to the east (left) in 1927/28 (addition, 1946).

Since the twenties the Salem Hospital's physical plant has been substantially enlarged to meet the growing medical needs of the North Shore. The firm of Stevens, Curtin, and Mason of Boston designed two additions to the original main building—an administrative wing, built in 1938, and the Macomber building for maternity and pediatric care, erected in 1940/41. The new two-story Ara N. Sargent Memorial Laboratory ell, planned by Curtin and Riley, Architects, was appended to the main building in 1948/49. In 1957/58, under the supervision of architects Valtz and Kimberly, the four-story Walter Gray Phippen building was attached to the south-

east corner of the complex, thereby expanding existing laboratory, operating room, and patient bed space. A separate medical office building was developed next in two stages, with James H. Ritchie and Associates (first portion, 1961), and Marcus and Nocka (second portion, 1967/68) serving as architects. The Ritchie firm was also responsible for the plans of the North Shore Babies' and Children's Hospital, which became part of the complex in 1960/61. The most recent major ell on the main structure, a good example of Brutalist contemporary architecture, is the Davenport building (see photo H-2r), constructed in 1972/73 from plans drafted by Tom Payette of the Boston firm of Payette Associates. The construction of the Shaughnessy Hospital, of similar materials and design, followed in 1976, with James Fitzgerald of Boston as the superintending architect.

H-3   SALEM HIGH SCHOOL

77 Willson Street at Highland Avenue

1972–1976

One of the largest, best-equipped, and most striking secondary-level educational facilities in Massachusetts, the new Salem High School was constructed between 1972 and 1976 at a cost of $18 million. This sprawling complex, like the Witchcraft Heights Elementary School (see H-4) built just before it, consists of a series of inter-connected rectangular modules spread across a rocky, contoured hilltop site. The instructional media center serves as the nucleus of the structure around which are situated three academic "houses," an arts center, an auditorium, a field house, a cafeteria, a voca-tional education center, and other supportive units. Constructed of reinforced concrete, brick, steel, and plate glass, this massive and weighty facility is of the Brutalist contemporary style, with asym-metrical elevations, sculptured stair towers, recessed window and door apertures, and broad, rough, wall surfaces interrupted by dark-appearing penetrations of varying sizes and shapes. The architect for the complex was the firm of Haldeman and Goransson Associated, Boston, while the contractor was B.G. Danis of New England, North Attleboro, Massachusetts.

H-4 WITCHCRAFT HEIGHTS ELEMENTARY SCHOOL

1971/72

1 Frederick Street off Belleview Avenue

One of the most modern and functional educational facilities on
the North Shore, the Witchcraft Heights Elementary School was
built in 1971/72 by the E.C. Blanchard Construction Company of
Lynn, Massachusetts, from plans prepared by the architectural firm
of Coletti Brothers of Hingham, Massachusetts. Positioned atop a
hill, but effectively hugging its contours, this low, rambling reinforced concrete, brick, steel, and plate-glass complex combines the
sculptural and "bare bones" quality of contemporary Brutalism, the
symmetrical elevations of the New Formalism, and the rectilinearity
and precision of the Miesian style. The various rectangular-box portions of the building, though of different shapes, proportions, and
embellishment, form a single forceful yet coherent architectural
statement. The main body of the structure contains administrative
offices, counseling stations, a media center, health care and
remedial reading rooms, a gymnasium, an auditorium/cafeteria,
teacher's rooms, and specialized art, music, and science rooms. In
the two-story, H-shaped south wing, twenty-one classrooms are arranged around a central library core.

H-5   JUNIPER POINT COTTAGES

1870s, etc.

Beach and Columbus avenues, Juniper Point on Salem Neck

Adjacent to the Willows, Salem's historic seaside park and amusement area, is the oldest residential section of Salem Neck, known as Juniper Point. Early in the city's history this rocky promontory contained fortifications, but it was later developed for farming by the Allen, Dustin, and other families. In the 1850s and 1860s the point served as a recreational "tenting ground." In 1870 the owner Daniel B. Gardner subdivided the area (approximately thirty acres) into house lots, and the point quickly developed into a desirable summer resort. For many years a large wooden hotel, the "Ocean House" (1879), was maintained here looking out onto Massachusetts Bay and its many islands.

The majority of the cottages on Juniper Point were built between 1870 and 1910, and although they were planned with an eye to economy, many are architecturally noteworthy. Of wood-frame construction and one-and-one-half or two stories tall, the best of these combine features usually associated with the Queen Anne, Stick, and Shingle styles. Today Juniper Point is almost exclusively a year-round residential community, and virtually all of the cottages have been winterized.

H-6 BAKER'S ISLAND LIGHTHOUSE   c. 1820
Baker's Island in Massachusetts Bay
NR

Approximately five miles out into Massachusetts Bay from Salem
Harbor, but officially part of the City of Salem, is Baker's Island, a
summer vacation colony rich in lore and tradition. Although the
island has been inhabited since the earliest years of New England
settlement, it was not until 1797/98, acting upon the authorization
of Congress, that a marine light station was established on the
north end. At first this station consisted of two wooden light towers
of unequal height, with a keeper's house in between. Then in 1820,
the Salem Town Meeting requested an appropriation from Congress
for a more permanent lighthouse; this action resulted in the construction of two new lighthouses soon thereafter. Since 1870, however, the station has displayed only one light, as the smaller of the
two towers was declared officially inactive in 1916 and removed in
1926. The conical-shaped, rubble-stone-masonry tower that has survived is still in service, although it is self-operating and has not had
a U.S. Coast Guard keeper in recent years. Nearby are the former
keeper's and assistant keeper's houses, that are but two of several
dozen modest and functional wood-frame dwellings which dot the
island and are in use each summer season.

BIBLIOGRAPHY

The below list contains a quality sampling of printed materials pertaining to Salem architecture; it is not intended to be a comprehensive bibliography. Only those works which include mention of Salem buildings appear. Purposely omitted are bibliographical reference listings, biographical dictionaries, architectural design books, and architectural dictionaries and style guides. To facilitate use, books, pamphlets, and periodical articles are arranged under thirteen categorical headings: general, guidebooks, Samuel McIntire, Essex County, Salem, and the eight Salem tour districts. The Institute's quarterly historical journal, the *Essex Institute Historical Collections*, is cited as *EIHC* in listings where it appears.

In addition to the printed titles in the bibliography, the following unpublished materials are essential sources for the study of Salem architecture: the Salem Historic District Study Committee Report (1968) (Essex Institute); Historic Salem, Inc. building research reports (Essex Institute); Essex County deeds and probate records (Essex County Registry of Deeds and Registry of Probate, Salem); City of Salem street books, assessors records, and tax records (City Hall; Essex Institute); City of Salem building permits (Essex Institute; City Hall; Building Inspector's Office); architectural drawings, specifications, and related documents (Samuel McIntire; Gridley J.F. Bryant; Emmerton and Foster; Enoch Fuller; William G. Rantoul; Philip Horton Smith, etc.) (Essex Institute); Salem architectural photographs (Frank Cousins, Samuel Chamberlain, Bryant F. Tolles, Jr., etc.) (Essex Institute); and various family papers and church and organizational records (Essex Institute, etc.). Important printed sources (Essex Institute) not listed include: Salem city directories (1837+); Salem city maps (1851+); Essex County view books; Salem city and education department reports; and, Essex County newspapers.

GENERAL

Abbott, Katherine M. *Old Paths and Legends of New England.* New York: G.P. Putnam's Sons, 1904. Salem, pp. 150–64.

Andrews, Wayne. *Architecture, Ambition and Americans: A Social History of American Architecture.* Rev. ed. New York: The Free Press, 1964.

Andrews, Wayne. *Architecture in New England: A Photographic History.* Brattleboro, Vermont: Stephen Greene Press, 1973.

Bailey, Henry Turner. "An Architect of the Old School." *New England Magazine* n.s. 25 (November 1901): 326–49. Treats the life and work of architect Gridley J.F. Bryant.

Briggs, Martin. *The Homes of the Pilgrim Fathers in England and America.* London and New York: Oxford University Press, 1932.

Bunnell, Gene. *Built to Last: A Handbook on Recycling Old Buildings.* Washington, D.C.: The Preservation Press for the National Trust for Historic Preservation, 1977. Section on Salem rehabilitation.

Carpenter, Ralph E., Jr. *The Fifty Best Historic American Houses.* New York: E.P. Dutton, 1955.

Chandler, Joseph E. *The Colonial House.* New York: Robert M. McBride, 1916. Treats 17th-century Salem houses.

Cummings, Abbott Lowell. *The Framed Houses of Massachusetts Bay, 1625-1725.* Cambridge and London: Belknap Press of Harvard University Press, 1979.

Cummings, Abbott Lowell. "Massachusetts and Its First Period Houses: A Statistical Survey," plus appendices, from Cummings, ed. *Architecture in Colonial Massachusetts.* Boston: Colonial Society of Massachusetts, 1979. Pp. 113–221.

Donnelly, Marion Card. *The New England Meetinghouse of the Seventeenth Century.* Middletown, Connecticut: Wesleyan University Press, 1968.

Davidson, Marshall, ed. *The American Heritage History of Notable American Houses.* New York: American Heritage Publishing Co., 1971.

Eberlein, Harold D. *The Architecture of Colonial America.* Boston: Little, Brown & Co., 1915.

Federal Writers Project. *Massachusetts: A Guide to its Places and People.* American Guide Series. Boston: Houghton Mifflin Co., 1937.

French, Leigh, Jr. *Colonial Interiors: Colonial and Early Federal—First Series.* New York: Bonanza Books, 1923.

Gowans, Alan. *Images of American Living: Four Centuries of Architecture and Furniture as Cultural Expression.* Philadelphia and New York: J.B. Lippincott Co., 1964.

Hamlin, Talbot F. *The American Spirit in Architecture. The Yale Pageant of America: A Pictorial History of the United States,* vol. 13, ed. by Ralph Henry Gabriel. New Haven: Yale University Press, 1926.

Hamlin, Talbot. *Greek Revival Architecture in America: Being an Account of Important Trends in American Architecture and American Life prior to the War Between the States.* New York: Oxford University Press, 1944. Reprinted, New York: Dover Publications, 1968.

Historic Buildings of Massachusetts: Photographs from the Historic American Buildings Survey. Scribner Historic Buildings Series. New York: Charles Scribner's Sons, 1976.

Hitchcock, Henry-Russell. *Architecture: Nineteenth and Twentieth Centuries.* Baltimore: Penguin Books, 1958. 3rd ed., 1968.

Howells, John Mead. *Lost Examples of Colonial Architecture: Buildings that have disappeared or been so altered as to be denatured.* New York: William Helburn, 1931. Reprinted, New York: Dover Publications, 1963.

Isham, Norman M. *Early American Homes and A Glossary of Colonial Architectural Terms.* Originally published as two separate works (1928; 1939) in limited editions by the Walpole Society. Reprinted, New York: DaCapo Press, 1967.

Jones, Alvin L. *Under Colonial Roofs.* Boston: C.B. Webster, 1894.

Kilham, Walter H. *Boston After Bulfinch: An Account of its Architecture, 1800-1900.* Cambridge: Harvard University Press, 1946.

Kimball, Fiske. *Domestic Architecture of the American Colonies and of the Early Republic.* New York: Charles Scribner's Sons, 1922. Reprinted, New York: Dover Publications, 1966.

Kirker, Harold. *The Architecture of Charles Bulfinch.* Cambridge: Harvard University Press, 1969.

Larkin, Oliver W. *Art and Life in America*. New York: Rinehart, 1949. Rev. ed., New York: Holt, Rinehart & Winston, 1966.

Lathrop, Elise L. *Historic Houses of Early America*. New York: Tudor Publishing Co., 1936.

Lathrop, Elise L. *Old New England Churches*. Rutland, Vermont: Tuttle Publishing Co., 1938.

McArdle, Alma deC. and Deirdre B. *Carpenter Gothic: 19th-Century Ornamented Houses of New England*. New York: Whitney Library of Design, 1978.

Mixer, Knowlton. *Old Houses of New England*. New York: The Macmillan Co., 1927.

Morrison, Hugh. *Early American Architecture: From the First Colonial Settlements to the National Period*. New York: Oxford University Press, 1952.

Nicholson, Arnold. *American Houses in History*. New York: Viking Press, 1965.

Northend, Mary H. *Historic Homes of New England*. Boston: Little, Brown & Co., 1914.

Pickering, Ernest. *The Homes of America*. New York: Thomas Y. Crowell Co., 1951.

Pierson, William H., Jr. *American Buildings and Their Architects*. Vol. 1, *The Colonial and Neo-Classical Styles*. Garden City, N.Y.: Doubleday & Co., 1970.

Polley, Robert F., ed. *American Historic Houses: The Living Past*. New York: G.P. Putnam's Sons, 1968.

Poppeliers, John C., ed. *Historic American Buildings Survey: Massachusetts Catalog*. Boston: Massachusetts Historical Commission, 1965.

Pratt, Richard. *The Golden Treasury of Early American Houses*. New York: Hawthorn Books, 1967.

Quinan, Jack. "Daniel Raynerd, Stucco Worker." *Old-Time New England* 65 (Winter-Spring 1975): 1–21.

Roth, Leland. *A Concise History of American Architecture*. New York: Harper & Row, 1979.

Shurtleff, Harold R. *The Log Cabin Myth: A Study of the Early Dwellings of the English Colonists in North America*. Cambridge: Harvard University Press, 1939. Reprinted, Gloucester, Mass.: Peter Smith, 1967.

Smith, George E.K. *A Pictorial History of Architecture in America*. 2 vols. New York: American Heritage Publishing Co., 1976.

Tallmadge, Thomas E. *The Story of Architecture in America*. New York: W.W. Norton & Co., 1927.

Three Centuries of Custom Houses. Washington, D.C.: National Society of the Colonial Dames of America, 1972.

Vanderbilt, Cornelius, Jr. *The Living Past of America: A Pictorial Treasury of our Historic Houses and Villages that have been Preserved and Restored*. New York: Crown Publishers, 1955.

Ware, William Rotch. *The Georgian Period*. 3 vols. New York: U.P.C. Book Co., 1923.

Whiffin, Marcus, and Koeper, Frederick. *American Architecture, 1607-1976*. Cambridge: M.I.T. Press, 1981.

GUIDEBOOKS

Along the Coast of Essex County: A Guidebook. Boston: Junior League of Boston, Inc., 1970.

Arvedson, George. *Salem With A Guide*. Salem: n.p., 1926.

Be-Witched in Historic Salem. Salem: Salem Chamber of Commerce, 1975. Several printings. Earlier edition under title, *Historic Salem, Massachusetts* (1967).

DaCosta, Beverley, ed. *Historic Houses of America Open to the Public.* New York: American Heritage Publishing Co., 1971.

Guide to Salem. Salem: Board of Park Commissioners, 1930.

Hill, Benjamin D., and Nevins, Winfield S. *The North Shore of Massachusetts Bay: A Guide and History of Marblehead, Salem Neck and Juniper Point, Beverly, and Cape Ann.* Salem: Salem Press, 1879. Successive editions to 1894.

Kimball, Henrietta D. *Old and New Salem, Historical.* Salem: George A. Kimball, 1891.

Messer, Nellie M. *Streets and Homes in Old Salem.* Salem: n.p., 1919. Successive editions to 1947.

Murray, Robert. *The Illustrated Salem Guide Book.* Salem: Salem Bicentennial Commission, 1975.

Pratt, Dorothy and Richard. *A Guide to Early American Homes, North and South.* New York: Bonanza Books, 1956.

Reader's Digest Illustrated Guide to the Treasures of America. Pleasantville, N.Y.: The Reader's Digest Association, 1974.

Reynolds, J. Frank. *The Compass: An Illustrated Souvenir Guide to Salem, Massachusetts.* Salem: n.p., 1926.

Smith, George E.K. *The Architecture of the United States: An Illustrated Guide to Notable Buildings, A.D. 1115 to the Present, Open to the Public,* vol. 1, *New England and the Mid-Atlantic States.* Garden City, N.Y.: Anchor Press, Doubleday Publishing Co., 1981.

Visitor's Guide to Salem. Salem: Essex Institute, 1895. Successive editions to 1953. Published by Henry P. Ives and Eben Putnam in six editions, 1880 to 1894.

SAMUEL McINTIRE

Butler, Jeanne F. "Competition 1792: Designing a Nation's Capitol." *Capitol Studies* 4, No. 1 (1976): 47–53. Section on McIntire.

Cousins, Frank, and Riley, Phil M. *The Wood-Carver of Salem: Samuel McIntire, His Life and Work.* Boston: Little, Brown & Co., 1916. Reprinted, New York: AMS Press, Inc., 1970.

Cummings, Abbott Lowell, "Samuel McIntire and His Sources." *EIHC* 93 (April-July 1957): 149–66.

Downs, Joseph. "Derby and McIntire." *Metropolitan Museum Bulletin* n.s. 6 (October 1947): 73–80.

Dyer, Walter A. *Early American Craftsmen.* New York: The Century Co., 1915. Chapter on McIntire, pp. 16–40.

Dyer, Walter A. "Samuel McIntire, Master Carpenter." *House Beautiful* 37 (February 1915): 65–69.

Hunt, W.H. "Samuel McIntire, housewright-architect, Salem, Mass." *American Architect* 119 (April 1921): 415–22, 428.

Kimball, Fiske. "The Elias Hasket Derby Mansion in Salem." *EIHC* 60 (October 1924): 273–92.

Kimball, Fiske. "Furniture Carvings by Samuel McIntire." *Antiques* 18 (November 1930): 388–92. References to interior carving.

Kimball, Fiske. *Mr. Samuel McIntire, Carver: The Architect of Salem.* Salem: Essex Institute, 1940. Reprinted, Gloucester, Mass.: Peter Smith, 1966.

Larkin, Oliver W. "Samuel McIntire and the Arts of Post-Colonial America." *EIHC* 93 (April-July 1957): 211–21.

Little, Nina Fletcher. "Carved Figures by Samuel McIntire and his Contemporaries." *EIHC* 93 (April-July 1957): 179–99.

Little, Nina Fletcher. "Corne, McIntire and the Hersey Derby Farm." *Antiques* 101 (June 1972): 226–29.

McDonald, Edith W. "The Woodcarver of Salem." *Stone and Webster Journal* 46 (January 1930): 53–65.

Mac Swiggan, Amelia E. "Samuel McIntire—Salem's Illustrious Carver." *Antiques Journal* 9 (January 1954): 14–17, 23.

Merrill, Walter M. "New Evidence that Samuel McIntire Designed Hamilton Hall." *EIHC* 91 (January 1955): 79.

Newcomb, Rexford. "Samuel McIntire, Early American Architect." *The Architect* 9 (October 1927): 37–43.

Pratt, Richard H. "McIntire, the Colonial Carpenter, he who made Salem Beautiful." *House and Garden* 51 (February 1927): 108, 158, 162, 164.

Stowe, Charles M. "Samuel McIntire of Salem." *Antiquarian* 12 (February 1929): 33–36, 66, 68.

Swan, Mabel M. "A Factual Estimate of Samuel McIntire." *EIHC* 93 (April-July 1957): 200–210.

"Tour of McIntire Houses, May 11–12, 1957." *EIHC* 93 (April-July 1957): 115–20. In special issue, "Samuel McIntire: A Bicentennial Symposium."

Walker, Ambrose. "Samuel McIntire—A Sketch." *EIHC* 68 (April 1932): 97–116.

ESSEX COUNTY

Arrington, Benjamin F. *Municipal History of Essex County, Massachusetts.* 4 vols. New York: Lewis Historical Publishing Co., 1922.

Belknap, Henry W. *Artists and Craftsmen of Essex County, Massachusetts.* Salem: Essex Institute, 1927.

Fuess, Claude M., ed., and Paradise, Scott H., comp. *The Story of Essex County.* 4 vols. New York: American Historical Society, 1935.

Hurd, Duane H., ed. *History of Essex County, Massachusetts.* 2 vols. Philadephia: J.W. Lewis, 1888.

Mac Donald, Albert J. *Selected Interiors of Old Houses in Salem and Vicinity.* Boston: Rogers and Manson Co., 1916.

[Tracy, Cyrus M.] *Standard History of Essex County, Massachusetts . . .,* ed. by H. Wheatland. Boston: C.F. Jewett & Co., 1878.

Webber, Charles H., and Nevins, Winfield S. *Old Naumkeag: An Historical Sketch of the City of Salem, and the Towns of Marblehead, Peabody, Beverly, Danvers, Wenham, Manchester, Topsfield, and Middleton.* Salem: A.A. Smith, 1877.

SALEM

Anderson Notter Associates, Inc., comp. *The Salem Handbook: A Renovation Guide for Homeowners.* Salem: Historic Salem, Inc., 1977.

Benjamin A.N. "Salem: Historic and Picturesque Features." *Outlook* 57 (6 November 1897): 591–98.

Bentley, William. "A Description and History of Salem." *Massachusetts Historical Society Collections* 6 (1799): 212–77.

Bentley, William. *The Diary of William Bentley, D.D.* 4 vols. Salem: Essex Institute, 1905–1914. Reprinted, Gloucester, Mass.: Peter Smith, 1962.

Belknap, Henry W. "Joseph True, Wood Carver of Salem, and his Account Book." *EIHC* 78 (April 1942): 117–57.

Bowditch, Harold, M.D. "The Buildings Associated with Nathaniel Bowditch (1773–1838)." *EIHC* 79 (July 1943): 205–21; 80 (January 1944): 92–93.

Bragdon, Claude F. "Six Hours in Salem." *American Architect and Building News* 39 (21 January 1893): 41–43.

"Brick Buildings in Salem [in 1806]." *EIHC* 1 (May 1859): 55–56. The so-called "Cushing list" from the *Salem Gazette.*

Brown, Frank Chouteau. "Salem, Massachusetts." *The Monograph Series: Records of Early American Architecture* 23: 17–32, ed. by Russell F. Whitehead. Included in *Pencil Points* 18 (May 1937): 305–322.

Buckham, John W. "Some Architectural Details as Illustrated in the Doorways of Old Salem." *Country Life in America* 2 (July 1902): 85–89.

Buckham, John W. "Some Old-Time Salem Houses and Celebrities." *Book World* 7 (1901): 799–804.

Chamberlain, Samuel. *Historic Salem in Four Seasons.* New York: Hastings House, 1938.

Chamberlain, Samuel. *Salem Interiors: Two Centuries of New England Taste and Decoration.* New York: Hastings House, 1950.

Chamberlain, Samuel. *A Stroll Through Historic Salem.* New York: Hastings House, 1969.

Cousins, Frank. *Colonial Architecture, Series One.* "Fifty Salem Doorways." New York: Doubleday, Page & Co., 1912.

Cousins, Frank, and Riley, Phil M. *The Colonial Architecture of Salem.* Boston: Little, Brown & Co., 1919.

Cousins, Frank, and Riley, Phil M. "Six Old Salem Doorways." *Architectural Record* 42 (October 1917): 393–99.

Cousins, Frank, and Riley, Phil M. "Windows of Old Salem." *Country Life in America* 28 (October 1915): 48–49.

Davenport, George F. *Homes and Hearths of Salem.* Salem: Observer Press, 1891.

Dow, George Francis. "Old Salem Houses." *Architectural Review* 15 (1908): 161–64.

Dow, Joy Wheeler. "A Salem Enchantment." *House Beautiful* 12 (November 1902): 334–44.

Felt, Joseph B. *Annals of Salem.* 2nd ed. 2 vols. Salem: W. & S.B. Ives, 1845 & 1849. 1st ed., one volume, 1827.

Franklin, M.S. "Recording the Architecture of Late Colonial Times in Salem, Massachusetts." *The Monograph Series: Records of Early American Architecture* 18: 198–212, ed. by Russell F. Whitehead. Included in *Pencil Points* 13 (June 1932): 407–422. Focuses on public buildings.

Gillespie, Charles B., comp. *Illustrated History of Salem and Environs . . .* Salem: Salem Evening News, 1897. Souvenir edition.

[Grebanier, Francis V.] *Puritan City: The Story of Salem.* New York: R.M. McBride, 1938.

Houseman, R.W. "Early New England Houses with 20th-Century Owners." *American Home* 66 (March 1963): 26–31.

Hunt, W.H. "Old Salem Houses." *American Architect* 109 (27 April 1921): 507–513, 522.

Kimball, Fiske, "Furniture Carvings by Samuel Field McIntire." *Antiques* 23 (February 1933): 56–58. Mentions Salem houses in which he did work.

Little, David M. "Documentary History of the Salem Custom House." *EIHC* 67 (January 1931): 1–26; 67 (April 1931): 145–60; 67 (July 1931): 265–80.

"List of Houses Built in Salem From 1750–1773." *EIHC* 58 (October 1922): 292–96. The so-called "Curwen list."

Loring, George B. "Some Account of Houses and other Buildings in Salem, From a Manuscript of the Late Col. Benj. Pickman." *EIHC* 6 (June 1864): 93–109.

Nevins, Winfield S. "The Houses and Haunts of Hawthorne." *New England Magazine* n.s. 9 (November 1893): 289–306.

Northend, Mary H. *Historic Doorways of Old Salem.* Cambridge: Riverside Press of Houghton Mifflin Co., 1926.

Northend, Mary H. *Memories of Old Salem . . . ..* New York: Moffat, Yard & Co., 1917.

Northend, Mary H. "Salem Porches; A Study in Architecture." *Boston Cooking-School Magazine* 11 (November 1906): 164–69.

Northend, Mary H. "Worthwhile Houses in Salem Built Since the Conflagration of June, 1914." *House Beautiful* 48 (September 1920): 193–95.

Osgood, Charles S., and Batchelder, Henry M. *Historical Sketch of Salem, 1626 [to] 1879.* Salem: Essex Institute, 1879.

"Our New Domain." *EIHC* 24 (October, November, December 1897): 241–74. Area in the vicinity of the Essex Institute.

Perley, Sidney. *The History of Salem, Massachusetts.* 3 vols. Salem: By the Author, 1924–1928.

Perley, Sidney. "Part of Salem in 1700." *Essex Antiquarian* 2 (November, 1898): 167–74. Followed by thirty-six articles on the same topic in the *Essex Antiquarian* to 1909.

Phillips, James Duncan. *Salem in the Eighteenth Century.* Boston: Houghton Mifflin Co., 1937.

Phillips, James Duncan. "Salem in the Nineties." *EIHC* 89 (October 1953): 295–328; 90 (January 1954): 17–57.

Phillips, James Duncan. *Salem in the Seventeenth Century.* Boston: Houghton Mifflin Co., 1933.

Pratt, Richard. "Salem." *Ladies Home Journal* 64 (April 1947): 46–51.

Riley, Phil M. "In the Spirit of Old Salem." *House Beautiful* 39 (February 1916): 72–74.

Robotti, Frances D. *Chronicles of Old Salem: A History in Miniature.* New York: Bonanza Books, 1948.

"Salem and her Architecture." *Brooklyn Institute of Arts and Sciences Bulletin* 10 (1913): 171–76.

"Salem, Mass., Historic Sites Threatened." *Historic Preservation* 17 (November-December 1965): 230–31.

Simpson, Jeffrey. "Salem Restored." *Antiques World* 1 (March 1979): 58–65.

Smith, Harris. "The Case of the Two 17th-Century Houses in Disguise." *Yankee* 32 (October 1968): 86–91, 145–46, 148. Gedney and Samuel Pickman houses.

Streeter, Gilbert L. "Some Historic Streets and Colonial Houses of Salem." *EIHC* 36 (July 1900): 185–213.

Sturgis, Walter K. "Arthur Little and the Colonial Revival." *Journal of the Society of Architectural Historians* 32 (May 1973): 147–63.

Upham, William P. "An Account of the Dwelling Houses of Francis Higginson, Samuel Skelton, Roger Williams and Hugh Peters." *EIHC* 8 (1866): 250–59.

Upham, William P. "First Houses in Salem." *Essex Institute Bulletin* 1 (1869): 37–41, 53–57, 73–81, 129–36, 145–50; 2 (1870): 33–39, 49–60.

White, George M. *Old Houses of Salem.* Salem: Salem Gazette, n.d.

A. SALEM COMMON

Belknap, Henry W. *The Seventeenth Century House.* Salem: Newcomb & Gauss, 1930. Treats the John Ward house.

Brown, Frank Chouteau. "The Gardner-Pingree-White House Built in Salem, Massachusetts, in 1804 by Samuel McIntire, Architect." *White Pine Monograph Series* 26: 145–60. Included in *Pencil Points* 21 (August 1940): 515–30.

Browne, Benjamin F. "An Account of Salem Common and the Levelling of the Same in 1802, With Short Notices of the Subscribers." *EIHC* 4 (February 1862): 2–13; 4 (April 1862): 76–88; 4 (June 1862): 129–40.

Browne, Benjamin F. "Youthful Recollections of Salem." *EIHC* 49 (July 1913):

193–209; (October 1913): 289–304. Also 50 (January 1914): 6–16; (October 1914): 289–96; and 51 (January 1915): 53–56; (October 1915): 297–315.

"The Crowninshield-Bentley House." *Historic Preservation* 11 (1959): 154–55.

Cummings, Abbott Lowell. "The House and Its People." In *The Crowninshield-Bentley House* (Salem: Essex Institute, 1976), pp. 5–20. Originally published in *EIHC* 97 (April 1961): 81–164.

Cummings, Abbott Lowell. "History in Houses: The Crowninshield-Bentley House in Salem, Massachusetts." *Antiques* 76 (October 1959): 328–29.

Essex Institute. *The Story of the First Meeting House Built in 1634-5 by the First Church, Gathered at Salem, July and August, 1629.* Salem: Salem Press, 1897.

Fales, Dean A., Jr. "The Crowninshield-Bentley House in Salem—A Documentary Restoration." *Antiques* 88 (October 1965): 486–93.

Farnam, Anne. "Dr. Bentley's Account Books: Documentation for the Creation of a Historical Setting." *EIHC* 116 (October 1980): 206–222. The Crowninshield-Bentley house.

Lahikainen, Dean L. "New Insights into the Early History of the Gardner-Pingree House in Salem, Massachusetts." *EIHC* 116 (October 1980): 223–47.

Merrill, Walter M. *New England Treasury of American Beginnings: Essex Institute.* New York: Newcomen Society, 1957.

"Pingree House." *Interior Decorator* 99 (February 1940): 11–17.

Plummer Hall, Salem: Its Libraries, Collections, Historical Associations. Salem: Salem Press, 1882.

Putnam, Eben. "An Inquiry into the Authenticity of the so-called First Meeting House at Salem, Mass." *Putnam's Monthly Historical Magazine* n.s. 7 (1899): 207–23.

Tolles, Carolyn K., and Wheaton, Elizabeth. "The Thomas March Woodbridge House—In Time and Place." In *Antiques in the Country* (Salem: The Children's Friend and Family Service Society of the North Shore, Inc., 1982), pp. 8–11.

Tolles, Bryant F., Jr. *The John Tucker Daland House.* Salem: Essex Institute, 1978. Originally published in *EIHC* 114 (January 1978): 1–23.

Upham, William P. "Notes on the Report as to the Authenticity of the First Meeting House in Salem." *EIHC* 40 (January 1904): 17–32.

Ward, Gerald W.R. "Additional Notes on the Crowninshield-Bentley House." In *The Crowninshield-Bentley House* (Salem: Essex Institute, 1976), pp. 21–30. Originally published in *EIHC* 111 (January 1975): 1–11.

Ward, Gerald W.R. *The Andrew-Safford House.* Salem: Essex Institute, 1976. Originally published in *EIHC* 112 (April 1976): 159–88.

Ward, Gerald W.R. *The Gardner-Pingree House.* Salem: Essex Institute, 1976. Originally published in *EIHC* 111 (April 1975): 81–98.

Ward, Gerald W.R. and Barbara M. *The John Ward House.* Salem: Essex Institute, 1976. Originally published in *EIHC* 110 (January 1974): 3–32.

Winchester, Alice. "The Pingree House in Salem." *Antiques* 49 (March 1946): 174–77.

B. DERBY STREET

Chadwell, Pauline S. "The Richard Derby House." *Antiques* 47 (May 1945): 282–83.

Cummings, Abbott Lowell. "Nathaniel Hawthorne's Birthplace: An Architectural Study." *EIHC* 114 (July 1958): 196–204.

[Dobrovolny, H. John]. *Master Plan: Salem Maritime National Historic Site.* Washington, D.C.: National Park Service, 1978.

Emmerton, Caroline O. *The Chronicles of Three Old Houses.* Boston: Thomas

Todd Co., 1935. House of Seven Gables, Hooper-Hathaway, and Retire Becket houses.

Lancaster, Clay. "Some Secret Spaces and Private Places in Early American Architecture." *Antiques* 50 (November 1946): 324–27. House of Seven Gables.

"The Old Bakery." *Old-Time New England* 2 (August 1911): 13–15. See also 3 (July 1912): 14–15. Hooper-Hathaway house.

Small, Edwin W. "The Derby House." *Old-Time New England* 47 (Spring 1957): 101–107.

Small, Edwin W. "A National Historic Site at Salem, Massachusetts." *Planning and Civic Comment* 4 (October-December 1938): 14–15.

Stevenson, Edward M., comp. *The House of Seven Gables.* Salem: House of Seven Gables, 1979. The most recent in a series of promotional booklets.

C. CITY CENTER

Annable, Irving K. "Historical Notes on the Crombie Street Congregational Church, Salem, Massachusetts." *EIHC* 77 (July 1941): 203–217.

Bogart, Olive. "How the Witch House Was Restored." *Yankee* 15 (November 1951): 36–37.

Dennis, Albert W. *The Merchants National Bank of Salem, Massachusetts: An Historical Sketch.* Salem: Salem Press, Co., 1908.

Dodge, Ernest S. *Salem Five Cents Savings Bank, 1855-1955: The Story of its First Hundred Years.* Portland, Me.: Anthoensen Press, 1955.

The First Baptist Church 150th Anniversary, 1804-1954. Salem: n.p., 1954.

The First Centenary of the North Church and Society in Salem, Massachusetts. Salem: Printed for the Society, 1873.

Gavet, William F. *Historical Sketch of Saint Peter's Church, Salem, Mass.* Salem: n.p., 1908.

Hayden, Barbara E. "Central Street, Salem, and the Ingalls House." *EIHC* 85 (January 1949): 58–91.

Jenkins, Lawrence W., and Whitehill, Walter Muir. *The Restoration of East India Marine Hall.* Salem: Peabody Museum, 1948.

Macy, Clinton T. *Brief History of St. Peter's Church.* Salem: St. Peter's Church, 1958.

"Market House in Derby Square." *EIHC* 62 (October 1926): 296–97. Description from *Salem Gazette,* November 26, 1816.

Messer, Nellie S. *Historical Sketch of the Tabernacle Church, Salem, Mass.* Salem: Tabernacle Church, 1930.

The New Holyoke Building . . . Salem, Mass. Salem: Holyoke Mutual Fire Insurance Co., 1936.

The One Hundred Years of the Salem Savings Bank. Salem: Salem Savings Bank, 1918.

Osgood, Charles S. "The Court Houses of Salem." *The Visitor* 1 (February 11, 1891): 169–74.

Perley, Sidney. "The Court Houses in Salem." *EIHC* 47 (April 1911): 101–123.

Phillips, James Duncan. *Town House Square in the Nineties, and Some of the People Who Crossed It.* Boston: Thomas Todd Co., 1940.

Phippen, Arthur H. *"The Tabernacle" in 1735-1935 . . . ..* Salem: Tabernacle Church, 1935.

Smith, Philip C.F. *East India Marine Hall: 1824-1974.* Salem: Peabody Museum, 1974.

Smith, Philip C.F. "The Metamorphosis of East India Marine Hall." *Historic Preservation* 27 (October-December 1975): 10–13.

Whitehill, Walter Muir. *The East India Marine Society and the Peabody Museum of Salem: A Sesquicentennial History.* Salem: Peabody Museum, 1949.

Willis, Lemuel. *A Semi-Centennial Address Delivered in the Universalist Church, Salem, Mass.* . . . Salem: Register Press, 1859.

D. UPPER FEDERAL AND UPPER ESSEX STREETS

Abbott, Lilly, S. *Grace Church in Salem: The First One Hundred Years, 1858-1958.* Salem: Grace Church Centennial Committee, 1958.

Andrews, J.P. "Reminiscences of Federal Street: Written in 1885 by J.P. Andrews." *EIHC* 83 (April 1947): 86–87.

Ashton, Joseph N. *The Salem Athenaeum, 1810-1910.* Salem: Berkeley Press, 1917.

"The Authenticity of the Roger Williams House." *EIHC* 25, Nos. 4-6 (April-June, 1888): 162–64.

Dow, George Francis. "Building Agreements in Seventeenth-Century Massachusetts . . .." *Old-Time New England* 13 (January 1923): 131–34. Refers to the Jonathan Corwin house.

Drake, Samuel Adams. "The Old Witch-House at Salem." *Appleton's Journal* 10 (1873): 673–75.

Messer, Nellis S. "The Ropes Memorial at Salem, Massachusetts." *Old-Time New England* 14 (April 1924): 149–63.

Northend, Mary H. "Old Cook-Oliver House in Salem." *American Homes and Gardens* 11 (September 1914): 308–11.

Northend, Mary H. "Peirce-Nichols House at Salem." *American Homes and Gardens* 12 (June 1915): 183–87.

"An Old Salem House of Romantic Memories and Historic Interest." *Craftsman* 26 (May 1914): 192–99. The Peirce-Nichols house.

Oliver, Henry K. "Henry K. Oliver's Reminiscences of Federal Street, Written in 1885." *EIHC* 82 (April 1946): 179–85.

Perley, Sidney. "Where Roger Williams Lived in Salem." *EIHC* 52 (April 1916): 97–111.

Rantoul, Robert S. "A Historic Ball Room." *EIHC* 31 (August-December 1894): 69–87. Assembly House.

Rantoul, Robert S. "The Nathaniel Ropes Estate." *EIHC* 40 (January 1904): 1–14.

Ryan, Margaret. "The Assembly House at Salem . . .." *House Beautiful* 50 (August 1921): 89–92.

Thayer, Oliver. "Early Recollections of the Upper Portion of Essex Street." *EIHC* 21 (July, August, September 1884): 211–24.

Ward, Gerald W.R. *The Assembly House.* Salem: Essex Institute, 1976. Originally published in *EIHC* 111 (October 1975): 241–66.

Ward, Gerald W.R. *The Peirce-Nichols House.* Salem: Essex Institute, 1976. Originally published in *EIHC* 111 (July 1975): 161–95.

Walsh, Louis S. *Origin of the Catholic Church in Salem and Its Growth in St. Mary's Parish and the Parish of the Immaculate Conception.* Boston: Cashman, Keating & Co., 1890.

Waters, William S. "Some Old Estates." *EIHC* 16 (January 1879): 37–54. Dean, Beckford, and Essex streets area.

Wiggin, Cynthia A. *Salem Athenaeum: A Short History.* Salem: Salem Athenaeum, 1964.

E. CHESTNUT AND BROAD STREETS

Corning, C.H. "Chestnut Street Associates, Salem, Mass." *Old-Time New England* 42 (April 1952): 102–105.

Oliver, Henry K. *An Address Delivered at the Dedication of the School-House on Broad Street, In Salem, March 18, 1856* . . . .. Salem: Wm. Ives and Geo. W. Pease, Printers, 1856.

Phillips, James Duncan. "Captain Stephen Phillips, 1764–1838." *EIHC* 76 (April 1940): 97–135.

Phillips, James Duncan. *Chestnut Street 40 Years Ago and the People Who Lived In and Around It . . ..* Boston: Thomas Todd Co., 1938.

Phillips, James Duncan. "Hamilton Hall: The Hall of the Federalists . . .." *EIHC* 83 (October 1947): 295–307.

The Pickering House, 1651. Salem: Pickering Foundation, 1972.

Sturgis, Elizabeth O.P. "Recollections of the 'Old Tucker House,' 28 Chestnut Street, Salem." *EIHC* 74 (1938): 109–141.

Winchester, Alice. "Living with Antiques: The Pickering House in Salem, Massachusetts." *Antiques* 61 (May 1952): 429–32.

Wiswall, Richard H. "Notes on the Building of Chestnut Street." *EIHC* 75 (July 1939): 203–233. With annotations by Henry W. Belknap. Reprinted, Salem: Newcomb & Gauss Co., 1939.

F. SOUTH SALEM

Dick, Rudolph C. *Nathaniel Griffin (1796-1876) of Salem—and his Naumkeag Steam Cotton Company.* New York: Newcomen Society, 1951.

Dow, George Francis. "The Colonial Village Built at Salem, Massachusetts in the Spring of 1930." *Old-Time New England* 22 (July 1931): 3–14.

Jarvis, Clive. *The Story of Pequot.* Salem: Naumkeag Steam Cotton Co., 1929.

Johnson, Claire D. "Domestic Architecture in Victorian Salem: A Lafayette Street Sampling." *EIHC* 115 (July 1979): 172–82.

A Reference Guide to Salem, 1630, Forest River Park . . .. Rev. ed. Salem: Board of Park Commissioners, 1935.

Saint Joseph Parish, Salem, Mass., 1873-1973. Salem: Compass Press, 1973.

G. NORTH SALEM

50th Anniversary, St. Thomas the Apostle Parish, Salem-Peabody, Mass.: 1927-1977. Peabody: By the Parish, 1977.

Harmony Grove Cemetery, Salem, Mass. Salem: G.M. Whipple and A.A. Smith, 1866.

Pitcoff, Rita L. "Greenlawn Cemetery: Salem's 'Botanical Garden'." *EIHC* 117 (January 1981): 43–53.

H. OUTLYING BUILDINGS

Phippen, Walter G. "From Charter Street to the Lookout: The Salem Hospital—A Brief History." *EIHC* 102 (April 1966): 91–162.

Streeter, Gilbert L. "The Story of Winter Island and Salem Neck." *EIHC* 33 (January-June 1897): 105–128.

Welch, William L. "Salem Neck and Winter Island." *EIHC* 33 (January-June 1897): 81–104.

Wise, Dewitt D. *Now, Then, Baker's Island.* Salem: Baker's Island Association, 1964.

Appendix I
BUILDINGS OPEN TO THE PUBLIC

The following buildings and complexes are open to the public on varying schedules, some for payment of an admission fee, and others on a non-fee basis. Additional public, church, and commercial buildings may be visited by special permission. Most of the architecture described in this book, however, is privately owned and closed to the public, and the owners' rights to privacy should be respected.

A-1   Essex Institute (1851/52; 1856/57, etc.), 132 Essex Street

A-2   Gardner-Pingree house (1804–1805) (Essex Institute), 128 Essex Street

A-3   Crowninshield-Bentley house (c. 1727–30, etc.) (Essex Institute), 126 Essex Street at Washington Square West

A-4   Andrew-Safford house (1818/19) (Essex Institute), 13 Washington Square West

A-5   John Ward house (after 1684, etc.) (Essex Institute), Brown Street opposite Howard

A-7   East Church (Salem Witch Museum) (1844–46), 19½ Washington Square North at Brown Street

A-32 Narbonne house (c. 1672, etc.) (Salem Maritime National Historic Site), 71 Essex Street (by special appointment)

B-8   Custom House (1818/19; 1853/54) (Salem Maritime National Historic Site), 178 Derby Street at Orange

B-10 Derby house (1761/62; 1790) (Salem Maritime National Historic Site), 168 Derby Street

B-13 House of Seven Gables (1668; c. 1678, etc.) (House of Seven Gables Settlement Association), 54 Turner Street

B-14 Retire Becket house (c. 1655) (House of Seven Gables Settlement Association), 54 Turner Street

B-15 Hooper-Hathaway house (c. 1682) (House of Seven Gables Settlement Association), 54 Turner Street

B-16 Nathaniel Hawthorne birthplace (between 1730 and 1745) (House of Seven Gables Settlement Association), 27 Hardy Street, accessible from 54 Turner Street

C-3   Peabody Museum of Salem (1824/25, etc.), 161 Essex Street Mall at Liberty and Charter streets

C-5   East India Mall and Parking Garage (1973–75; 1977–79), Essex Street Mall; Brown and Liberty streets and St. Peter Square

C-12 Old Town Hall and Market House (1816), 32 Derby Square between Essex Street Mall and Front Street

C-22   United States Post Office building (1932–33), 2 Margin Street between Gedney and Norman

C-24   Gedney house (c. 1665) (S.P.N.E.A.), 21 High Street (by special appointment)

C-31   City Hall (1836/37), 93 Washington Street

C-34   First District Court of Essex County (1976–77), 60 Washington Street at Church

C-42   Essex Street courthouses (1839–41, etc.), 32-36-43 Federal Street

D-1   Peirce-Nichols house (c. 1782; 1801, etc.) (Essex Institute), 80 Federal Street

D-15   Assembly House (1783; c. 1797/98, etc.) (Essex Institute), 138 Federal Street

D-31   Bertram-Waters house (Salem Public Library) (1855; 1888/89; 1911/12), 370 Essex Street at Monroe

D-45   Putnam-Balch house ("Greymoor") (1871/72), 329 Essex Street at Cambridge

D-46   Ropes Memorial (Ropes Mansion) (late 1720s, etc.) (managed by the Essex Institute), 318 Essex Street opposite Cambridge

D-49   Jonathan Corwin house ("Witch House") (c. 1675), 310½ Essex Street at North

E-21   Stephen Phillips Memorial Trust house (West-Phillips house) (early 19th century; 1824, etc.), 34 Chestnut Street

E-36   Pickering house (c. 1651, etc.), 18 Broad Street at Pickering

F-16   Pioneer Village (1930; replica), Forest River Park, accessible from Clifton and West avenues

BUILDINGS LISTED BY NAME

Numbers in parentheses refer to entries in which building is mentioned only, not extensively described or illustrated.

Newmark building; Old Custom House; One Salem Green; Peabody building; Pickering Wharf; Pickman building; Pickman-Derby block; Power block; Proctor block; Rust brick store; Shepard block; Shribman building; Stearns block; Union building; Varney-Reynolds-Ropes building; West India Goods Store (Rum Shop); Y.M.C.A. building

Cook (Robert) house, A-18

Cook-Daland house, D-39

Cook-Kimball house, A-18

Cook-Oliver house, D-17

Corwin (Jonathan) house ("Witch House"), (C-45), D-49

Cox, (Francis) house, E-1

Crombie Street Church (Congregational), C-29

Crosby (Capt. Nicholas) house, D-33

Crowninshield (Benjamin W.) house (Home for Aged Women), B-7

Crowninshield (Clifford) house, A-29

Crowninshield (George) house, (B-8)

Crowninshield (John) house, (A-7)

Crowninshield-Bentley house, A-3

Culliton (John) house, D-18

Curtis (Nancy) house, D-8

Curwen/Gillis double house, D-42

Curwen/Webb double house, E-26

Custom House, B-8, (B-9), (D-14)

Custom houses. *See* Custom House; Old Custom House

Cutts-Frye-Chipman house, D-16

Daland (John Tucker) house, A-1, (D-31), (D-37), (D-42)

Danforth (Joseph) house, A-33

Daniel Low building. *See* First Church

Daniels house, A-30

Davenport building. *See* Salem Hospital

Davis (Capt. Tobias) house, C-26

Dean-Sprague-Stearns house ("The East India House"), D-25, (D-27)

Dennis (Devereux) house, G-9

Derby farm, (F-10), (F-18)

Derby (Ezekial Hersey) house, (C-15)

Derby (Richard) house, (B-9), B-10, (E-27), (E-30)

Derby (Elias Hasket) mansion, (C-11), (C-12), (C-17)

Derby-Ward house, B-5

Devereux-Hoffman-Simpson house, E-15

Devine (Mary A.) house, F-10, (F-12)

Dickson Memorial Chapel and Conservatory (Greenlawn Cemetery), G-15

Dodge (Ernest S.) wing. *See* Peabody Museum of Salem

Dodge-Barstow-West house, E-14

Dodge-Bertram-Whipple house, G-13

Dodge-Shreve house, (A-4), (D-44), (E-13), E-18, (E-30), (F-4), (G-13)

Dow (Enoch) house, (D-13)

Downing block, C-6

Driver-Mansfield-Nichols house, E-34

Dugan (James) house, G-12

Dunckley-Sargent house, G-6

East Church (Salem Witch Museum), A-7

East Hall. *See* Peabody Museum of Salem

Hale (Mercantile) building, C-16
Hamilton Hall, E-4
Hanson (Job V.) house, G-2, (G-7)
Hanson (John) house, (G-2), G-7
Hanson (Joseph H.) house, D-37
Harrington (Leonard) house, E-29
Harrington (Richard) house, D-16
Harris house, (G-14)
Harris/Webb double house, F-7
Hathaway (Benjamin G.) house, F-20
Hawkes (Benjamin) house, B-9
Hawthorne (Nathaniel) birthplace, B-16
Hawthorne Inn, (A-3), A-36
Heard (Nathaniel) cottage, G-10
Henfield building. See Pickman and Henfield buildings
Heritage Cooperative Bank (Cate's block), C-32
Higbee (Lemuel) house, D-24
Hodges (John) house, A-33, (F-3)
Hodges (Jonathan) house, E-6
Holman-Price house, (D-32), D-43
Holyoke Mutual (Fire) Insurance Company building, C-25
Home for Aged Women. See Crowninshield (Benjamin W.) house
Hooper (George W.) house, F-4
Hooper-Hathaway house (The Old Bakery), B-15
Horton (Nathaniel) house, (G-9)
Hose Company Number 6 firehouse. See North Street firehouse
Hose No. 2 firehouse, A-16
Hosmer-Townsend-Waters house, A-24
Hotels and inns. See Arrington block; Barton's Hotel; Daniels house;
    Hawthorne Inn; Washington Hotel
House of Seven Gables (Turner house), B-13, (B-14), (B-15), (B-16)
House of Seven Gables Settlement Association houses. See Becket (Retire)
    house; Emmerton (Caroline) Hall; Hawthorne (Nathaniel) birthplace;
    Hooper-Hathaway house; House of Seven Gables; Phippen (Joshua) house
Howard Street Church, (C-29)
Howard-Downing house, A-6
Hoyt block. See Naumkeag Trust Company building
Huse (John) house, D-20

Independent Congregational Church, (Barton Square Church), (C-3)
Ireland-Emery house, D-12
Ives-Putnam house, D-23
Ives-Webb house, A-6

Jailer's (sheriff's) house, C-38, (D-14)
Jelley (William M.) house, D-39
Johnson (Emery S.) house, D-34
Jones (Gardner Maynard) Memorial Library, (A-31)
Juniper Point cottages, H-5

Kelsey (Harlan P.) house, E-36
Kiley (David) house, D-24
Kimball-Fogg house, E-28
King (Miss Elizabeth) house, E-5

Salem Five Cents Savings Bank building (Gardner building), C-15
Salem Fraternity. *See* Essex Bank building
Salem High School, (H-1), H-3
Salem Hospital, H-2
Salem Jail, C-38, (D-14)
Salem Maritime National Historic Site. *See* Custom House; Derby (Richard)
    house; Hawkes (Benjamin) house; West India Goods Store (Rum Shop)
Salem Police Station, C-9, (C-34)
Salem Public Library. *See* Bertram-Waters house
Salem (Eastern) Savings Bank (Asiatic building), C-18
Salem State College. *See* O'Keefe (Richard B.) Physical Education/Athletic
    Center; Salem State College Library
Salem State College Library, F-17
Salem Steam Fire Engine house, C-35
Salem Witch Museum. *See* East Church
Sanders homestead, (C-28)
Sanderson (Jacob and Elijah) double house, D-10
Saunders (Capt. Thomas) house, E-24, (E-25), (E-31)
Saunders-Saltonstall-Tuckerman double house, E-25
Saunders-Ward house, D-9
Savage (Ezekiel) house, E-33
Scale house, (B-8)
School of Nursing building. *See* Salem Hospital
Schools. *See* Bentley School; Broad Street School; Classical and High
    School; Latin Grammar and English High School (Broad Street School;
    Oliver Primary School); Mack Industrial School; Old Salem High School;
    Salem High School; School of Nursing building; State Normal School;
    Witchcraft Heights Elementary School
Scott (Joseph) House, C-8
Seamans (Francis A.) house, E-27
Second Corps Cadets Armory, C-1
Shaughnessy Hospital. *See* Salem Hospital
Sheriff's house. *See* Jailer's house
Shepard block, C-27
Shillaber (Ebenezer) house, D-11
Shribman building. *See* Neal and Newhall building
Silsbee (Capt. Nathaniel) house, B-11
Silsbee (Nathaniel) house, A-21
Silsbee (Nathaniel, Jr.) house, A-21
Silsbee (Sarah) house, B-11
Smith (Caleb A.) house, G-5
Smith (Ebenezer) house (Burrill house), D-26
Smith (Capt. Isaac) house, A-16
Smith (Jabez) house, D-21
Smith-Crosby-Endicott house, D-33
South Branch Library, (F-11)
South Church, (E-3)
Sprague (Joseph) house, (D-29)
Sprague-Peabody-Silsbee house, D-27
State Normal School, E-39
Stearns block, (C-7), (C-18), (D-15), (D-25)
Stevens (William) house, E-37
Stone (Deacon John) double house, E-1
Story (Joseph) house, A-12

GENERAL INDEX

This index does not include the names of buildings and complexes, all of which are listed in the special sections above. Nor does it include individual or family names associated with building histories. The prime focus of the index is on architects', builders', contractors', and artisans' names, building types, and architectural styles.

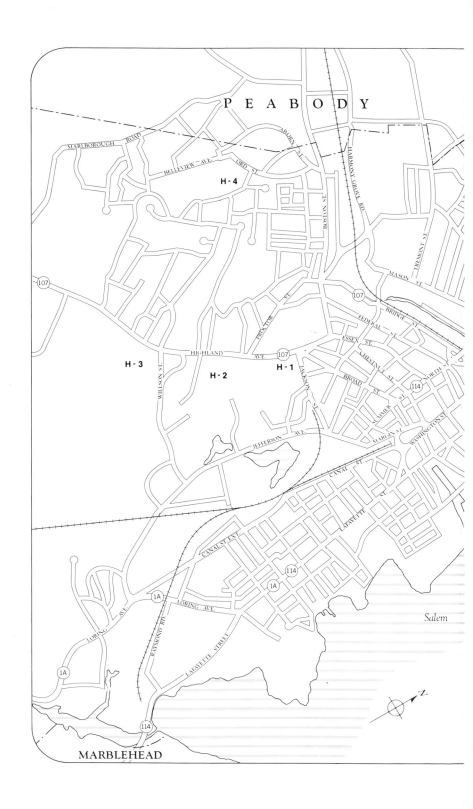